RUNAWAYS

TRUE BELIEVERS

WRITER: **BRIAN K. VAUGHAN**
PENCILS: **ADRIAN ALPHONA**
INKS: **CRAIG YEUNG**
COLORS: **CHRISTINA STRAIN**
LETTERS: **VC'S RANDY GENTILE**
& **DAVE SHARPE**
COVER ART: **JO CHEN**
EDITORS: **MACKENZIE CADENHEAD**
& **C.B. CEBULSKI**

RUNAWAYS CREATED BY **BRIAN K. VAUGHAN**
& **ADRIAN ALPHONA**

COLLECTION EDITOR: JENNIFER GRÜNWALD
ASSISTANT EDITOR: JOHN DENNING
EDITOR, SPECIAL PROJECTS:
SENIOR EDITOR, SPECIAL PROJECTS:
SENIOR VICE PRESIDENT OF SALES: DAVID GABRIEL
BOOK DESIGNER: **RODOLFO MURAGUCHI**

EDITOR IN CHIEF: **JOE QUESADA**
PUBLISHER: **DAN BUCKLEY**
EXECUTIVE PRODUCER: **ALAN FINE**

30131 04502187 7
London Borough of Barnet

RUNAWAYS: TRUE BELIEVERS. Contains material originally published in magazine form as RUNAWAYS #1-6. First printing 2009. Hardcover ISBN# 978-0-7851-4144-0. Softcover ISBN# 978-0-7851-4145-7. Published by MARVEL PUBLISHING, INC., a subsidiary of MARVEL ENTERTAINMENT, INC. OFFICE OF PUBLICATION: 417 5th Avenue, New York, NY 10016. Copyright © 2005 and 2009 Marvel Characters, Inc. All rights reserved. Hardcover: $19.99 per copy in the U.S. (GST #R127032852). Softcover: $14.99 per copy in the U.S. (GST #R127032852). Canadian Agreement #40668537. All characters featured in this issue and the distinctive names and likenesses thereof, and all related indicia are trademarks of Marvel Characters, Inc. No similarity between any of the names, characters, persons, and/or institutions in this magazine with those of any living or dead person or institution is intended, and any such similarity which may exist is purely coincidental. **Printed in the U.S.A.** ALAN FINE, EVP - Office Of The Chief Executive Marvel Entertainment, Inc. & CMO Marvel Characters B.V.; DAN BUCKLEY, Chief Executive Officer and Publisher - Print, Animation & Digital Media; JIM SOKOLOWSKI, Chief Operating Officer; DAVID GABRIEL, SVP of Publishing Sales & Circulation; DAVID BOGART, SVP of Business Affairs & Talent Management; MICHAEL PASCIULLO, VP Merchandising & Communications; JIM O'KEEFE, VP of Operations & Logistics; DAN CARR, Executive Director of Publishing Technology; JUSTIN F. GABRIE, Director of Publishing & Editorial Operations; SUSAN CRESPI, Editorial Operations Manager; ALEX MORALES, Publishing Operations Manager; STAN LEE, Chairman Emeritus. For information regarding advertising in Marvel Comics or on Marvel.com, please contact Mitch Dane, Advertising Director, at mdane@marvel.com. For Marvel subscription inquiries, please call 800-217-9158. **Manufactured between** 11/9/09 and 12/9/09 (hardcover), and 11/9/09 and 3/31/10 (softcover), by R.R. DONNELLEY, INC., SALEM, VA, USA.

10 9 8 7 6 5 4 3 2 1

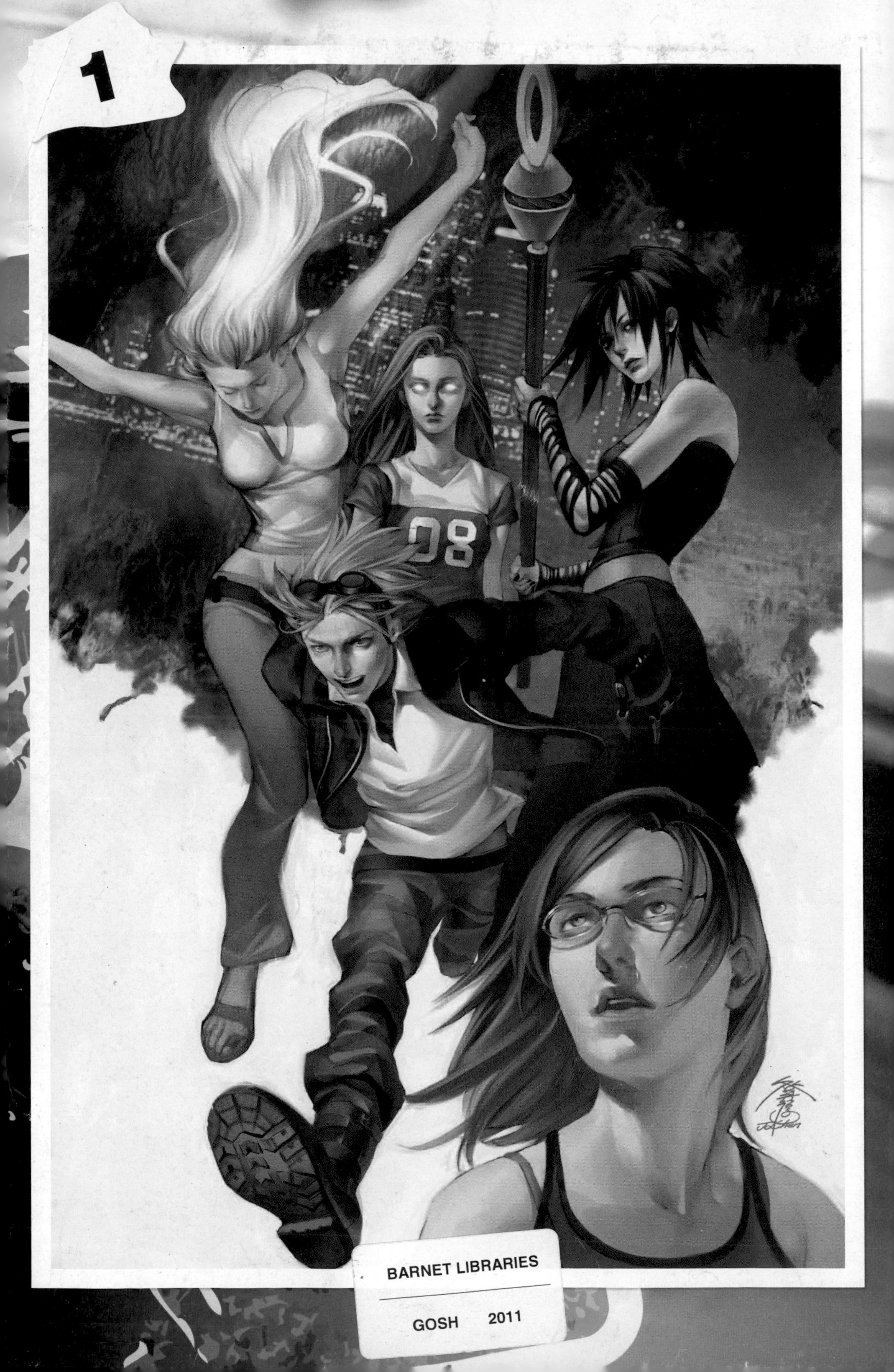
1
08

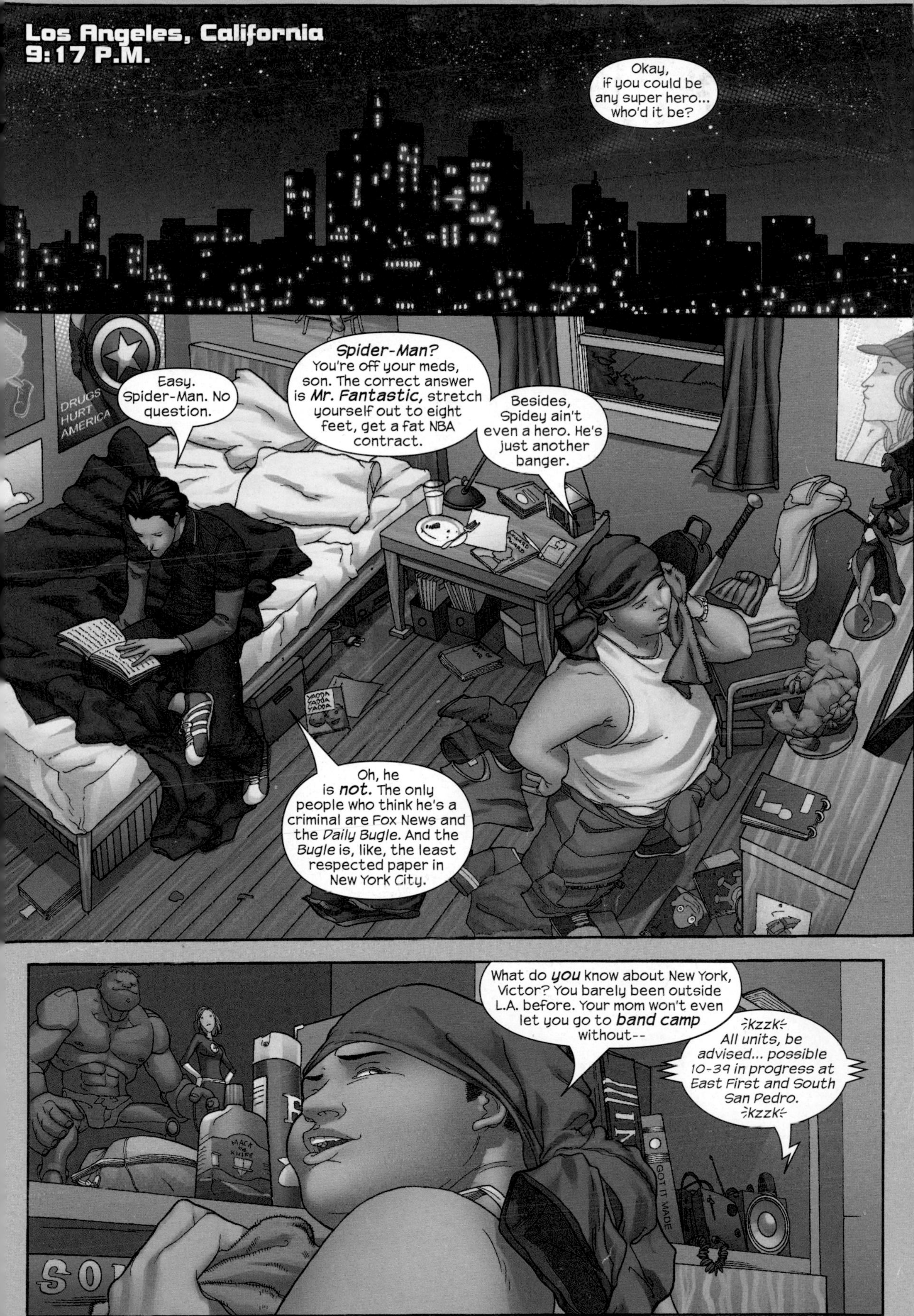
Los Angeles, California
9:17 P.M.
Okay, if you could be any super hero... who'd it be?
Easy. Spider-Man. No question.
DRUGS HURT AMERICA
Spider-Man? You're off your meds, son. The correct answer is ***Mr. Fantastic,*** stretch yourself out to eight feet, get a fat NBA contract.
Besides, Spidey ain't even a hero. He's just another banger.
Oh, he is ***not.*** The only people who think he's a criminal are Fox News and the *Daily Bugle*. And the *Bugle* is, like, the least respected paper in New York City.
What do ***you*** know about New York, Victor? You barely been outside L.A. before. Your mom won't even let you go to ***band camp*** without--
kzzk All units, be advised... possible 10-39 in progress at East First and South San Pedro. *kzzk*

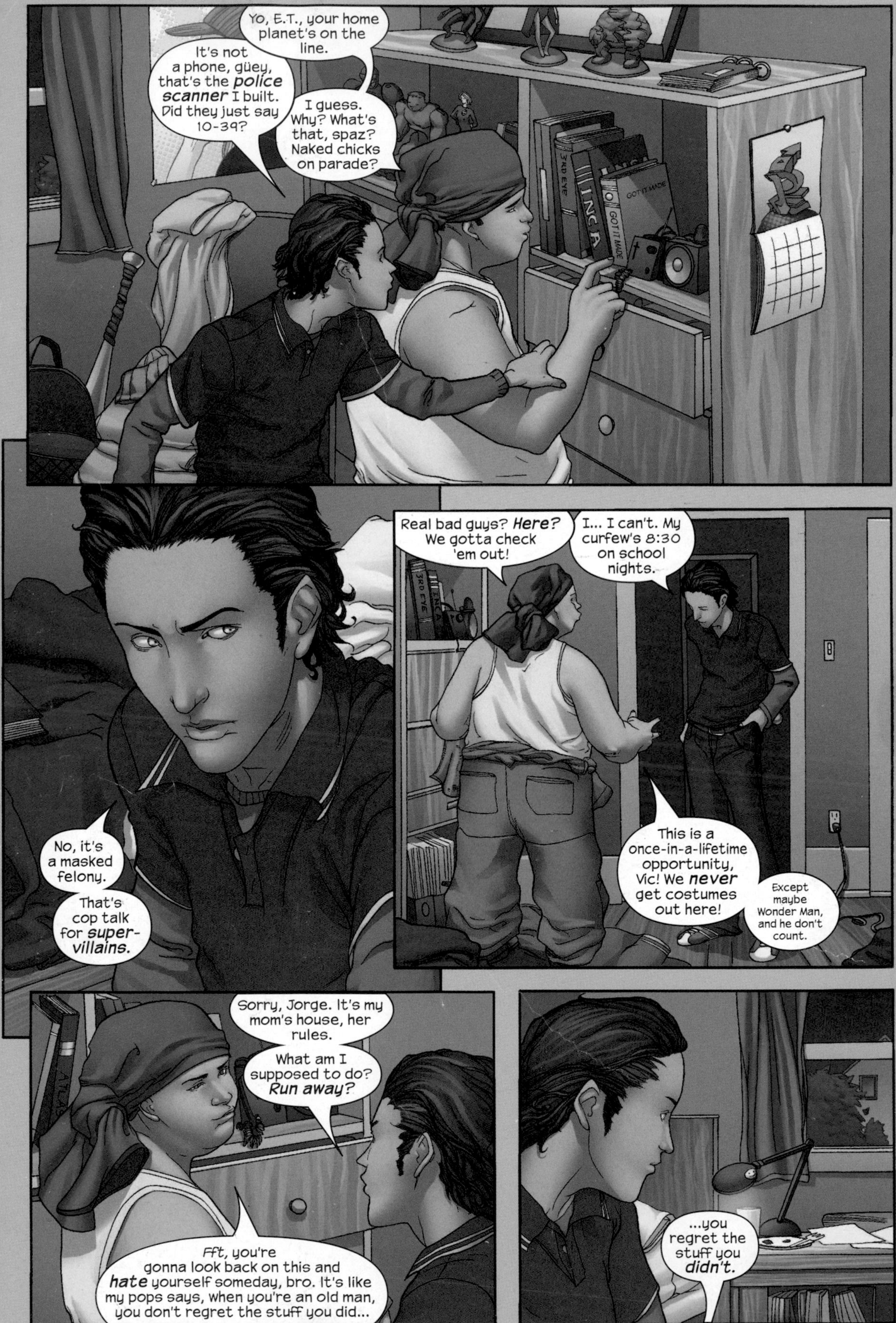
Yo, E.T., your home planet's on the line.
It's not a phone, güey, that's the *police scanner* I built. Did they just say 10-39?
I guess. Why? What's that, spaz? Naked chicks on parade?
3RD EYE
INCA
GOT IT MADE
No, it's a masked felony.
That's cop talk for ***super-villains.***
Real bad guys? ***Here?*** We gotta check 'em out!
I... I can't. My curfew's 8:30 on school nights.
This is a once-in-a-lifetime opportunity, Vic! We ***never*** get costumes out here!
Except maybe Wonder Man, and he don't count.
Sorry, Jorge. It's my mom's house, her rules.
What am I supposed to do? ***Run away?***
Fft, you're gonna look back on this and ***hate*** yourself someday, bro. It's like my pops says, when you're an old man, you don't regret the stuff you did...
...you regret the stuff you ***didn't.***

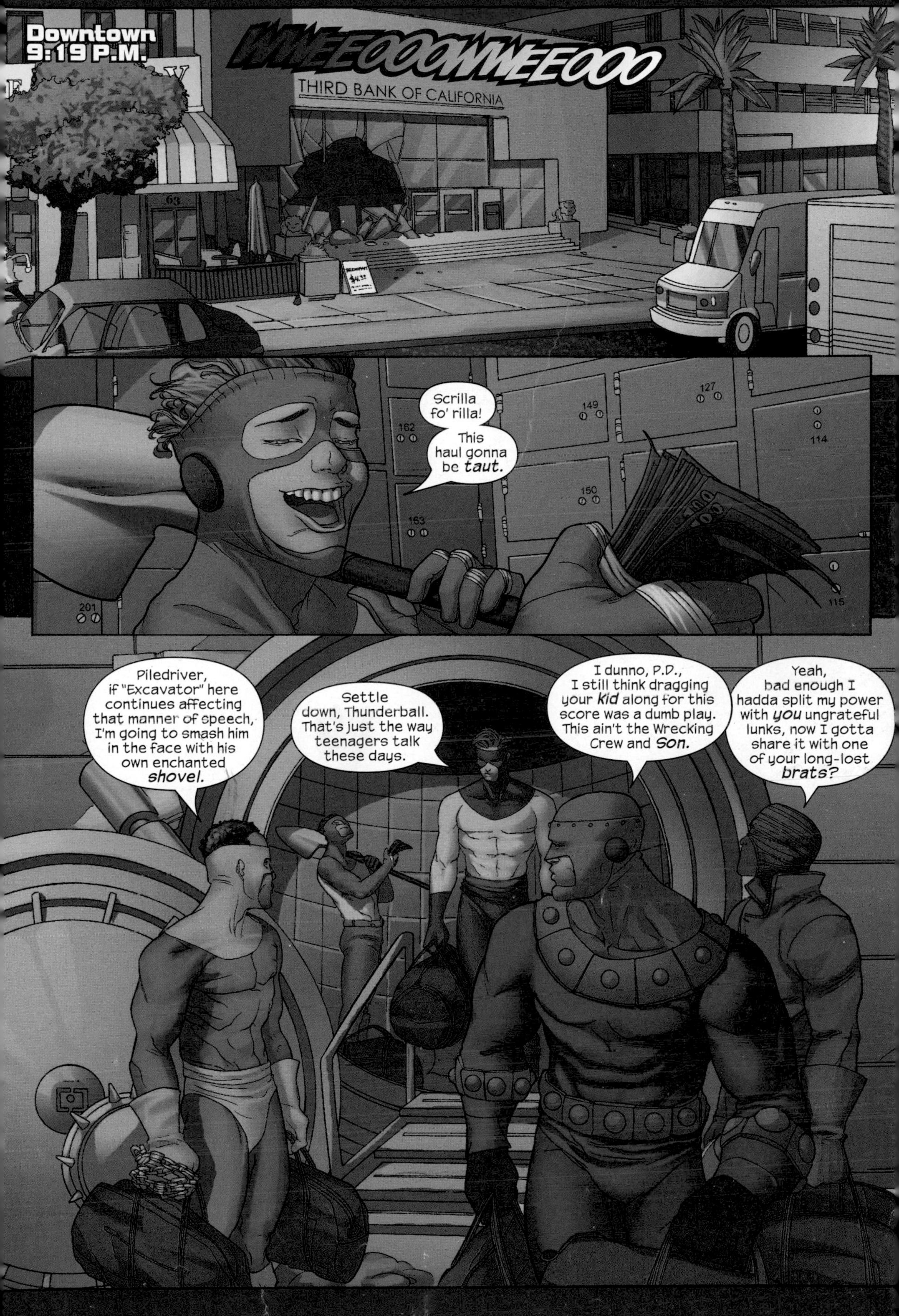
Downtown 9:19 P.M.
WWEEOOOWWEEOOO
THIRD BANK OF CALIFORNIA
Scrilla fo' rilla!
This haul gonna be taut.
Piledriver, if "Excavator" here continues affecting that manner of speech, I'm going to smash him in the face with his own enchanted shovel.
Settle down, Thunderball. That's just the way teenagers talk these days.
I dunno, P.D., I still think dragging your kid along for this score was a dumb play. This ain't the Wrecking Crew and Son.
Yeah, bad enough I hadda split my power with you ungrateful lunks, now I gotta share it with one of your long-lost brats?

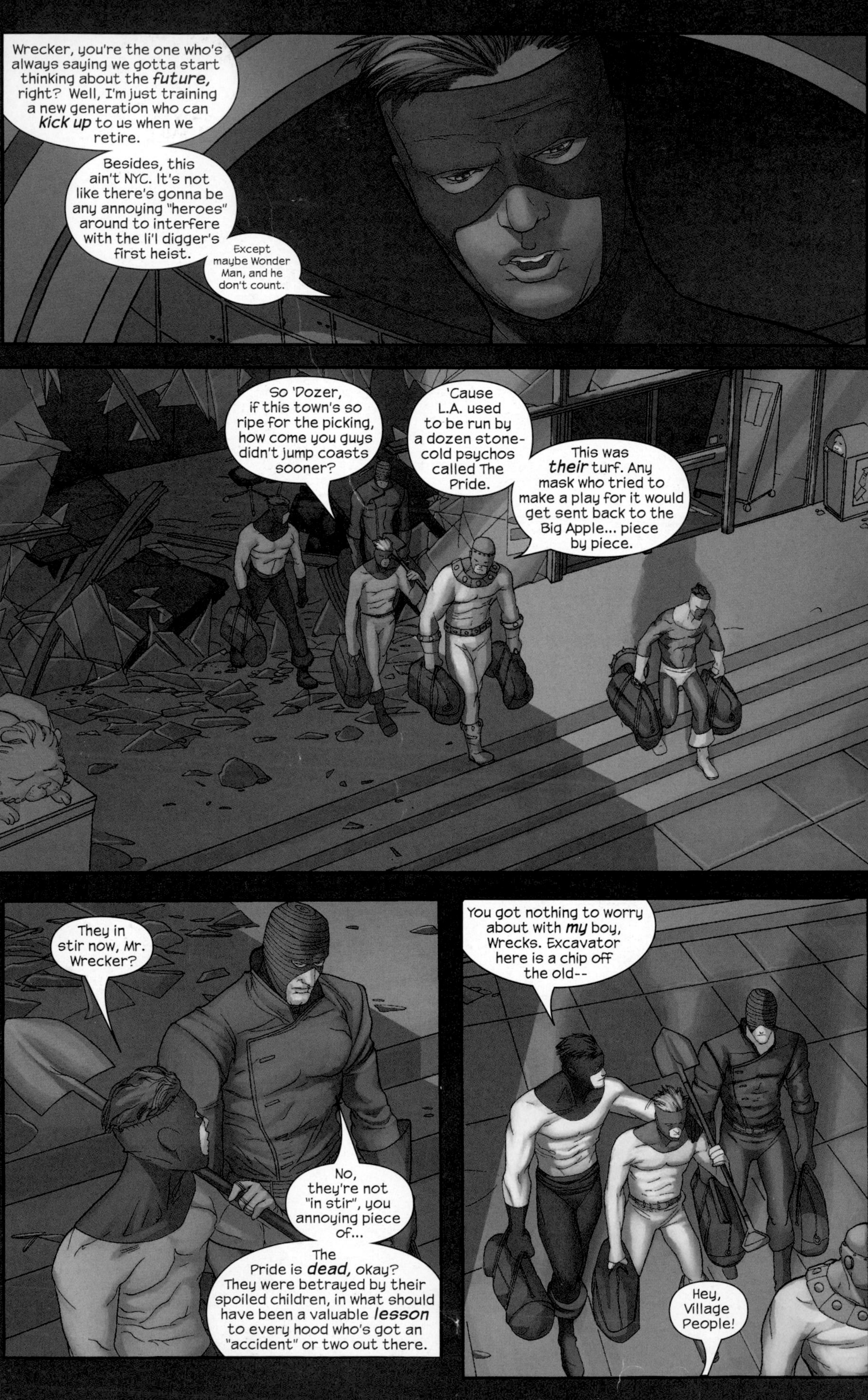

Wrecker, you're the one who's always saying we gotta start thinking about the *future,* right? Well, I'm just training a new generation who can *kick up* to us when we retire.
Besides, this ain't NYC. It's not like there's gonna be any annoying "heroes" around to interfere with the li'l digger's first heist.
Except maybe Wonder Man, and he don't count.
So 'Dozer, if this town's so ripe for the picking, how come you guys didn't jump coasts sooner?
'Cause L.A. used to be run by a dozen stone-cold psychos called The Pride.
This was *their* turf. Any mask who tried to make a play for it would get sent back to the Big Apple... piece by piece.
They in stir now, Mr. Wrecker?
No, they're not "in stir", you annoying piece of...
The Pride is *dead,* okay? They were betrayed by their spoiled children, in what should have been a valuable *lesson* to every hood who's got an "accident" or two out there.
You got nothing to worry about with *my* boy, Wrecks. Excavator here is a chip off the old--
Hey, Village People!

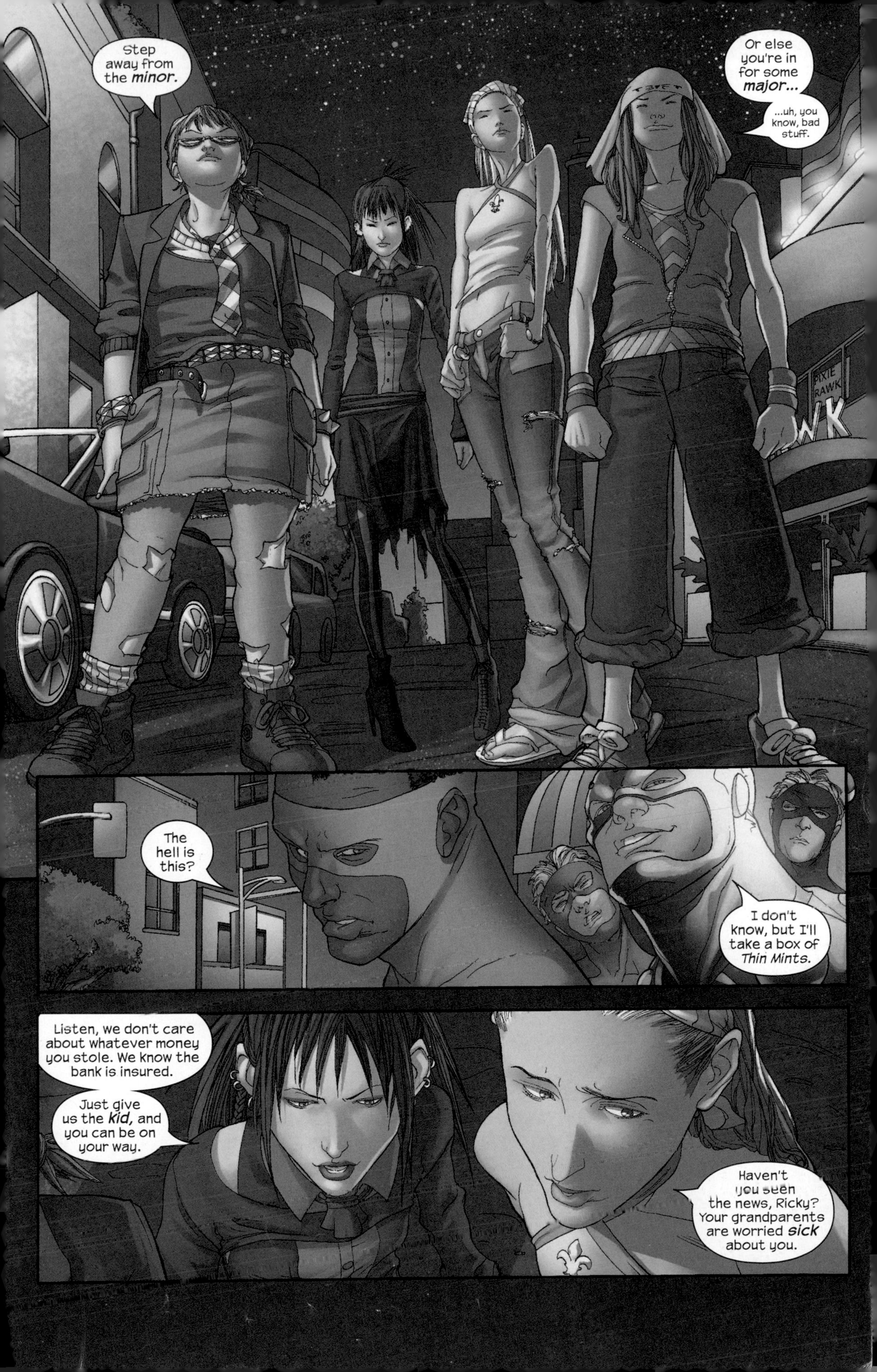
Step away from the *minor.*
Or else you're in for some *major...*
...uh, you know, bad stuff.
The hell is this?
I don't know, but I'll take a box of *Thin Mints.*
Listen, we don't care about whatever money you stole. We know the bank is insured.
Just give us the *kid,* and you can be on your way.
Haven't you seen the news, Ricky? Your grandparents are worried *sick* about you.

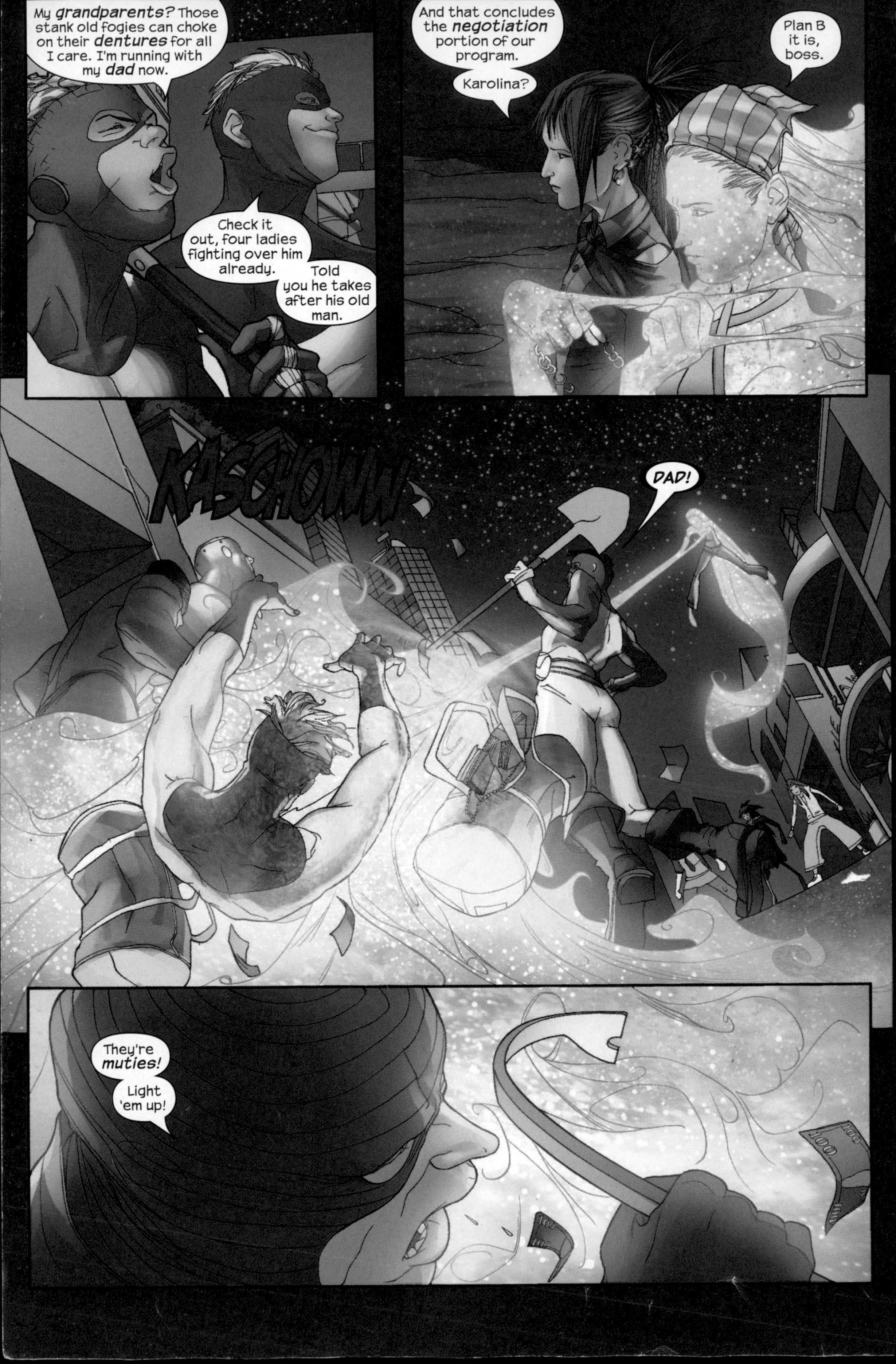
My grandparents? Those stank old fogies can choke on their dentures for all I care. I'm running with my dad now.
Check it out, four ladies fighting over him already.
Told you he takes after his old man.
And that concludes the negotiation portion of our program.
Karolina?
Plan B it is, boss.
KASCHOWW
DAD!
They're muties!
Light 'em up!

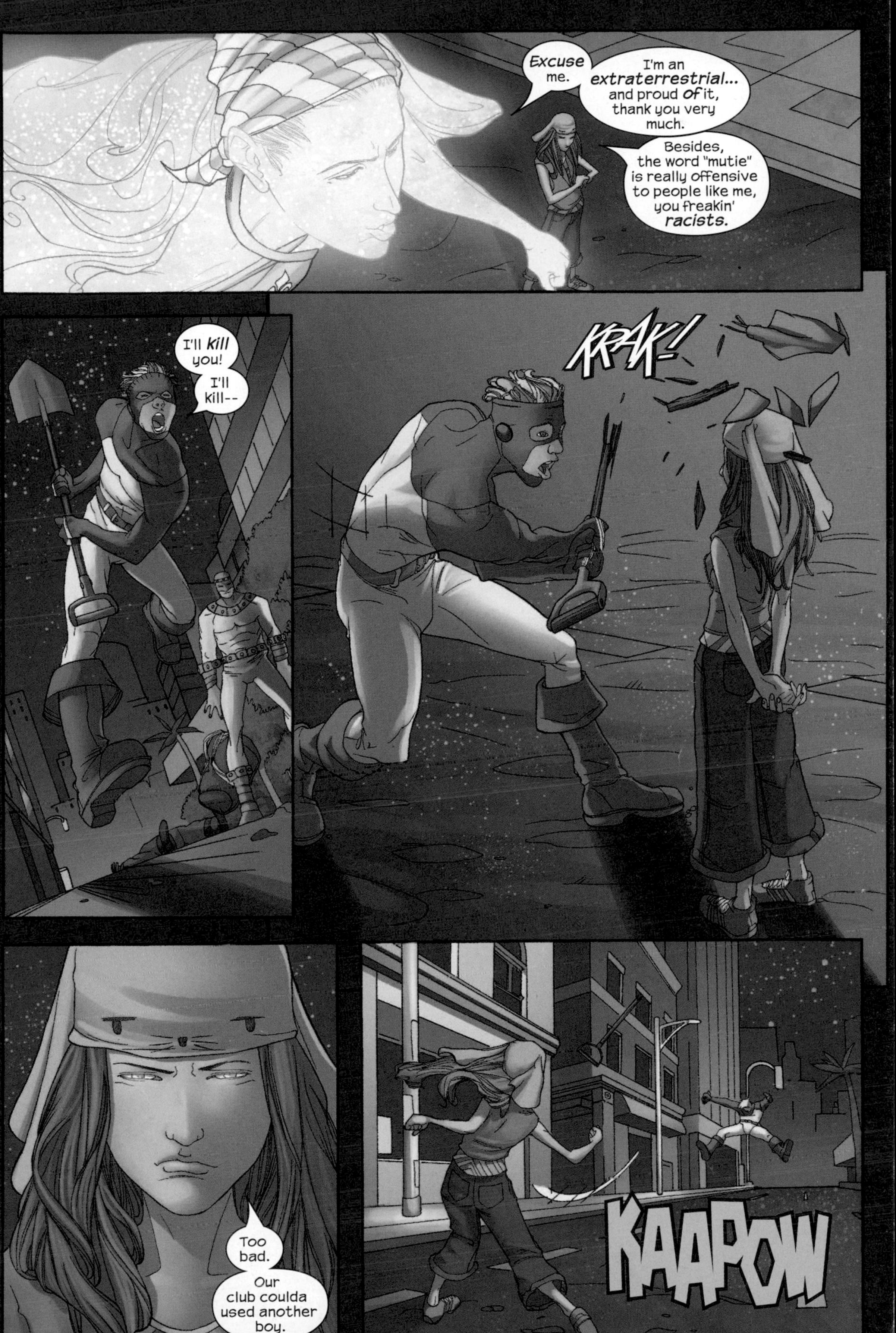
Excuse me.
I'm an extraterrestrial... and proud of it, thank you very much.
Besides, the word "mutie" is really offensive to people like me, you freakin' racists.
I'll kill you!
I'll kill--
KRAK!
Too bad.
Our club coulda used another boy.
KAAPOW

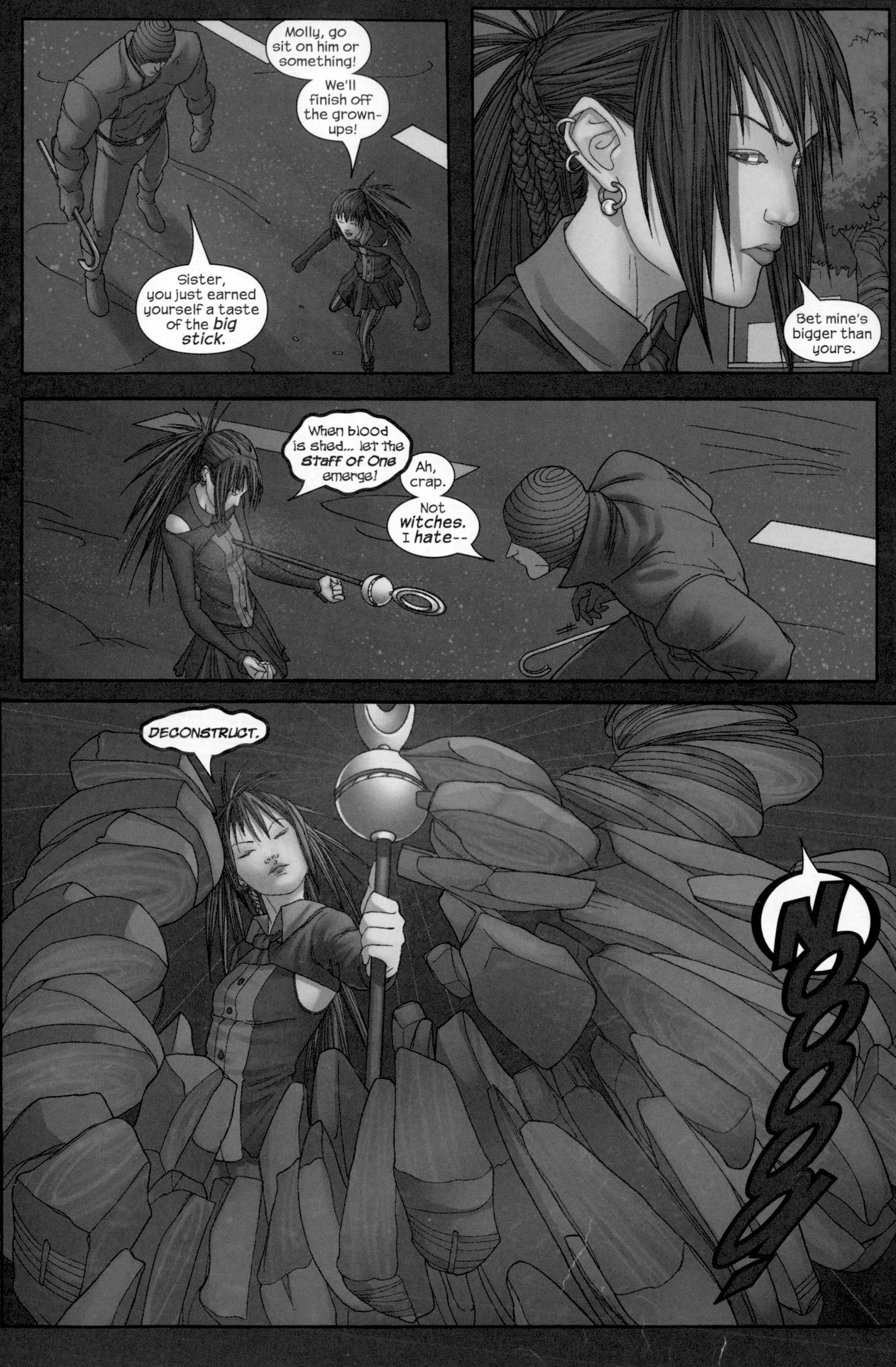

Molly, go sit on him or something!
We'll finish off the grown-ups!
Sister, you just earned yourself a taste of the *big stick.*
Bet mine's bigger than yours.
When blood is shed... let the *Staff of One* emerge!
Ah, crap.
Not *witches.* I *hate*--
DECONSTRUCT.
NOOOOOO

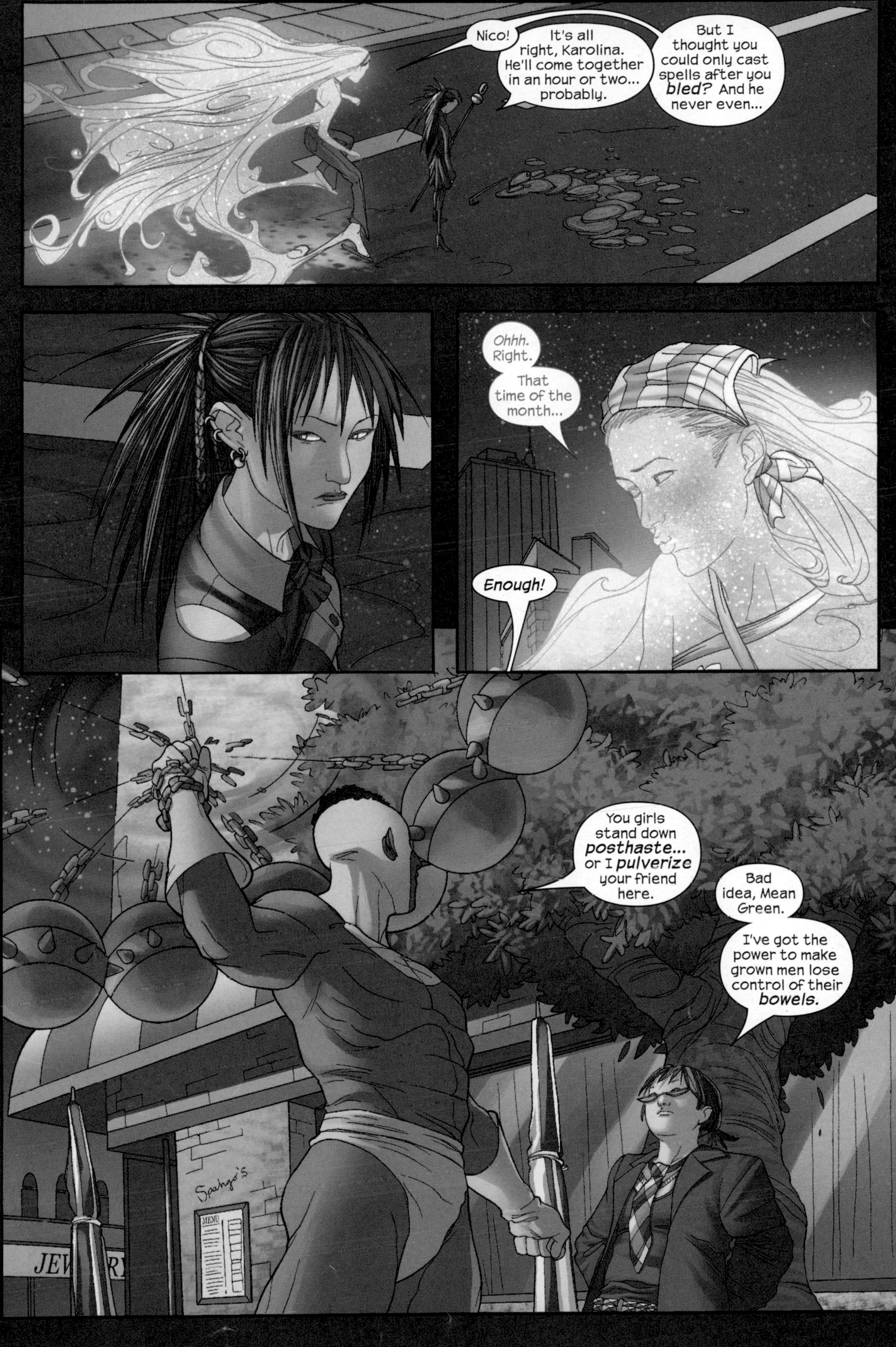
Nico!
It's all right, Karolina. He'll come together in an hour or two... probably.
But I thought you could only cast spells after you *bled?* And he never even...
Ohhh. Right.
That time of the month...
Enough!
You girls stand down ***posthaste...*** or I ***pulverize*** your friend here.
Bad idea, Mean Green.
I've got the power to make grown men lose control of their ***bowels.***
Spahgo's
MENU

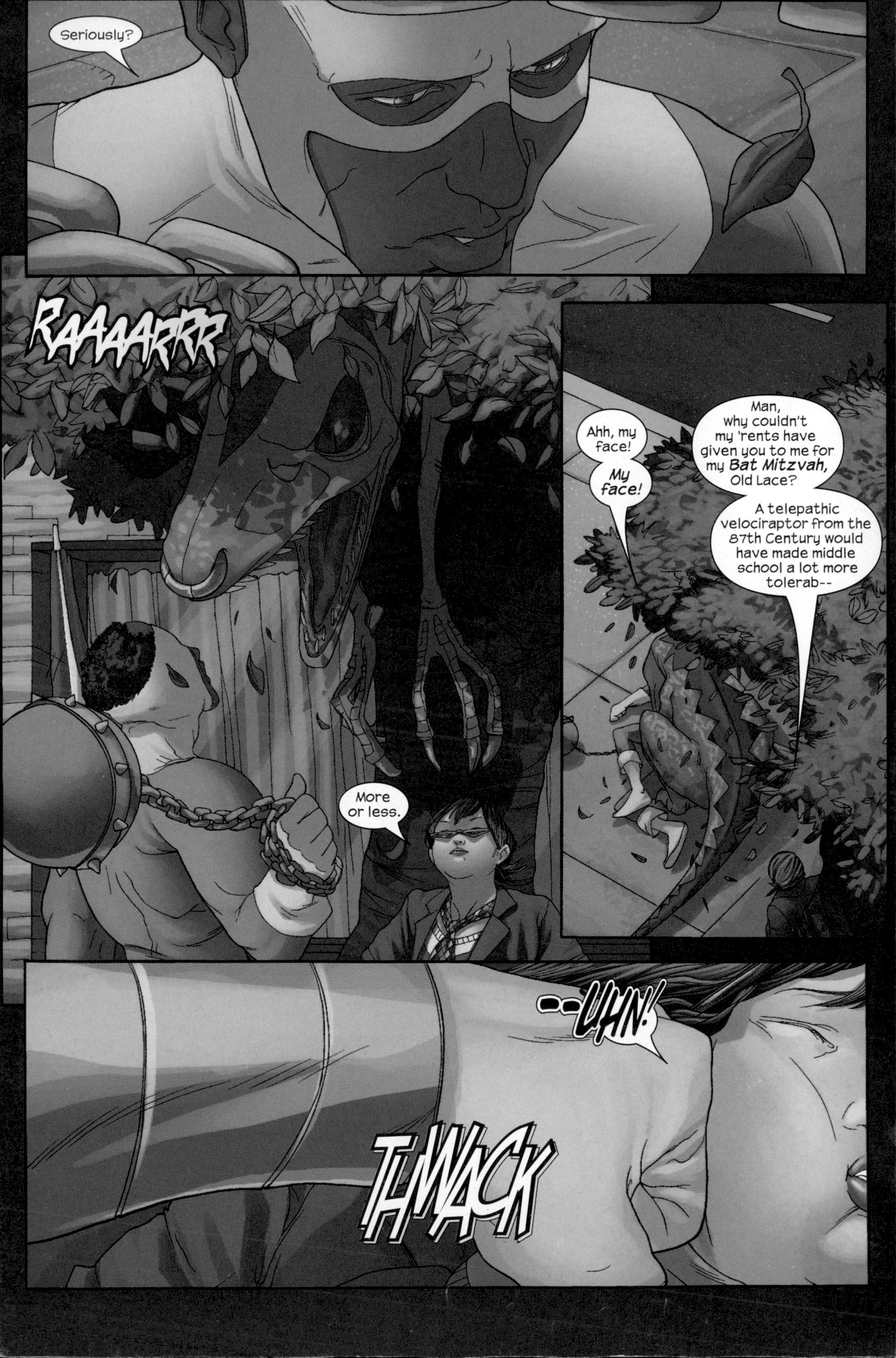
Seriously?
RAAAARRR
More or less.
Ahh, my face!
My face!
Man, why couldn't my 'rents have given you to me for my Bat Mitzvah, Old Lace?
A telepathic velociraptor from the 87th Century would have made middle school a lot more tolerab--
--UHN!
THWACK

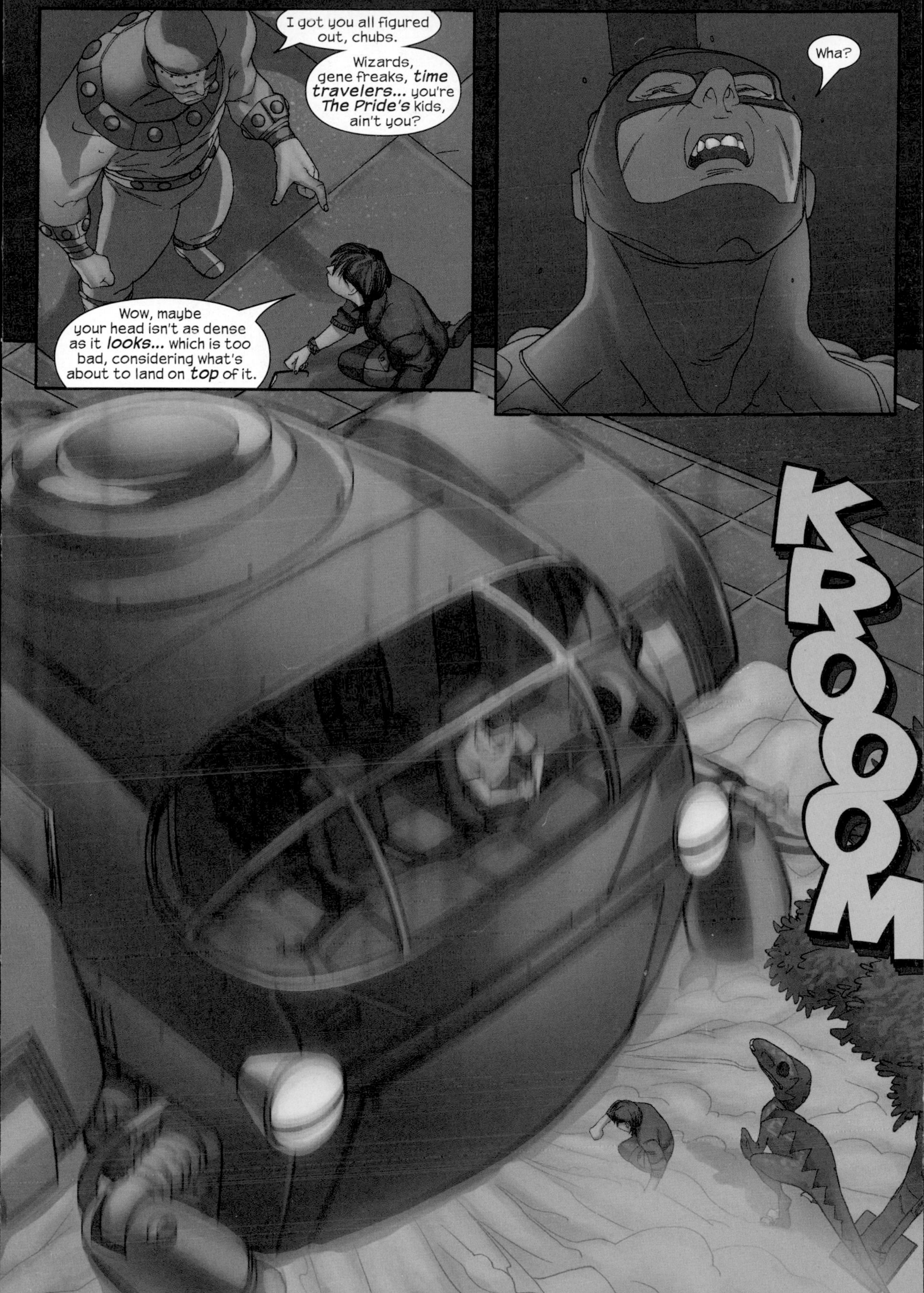
I got you all figured out, chubs.
Wizards, gene freaks, *time travelers...* you're *The Pride's* kids, ain't you?
Wow, maybe your head isn't as dense as it *looks...* which is too bad, considering what's about to land on *top* of it.
Wha?
KROOOM

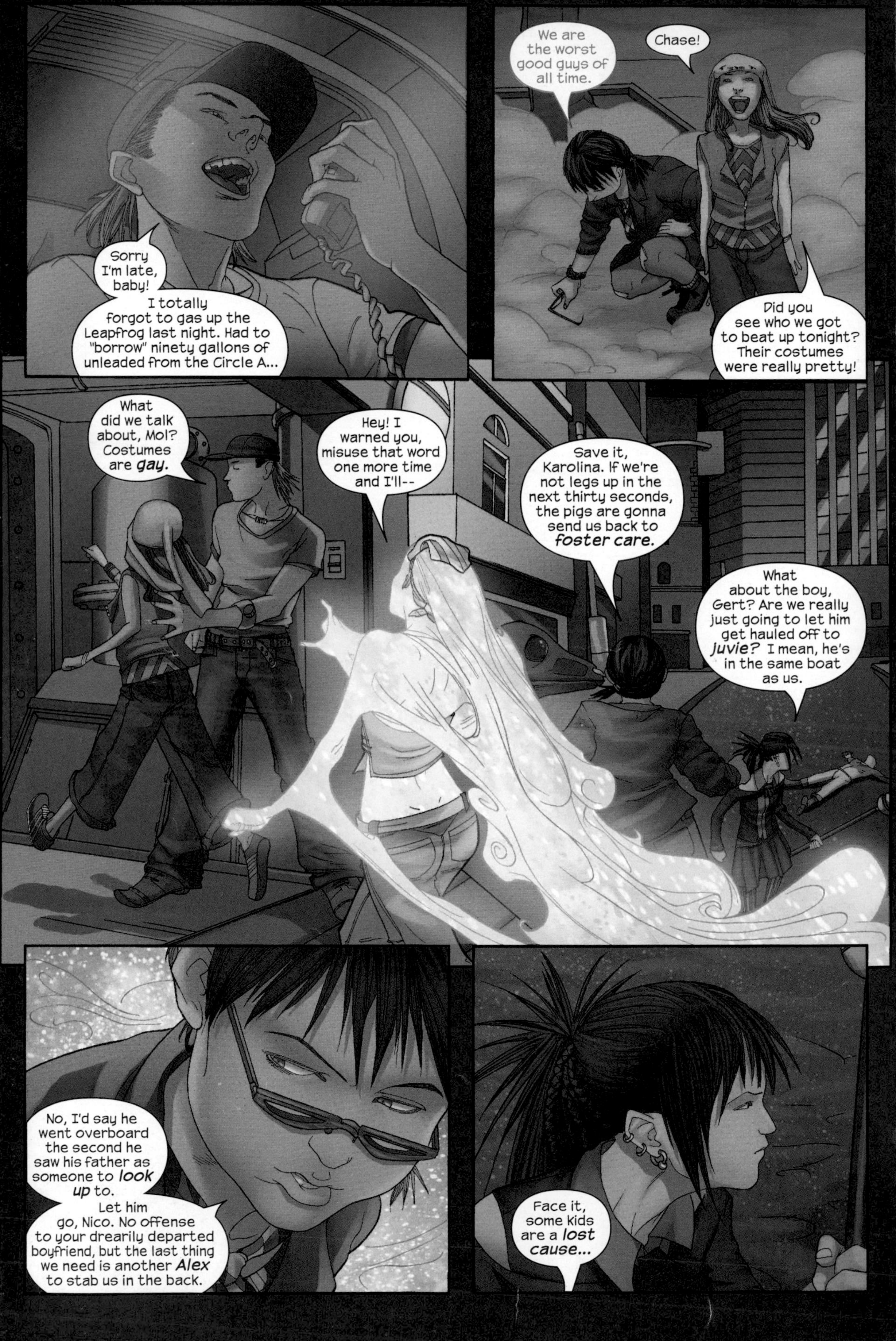
Sorry I'm late, baby!
I totally forgot to gas up the Leapfrog last night. Had to "borrow" ninety gallons of unleaded from the Circle A...
We are the worst good guys of all time.
Chase!
Did you see who we got to beat up tonight? Their costumes were really pretty!
What did we talk about, Mol? Costumes are gay.
Hey! I warned you, misuse that word one more time and I'll--
Save it, Karolina. If we're not legs up in the next thirty seconds, the pigs are gonna send us back to foster care.
What about the boy, Gert? Are we really just going to let him get hauled off to juvie? I mean, he's in the same boat as us.
No, I'd say he went overboard the second he saw his father as someone to look up to.
Let him go, Nico. No offense to your drearily departed boyfriend, but the last thing we need is another Alex to stab us in the back.
Face it, some kids are a lost cause...

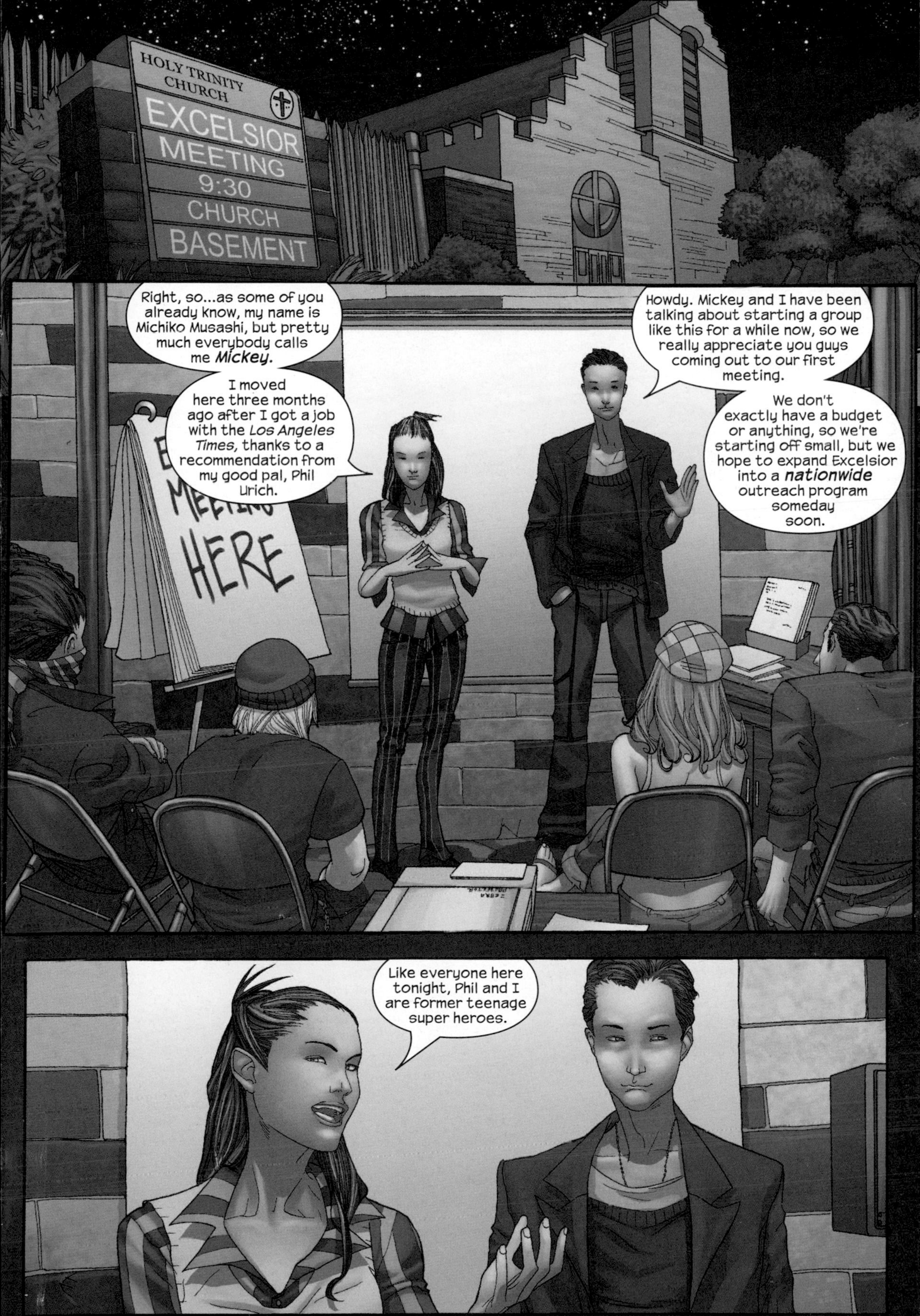
HOLY TRINITY CHURCH
EXCELSIOR MEETING 9:30 CHURCH BASEMENT
Right, so...as some of you already know, my name is Michiko Musashi, but pretty much everybody calls me *Mickey.*
I moved here three months ago after I got a job with the *Los Angeles Times,* thanks to a recommendation from my good pal, Phil Urich.
MEETING HERE
Howdy. Mickey and I have been talking about starting a group like this for a while now, so we really appreciate you guys coming out to our first meeting.
We don't exactly have a budget or anything, so we're starting off small, but we hope to expand Excelsior into a ***nationwide*** outreach program someday soon.
Like everyone here tonight, Phil and I are former teenage super heroes.

Anyway, I'm obviously not the only one here with a story like that. Chris, why don't you keep it going?

Oh, uh, sure. My name's Chris Powell, and I'm... well, I *used* to be *Darkhawk.*

I found this *amulet* back when I was in high school, and it changed me into this... this *thing.* You know the drill.

From the time I was a sophomore in college up until a few months ago, I'd been living a double life as the New Warriors' *Turbo.*

But late last year, I was fighting some Z-lister, and I had this... this *epiphany.* I realized that I could do more good with my *education* than I ever could with some hi-tech *costume.* That's when I decided to get back into investigative journalism.

I used the powers it gave me as a *vigilante* for a couple of years, which was cool and all, but I...

...I started having these *nightmares.* Really intense ones. I mean, I was in New York when some pretty bad stuff went down, and I... just had to get away.

I'm not cut out for seeing all the stuff I've seen, you know? I don't think *anyone* my age is. I'm sure I sound like a *coward,* but--

You're a brave guy, Chris. You always have been.

Julie, why don't you take the floor?

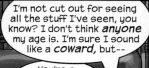

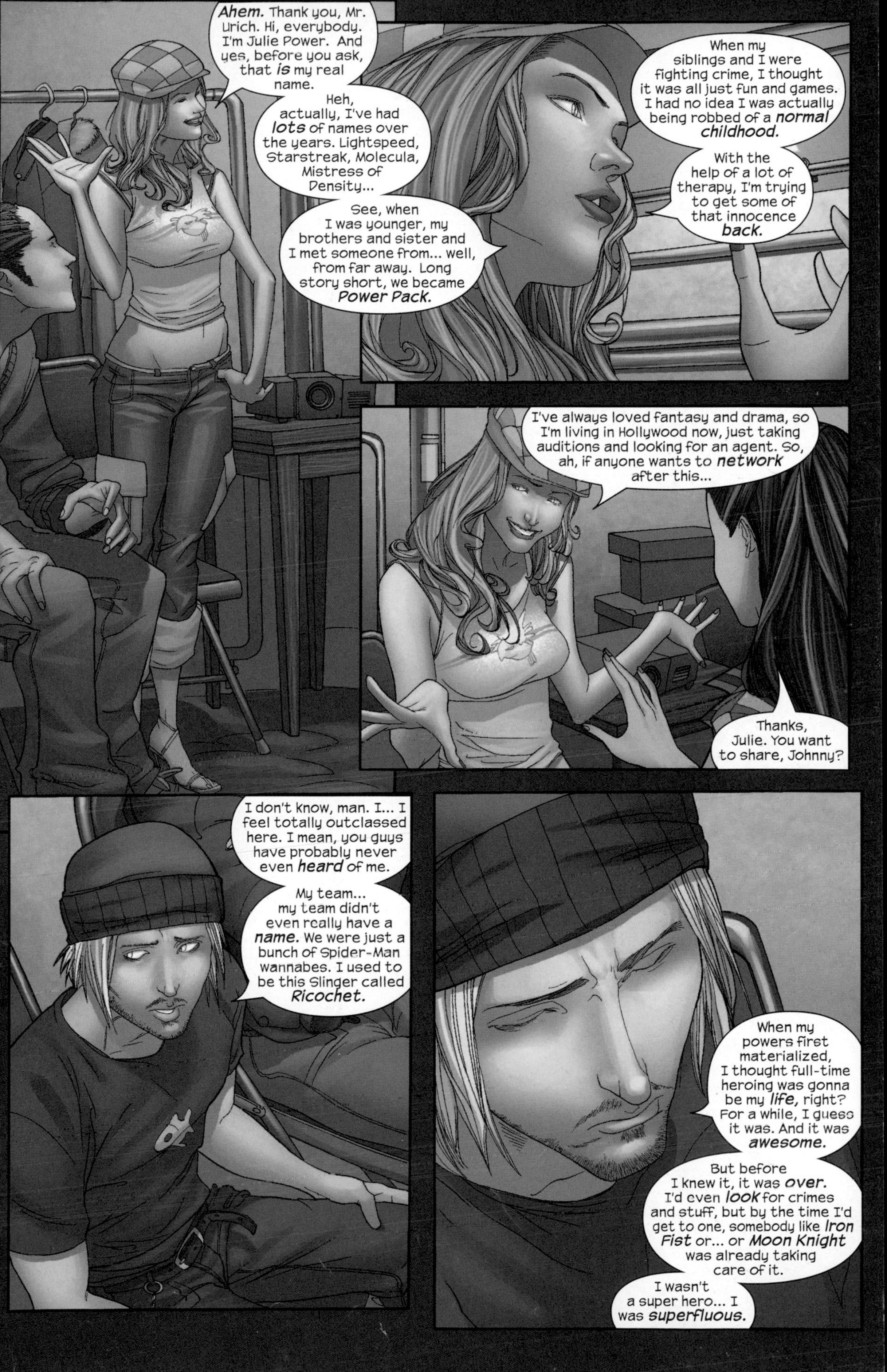

Ahem. Thank you, Mr. Urich. Hi, everybody. I'm Julie Power. And yes, before you ask, that is my real name.
Heh, actually, I've had lots of names over the years. Lightspeed, Starstreak, Molecula, Mistress of Density...
See, when I was younger, my brothers and sister and I met someone from... well, from far away. Long story short, we became Power Pack.
When my siblings and I were fighting crime, I thought it was all just fun and games. I had no idea I was actually being robbed of a normal childhood.
With the help of a lot of therapy, I'm trying to get some of that innocence back.
I've always loved fantasy and drama, so I'm living in Hollywood now, just taking auditions and looking for an agent. So, ah, if anyone wants to network after this...
Thanks, Julie. You want to share, Johnny?
I don't know, man. I... I feel totally outclassed here. I mean, you guys have probably never even heard of me.
My team... my team didn't even really have a name. We were just a bunch of Spider-Man wannabes. I used to be this Slinger called Ricochet.
When my powers first materialized, I thought full-time heroing was gonna be my life, right? For a while, I guess it was. And it was awesome.
But before I knew it, it was over. I'd even look for crimes and stuff, but by the time I'd get to one, somebody like Iron Fist or... or Moon Knight was already taking care of it.
I wasn't a super hero... I was superfluous.

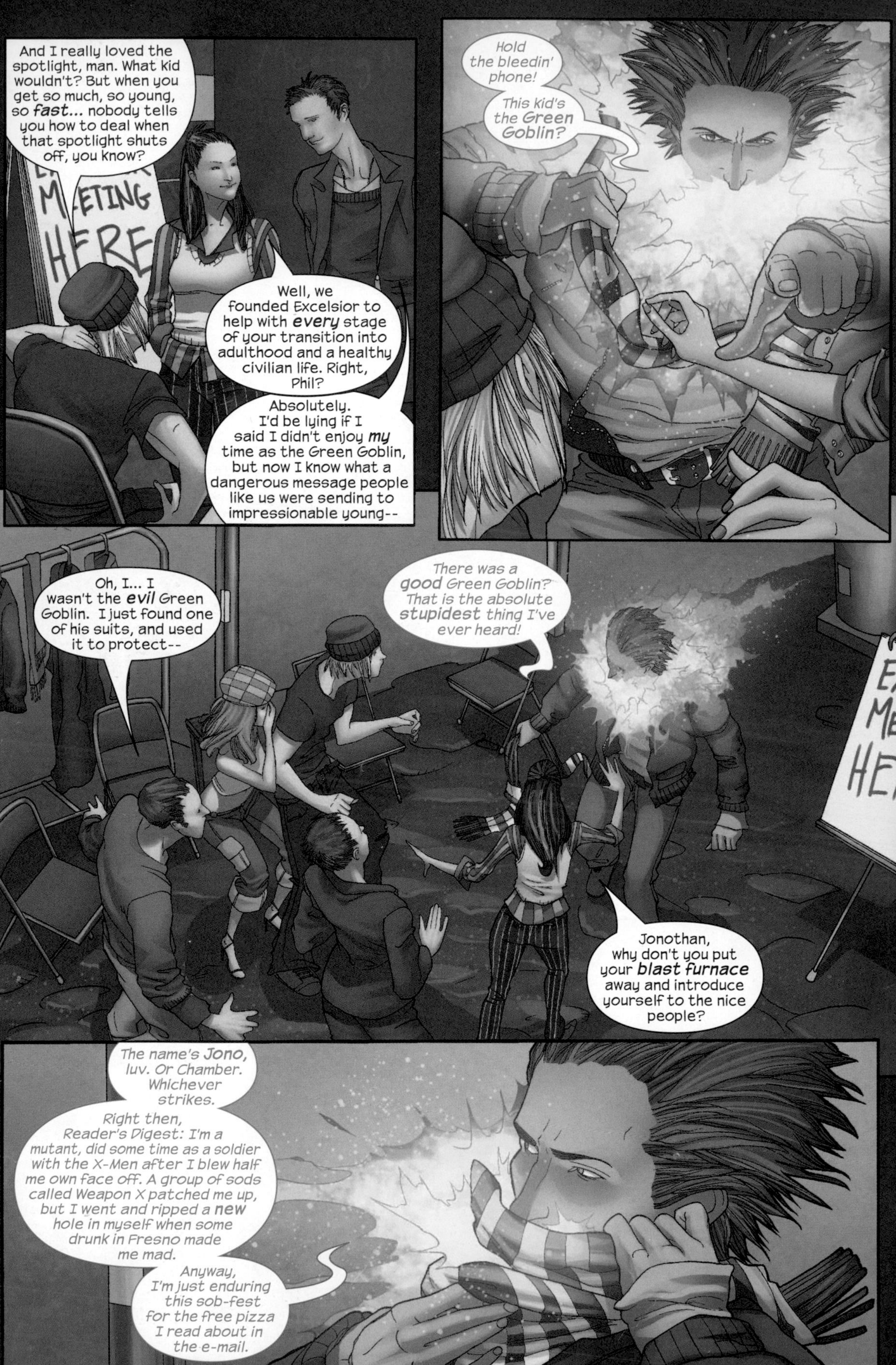
And I really loved the spotlight, man. What kid wouldn't? But when you get so much, so young, so *fast*... nobody tells you how to deal when that spotlight shuts off, you know?
M-ETING HERE
Well, we founded Excelsior to help with *every* stage of your transition into adulthood and a healthy civilian life. Right, Phil?
Absolutely. I'd be lying if I said I didn't enjoy *my* time as the Green Goblin, but now I know what a dangerous message people like us were sending to impressionable young--
Hold the bleedin' phone!
This kid's the *Green Goblin*?
Oh, I... I wasn't the *evil* Green Goblin. I just found one of his suits, and used it to protect--
There was a *good* Green Goblin? That is the absolute *stupidest* thing I've ever heard!
Jonothan, why don't you put your *blast furnace* away and introduce yourself to the nice people?
The name's *Jono*, luv. Or Chamber. Whichever strikes.
Right then, Reader's Digest: I'm a mutant, did some time as a soldier with the X-Men after I blew half me own face off. A group of sods called Weapon X patched me up, but I went and ripped a *new* hole in myself when some drunk in Fresno made me mad.
Anyway, I'm just enduring this sob-fest for the free pizza I read about in the e-mail.

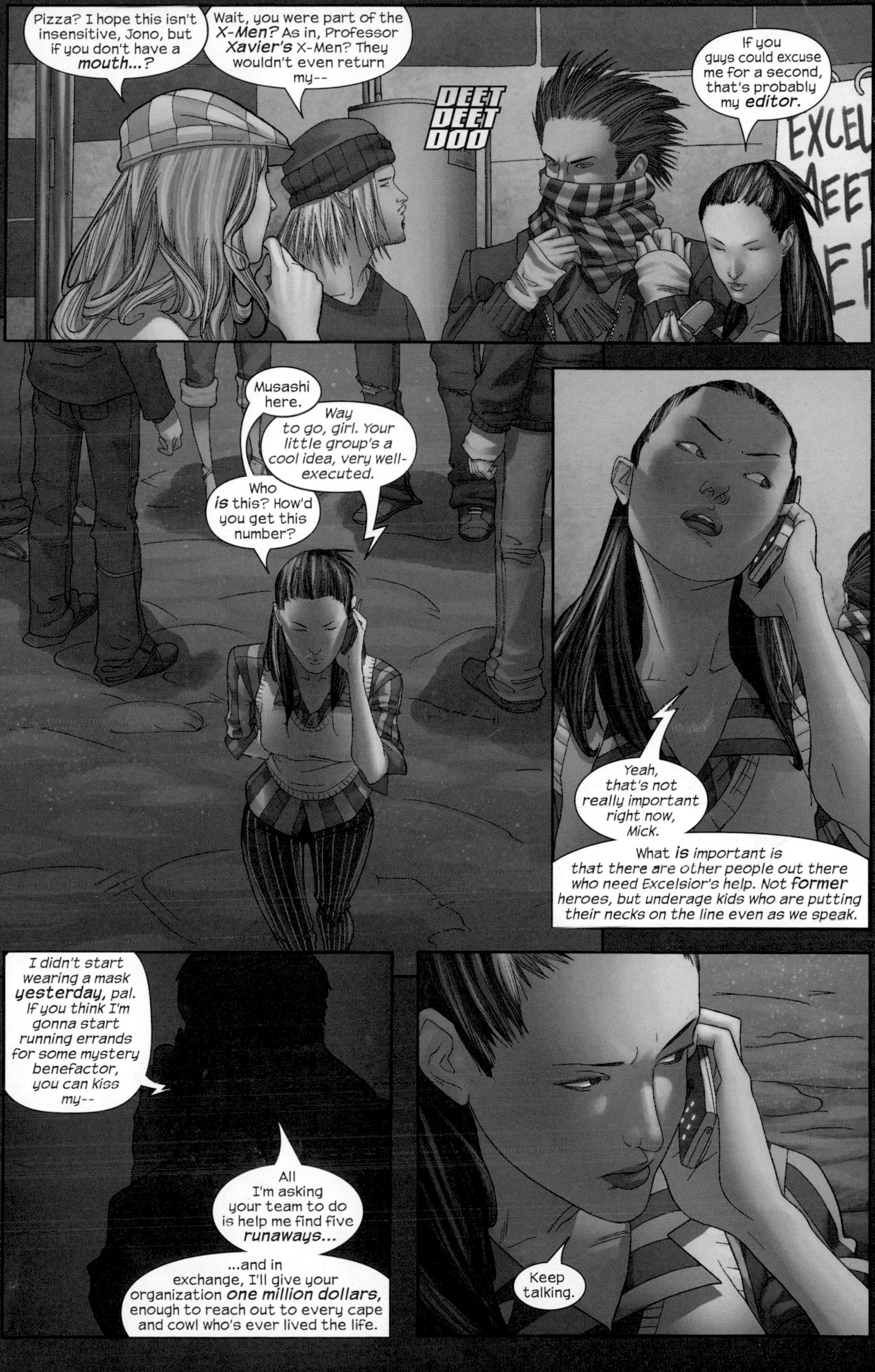
Pizza? I hope this isn't insensitive, Jono, but if you don't have a mouth...?
Wait, you were part of the X-Men? As in, Professor Xavier's X-Men? They wouldn't even return my--
DEET DEET DOO
If you guys could excuse me for a second, that's probably my editor.
EXCEL
MEET
Musashi here.
Way to go, girl. Your little group's a cool idea, very well-executed.
Who is this? How'd you get this number?
Yeah, that's not really important right now, Mick.
What is important is that there are other people out there who need Excelsior's help. Not former heroes, but underage kids who are putting their necks on the line even as we speak.
I didn't start wearing a mask yesterday, pal. If you think I'm gonna start running errands for some mystery benefactor, you can kiss my--
All I'm asking your team to do is help me find five runaways...
...and in exchange, I'll give your organization one million dollars, enough to reach out to every cape and cowl who's ever lived the life.
Keep talking.

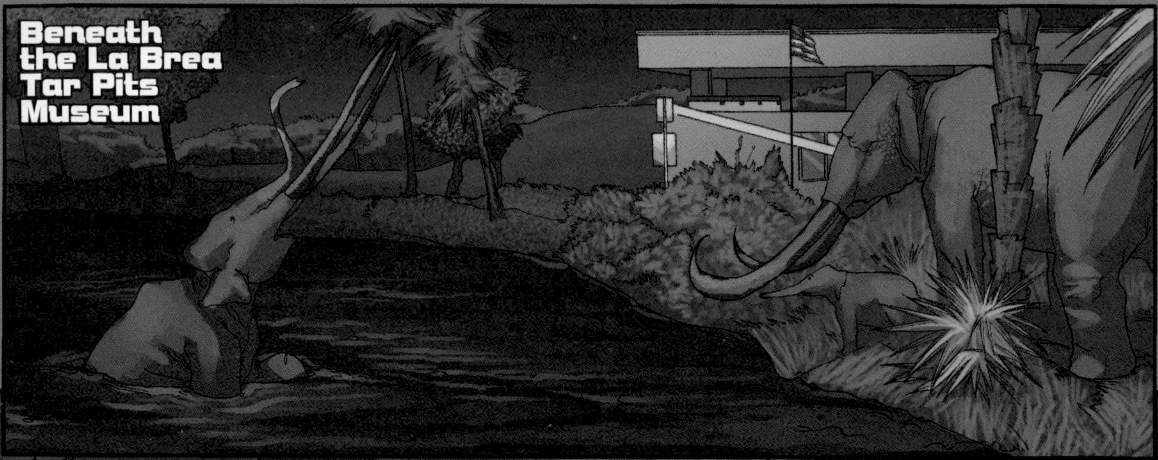
Beneath the La Brea Tar Pits Museum

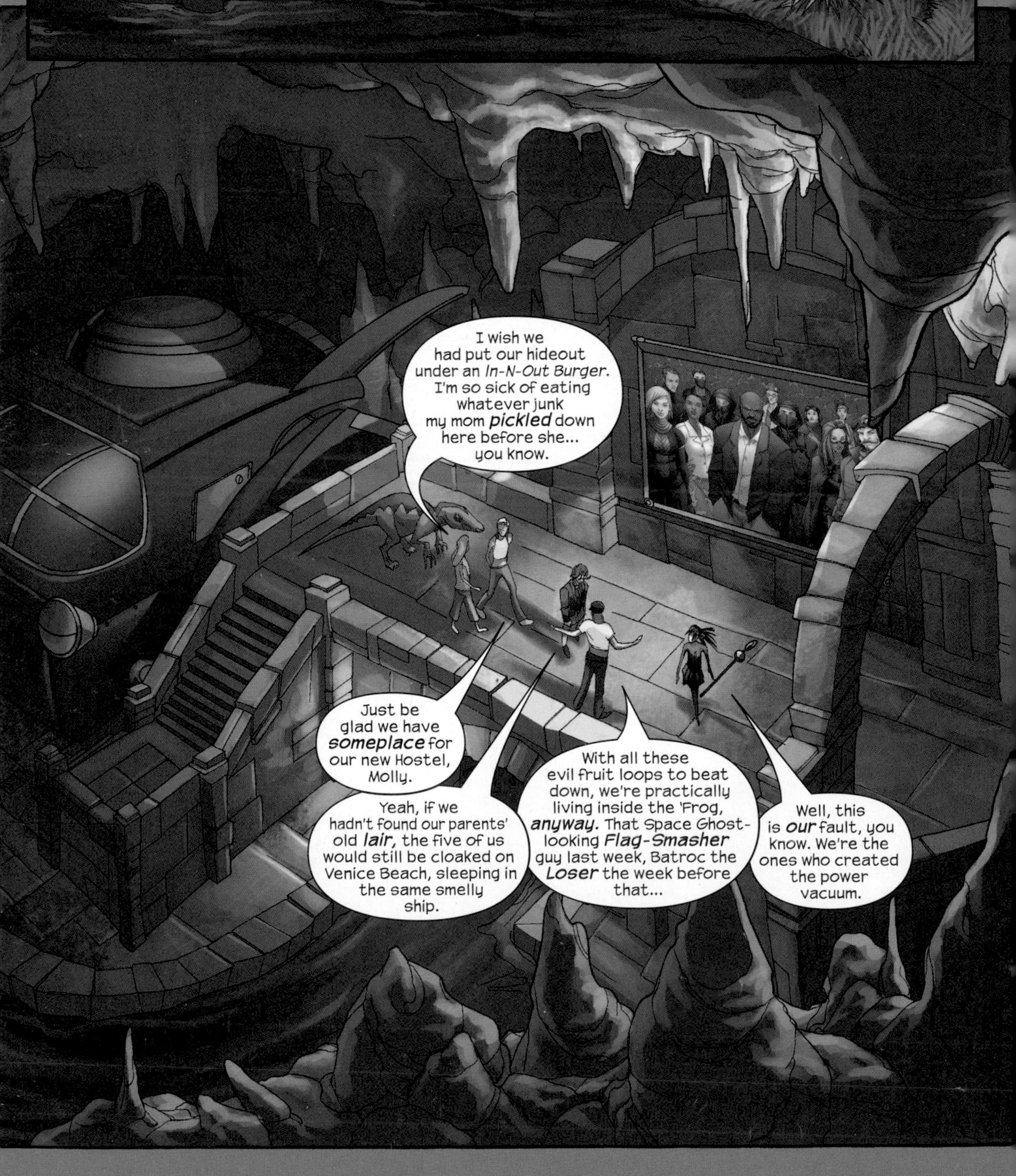
I wish we had put our hideout under an In-N-Out Burger. I'm so sick of eating whatever junk my mom pickled down here before she... you know.
Just be glad we have someplace for our new Hostel, Molly.
Yeah, if we hadn't found our parents' old lair, the five of us would still be cloaked on Venice Beach, sleeping in the same smelly ship.
With all these evil fruit loops to beat down, we're practically living inside the 'Frog, anyway. That Space Ghost-looking Flag-Smasher guy last week, Batroc the Loser the week before that...
Well, this is our fault, you know. We're the ones who created the power vacuum.

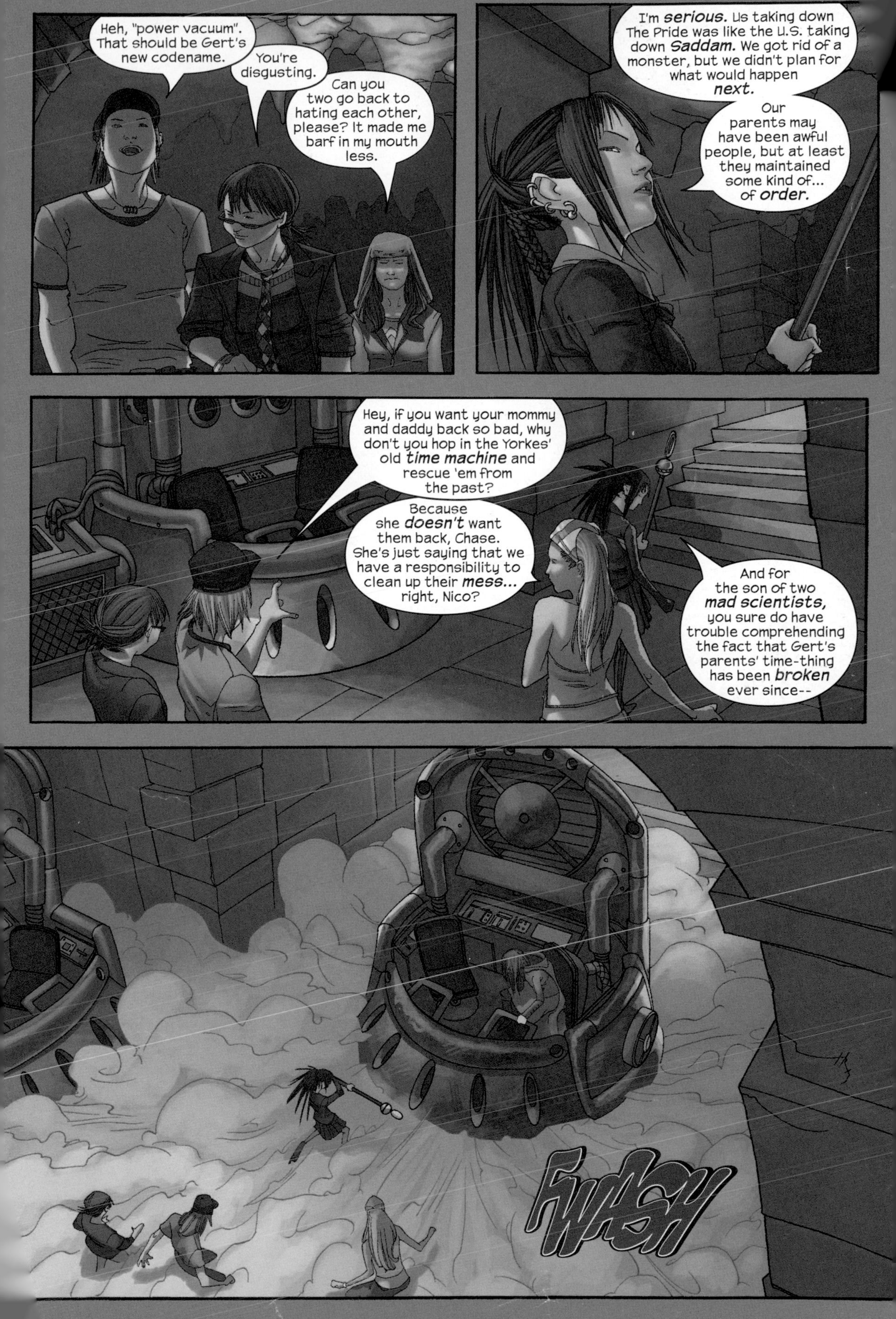
Heh, "power vacuum". That should be Gert's new codename.
You're disgusting.
Can you two go back to hating each other, please? It made me barf in my mouth less.
I'm *serious.* Us taking down The Pride was like the U.S. taking down *Saddam.* We got rid of a monster, but we didn't plan for what would happen *next.*
Our parents may have been awful people, but at least they maintained some kind of... of *order.*
Hey, if you want your mommy and daddy back so bad, why don't you hop in the Yorkes' old *time machine* and rescue 'em from the past?
Because she *doesn't* want them back, Chase. She's just saying that we have a responsibility to clean up their *mess...* right, Nico?
And for the son of two *mad scientists,* you sure do have trouble comprehending the fact that Gert's parents' time-thing has been *broken* ever since--
FWASH

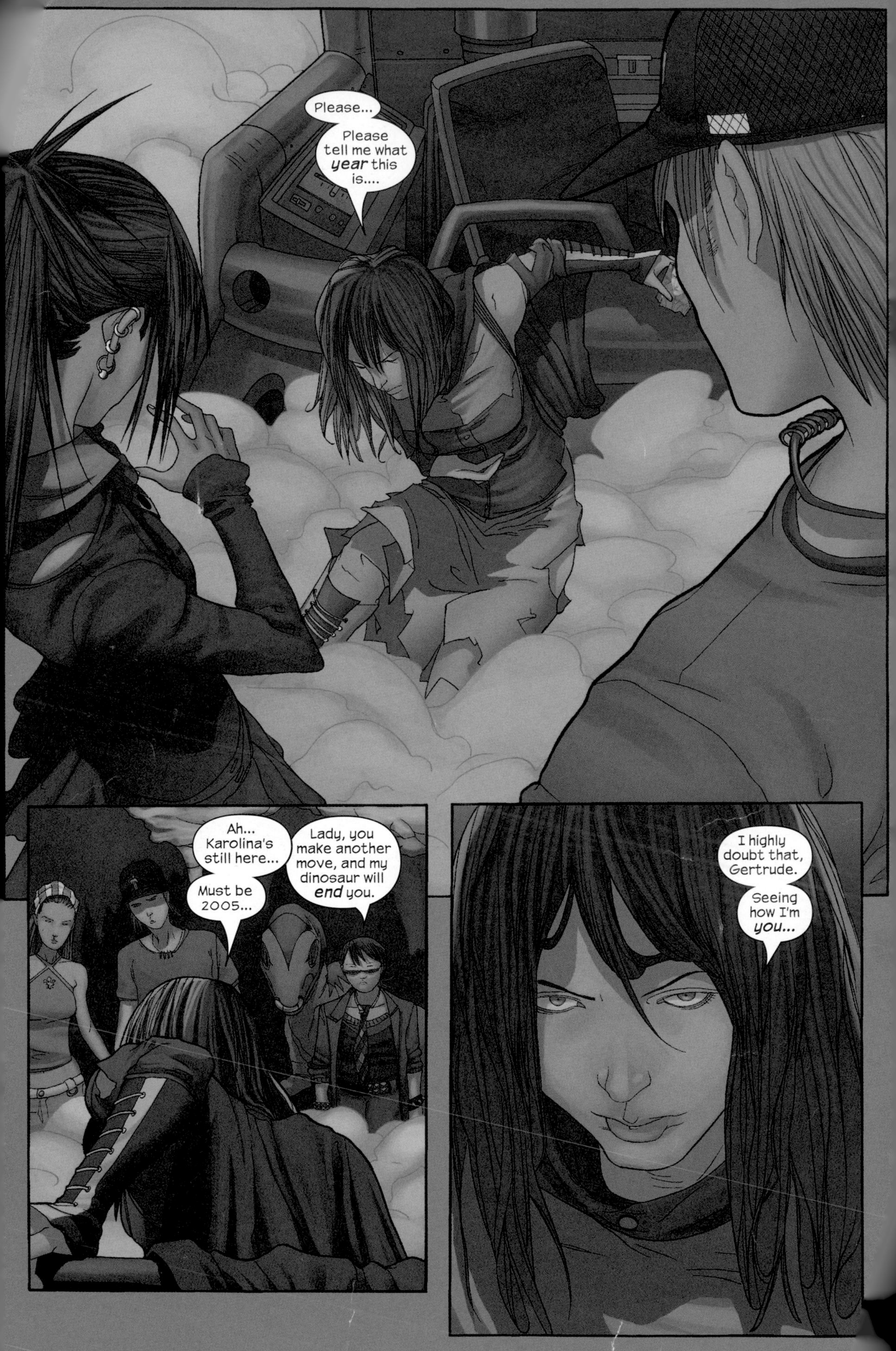
Please...
Please tell me what *year* this is....
Ah... Karolina's still here...
Must be 2005...
Lady, you make another move, and my dinosaur will *end* you.
I highly doubt that, Gertrude.
Seeing how I'm *you...*

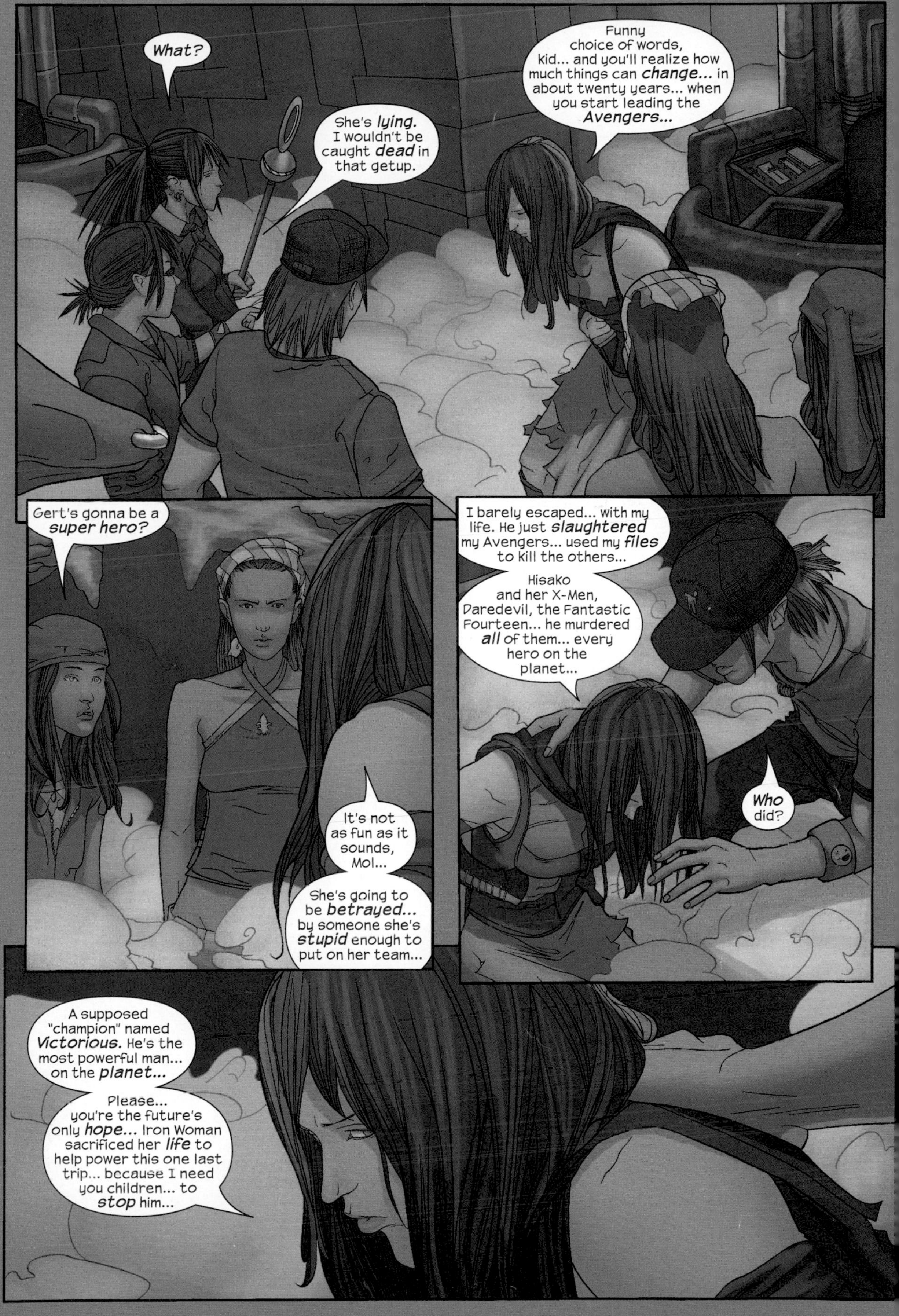
What?
She's lying. I wouldn't be caught dead in that getup.
Funny choice of words, kid... and you'll realize how much things can change... in about twenty years... when you start leading the Avengers...
Gert's gonna be a super hero?
It's not as fun as it sounds, Mol...
She's going to be betrayed... by someone she's stupid enough to put on her team...
I barely escaped... with my life. He just slaughtered my Avengers... used my files to kill the others...
Hisako and her X-Men, Daredevil, the Fantastic Fourteen... he murdered all of them... every hero on the planet...
Who did?
A supposed "champion" named Victorious. He's the most powerful man... on the planet...
Please... you're the future's only hope... Iron Woman sacrificed her life to help power this one last trip... because I need you children... to stop him...

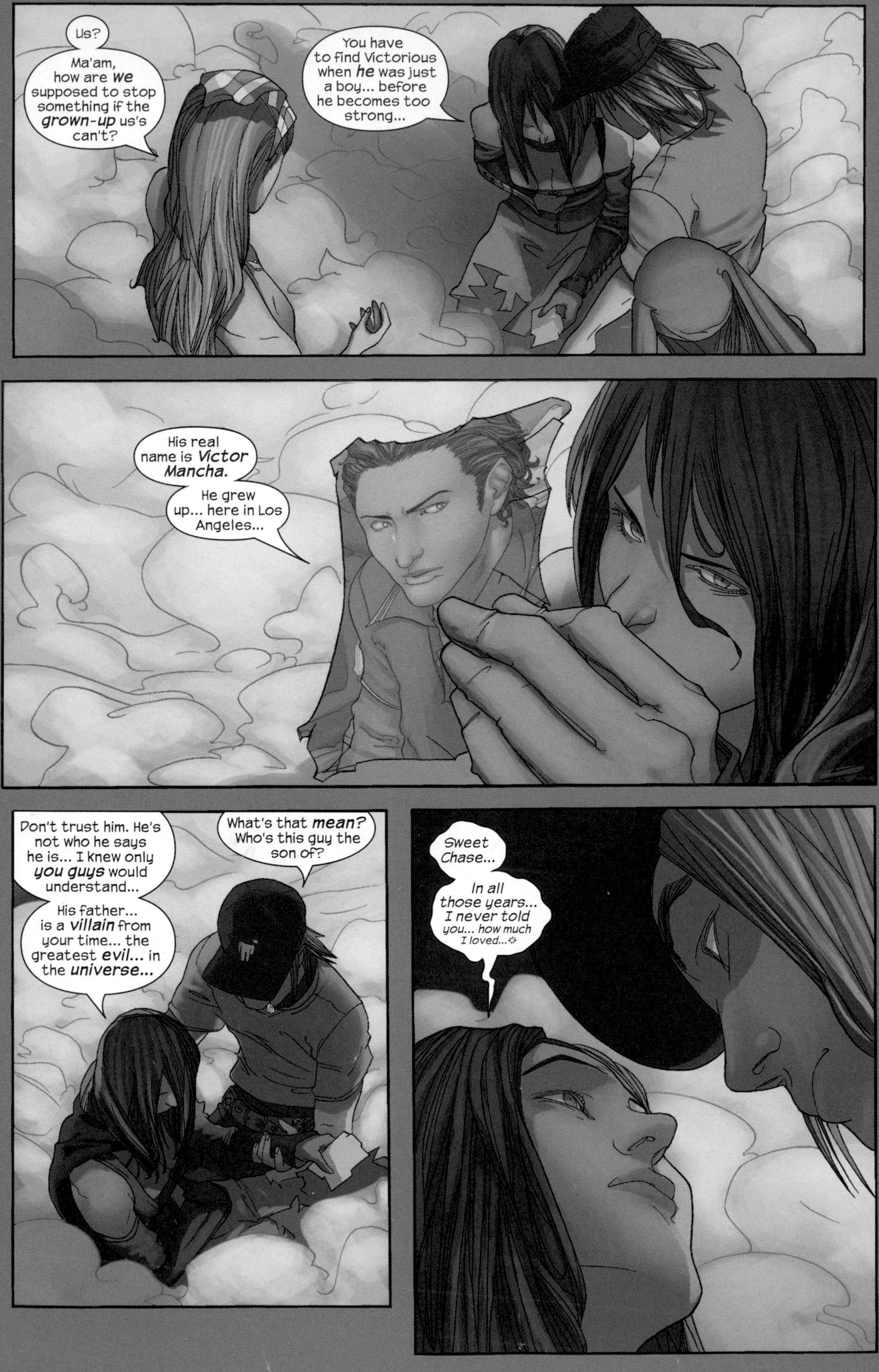
Us?
Ma'am, how are **we** supposed to stop something if the ***grown-up*** us's can't?
You have to find Victorious when ***he*** was just a boy... before he becomes too strong...
His real name is ***Victor Mancha.***
He grew up... here in Los Angeles...
Don't trust him. He's not who he says he is... I knew only ***you guys*** would understand...
His father... is a ***villain*** from your time... the greatest ***evil...*** in the ***universe...***
What's that ***mean?*** Who's this guy the son of?
Sweet Chase...
In all those years... I never told you... how much I loved...

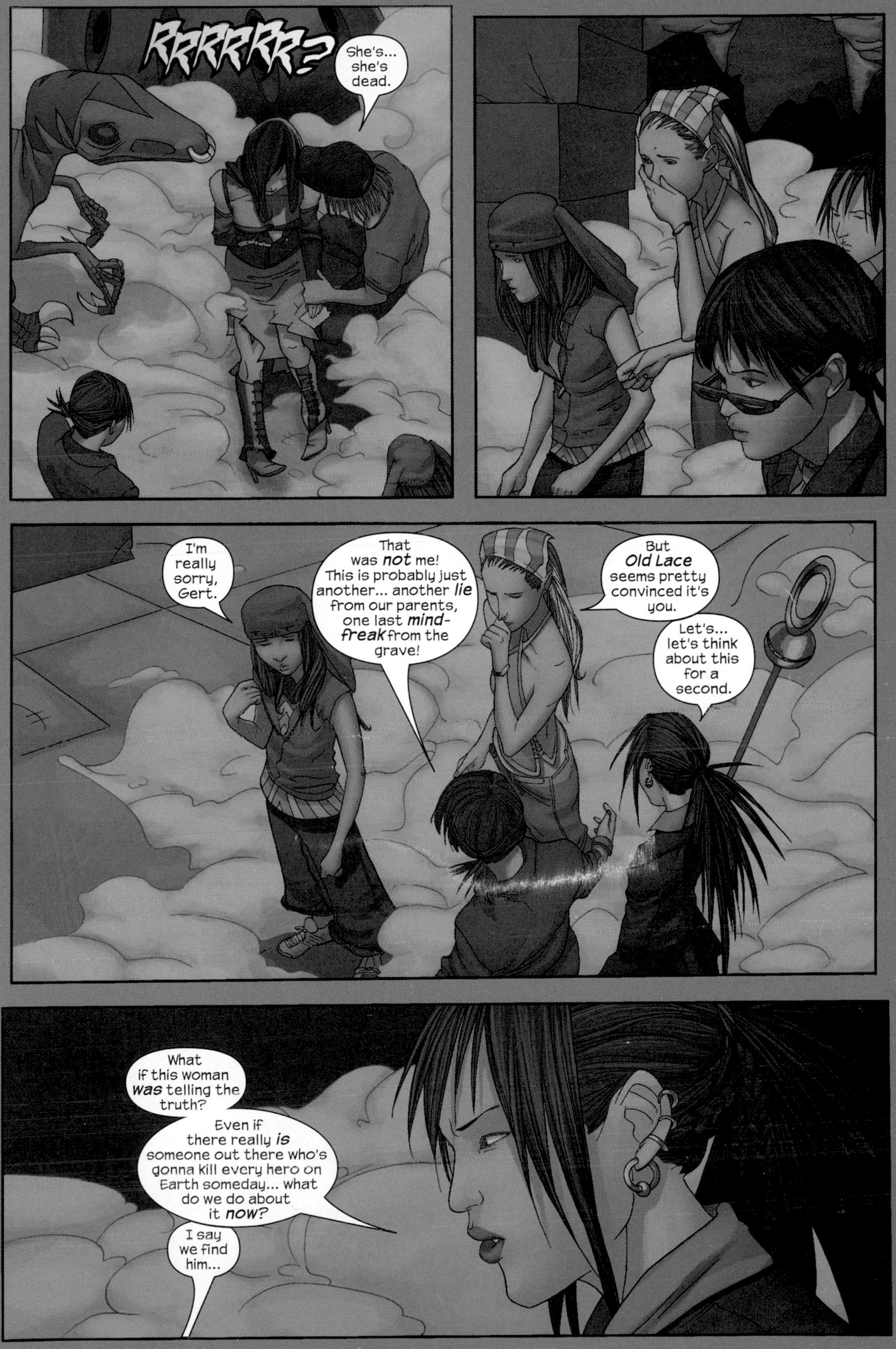
RRRRRR?
She's... she's dead.
I'm really sorry, Gert.
That was *not* me! This is probably just another... another *lie* from our parents, one last *mind-freak* from the grave!
But *Old Lace* seems pretty convinced it's you.
Let's... let's think about this for a second.
What if this woman *was* telling the truth?
Even if there really *is* someone out there who's gonna kill every hero on Earth someday... what do we do about it *now?*
I say we find him...

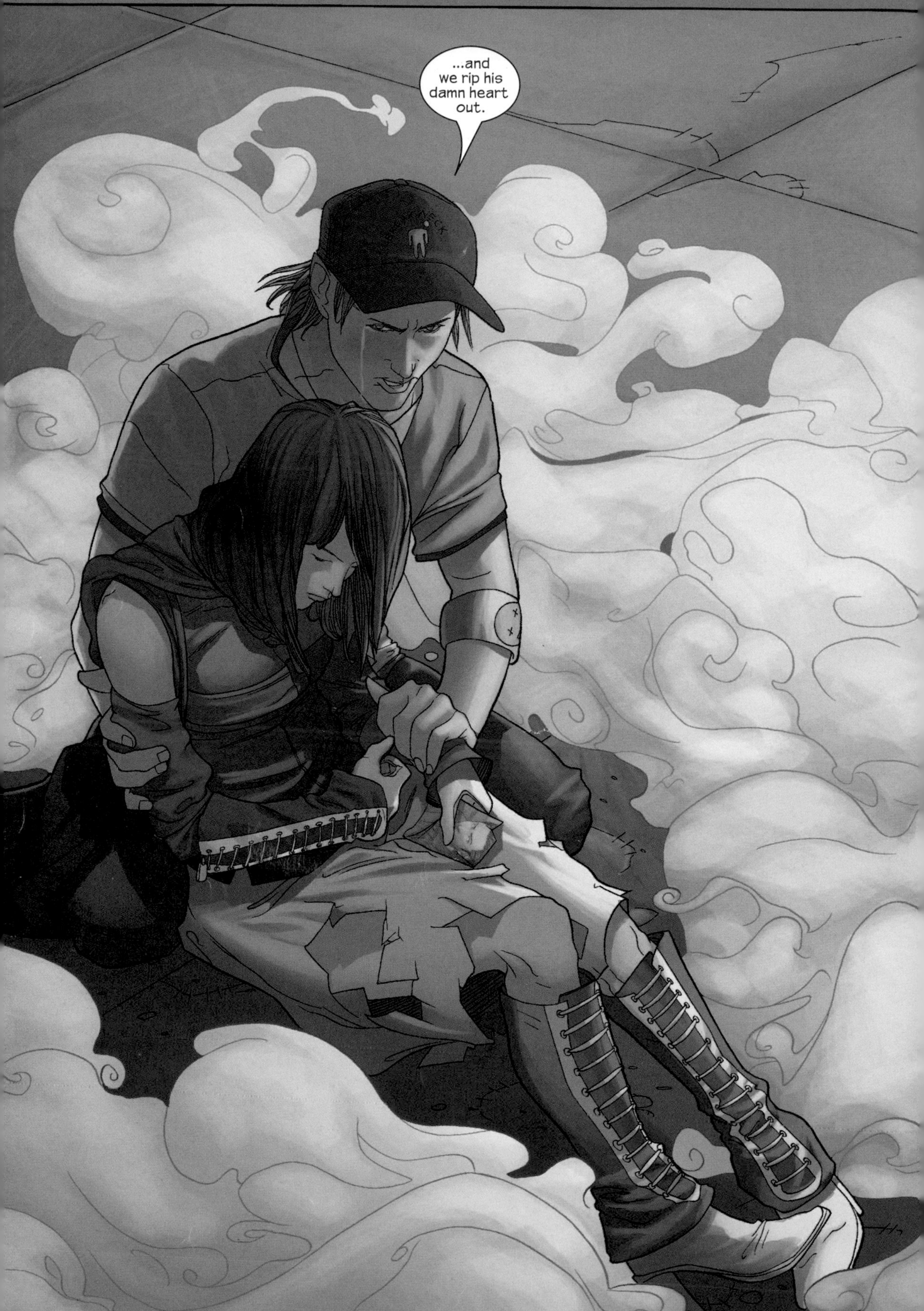
...and we rip his damn heart out.

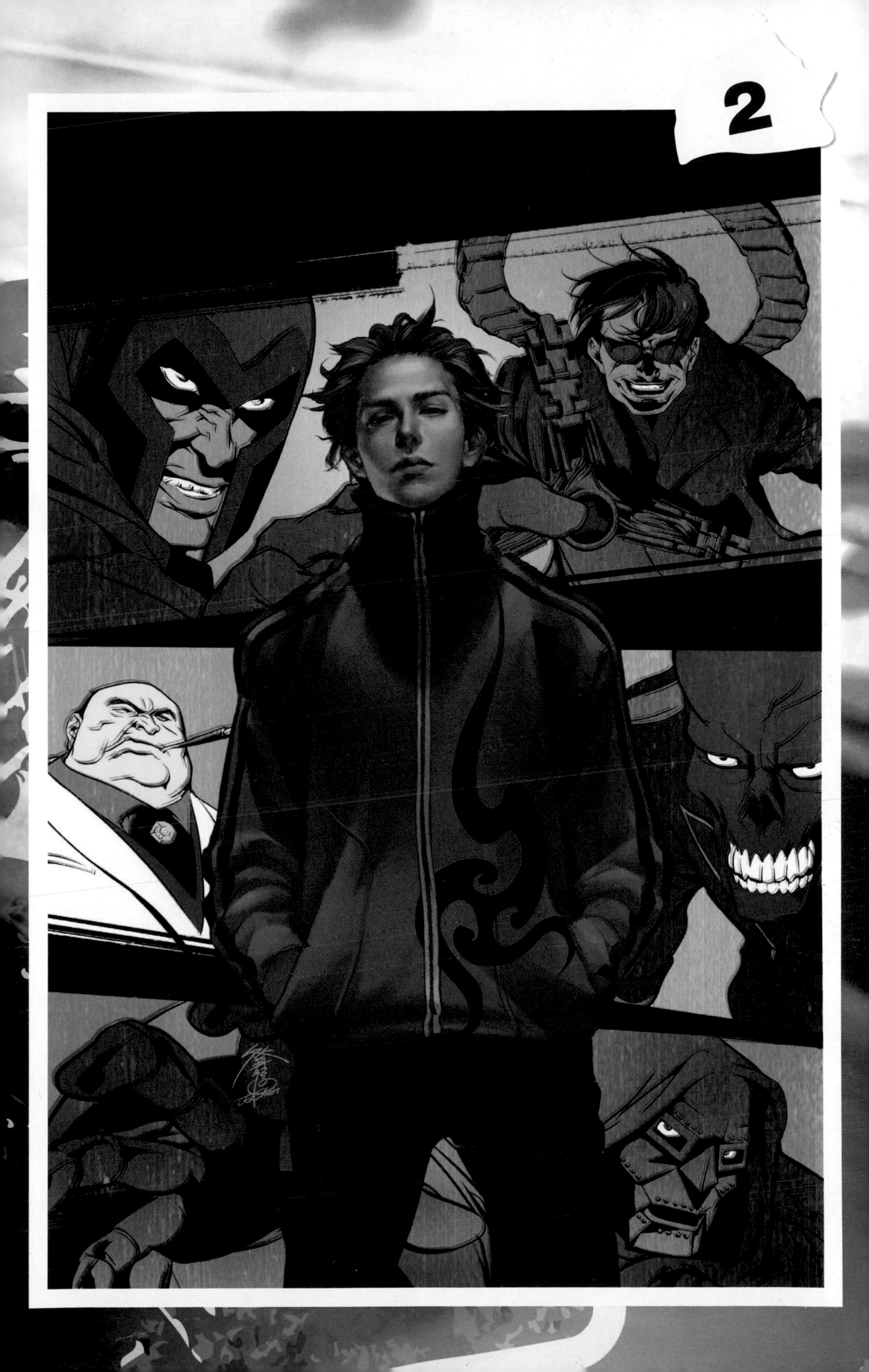
2

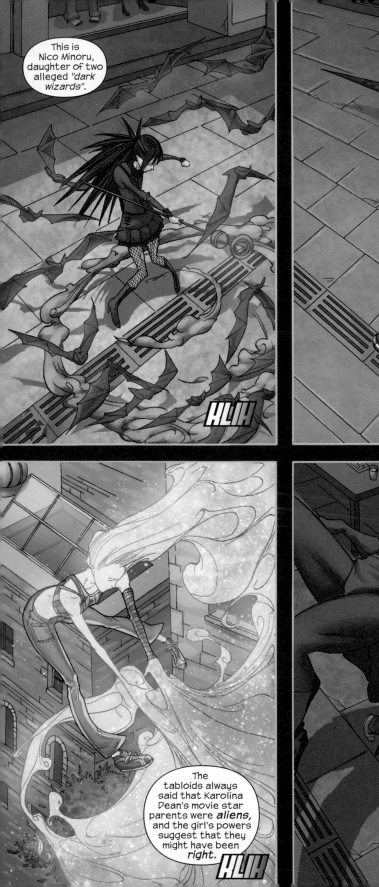

This is Nico Minoru, daughter of two alleged "dark wizards".

Gertrude Yorkes with her pet *velociraptor*, which was probably stolen from another era by her time-traveling mom and dad.

KLIK

KLIK

The tabloids always said that Karolina Dean's movie star parents were *aliens*, and the girl's powers suggest that they might have been *right*.

And Molly Hayes, the preternaturally strong child of evil mutants. Not that all mutants are *evil*, of course, but... you know.

KLIK

KLIK

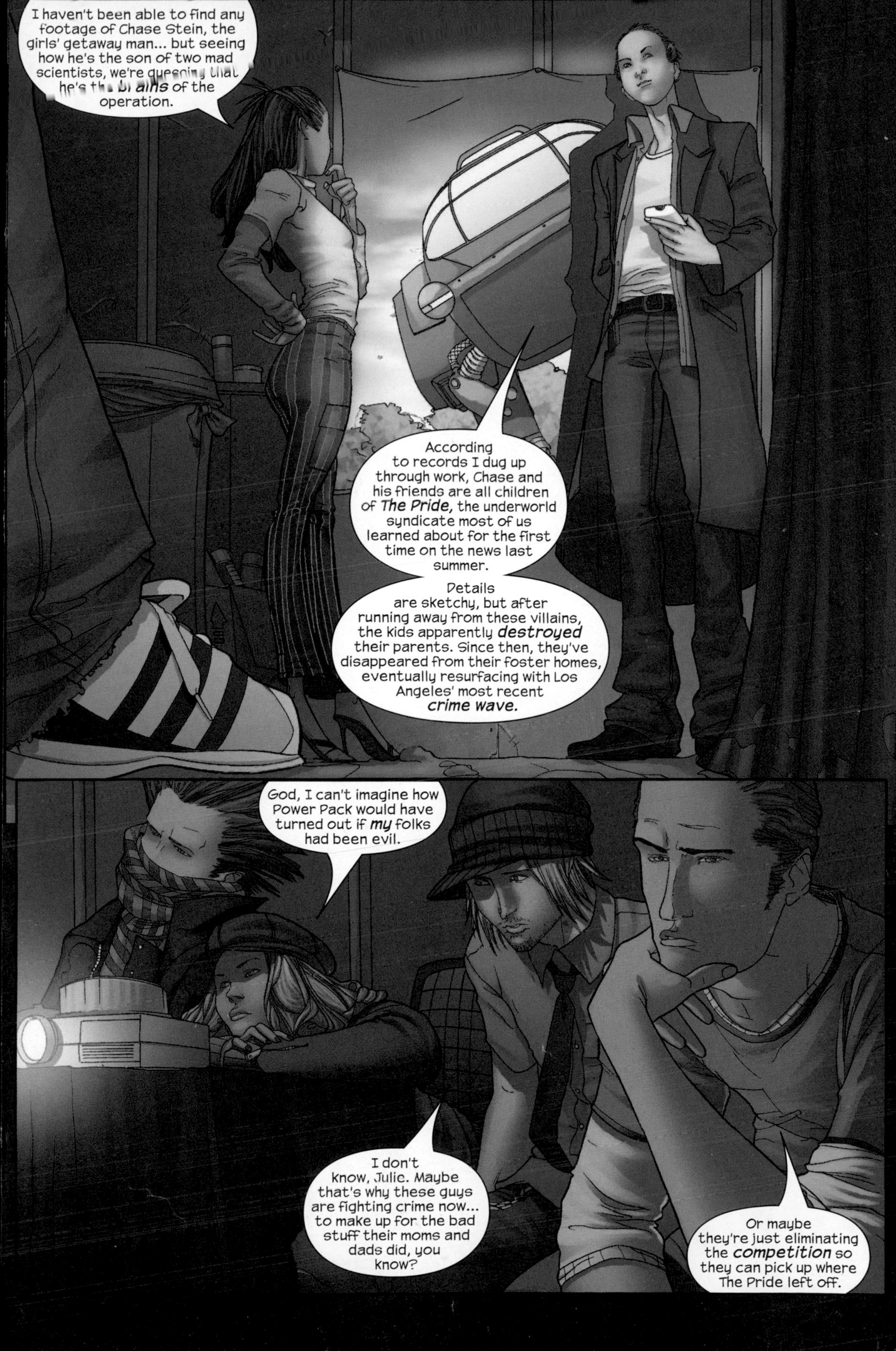
I haven't been able to find any footage of Chase Stein, the girls' getaway man... but seeing how he's the son of two mad scientists, we're guessing that he's the brains of the operation.
According to records I dug up through work, Chase and his friends are all children of The Pride, the underworld syndicate most of us learned about for the first time on the news last summer.
Details are sketchy, but after running away from these villains, the kids apparently destroyed their parents. Since then, they've disappeared from their foster homes, eventually resurfacing with Los Angeles' most recent crime wave.
God, I can't imagine how Power Pack would have turned out if my folks had been evil.
I don't know, Julie. Maybe that's why these guys are fighting crime now... to make up for the bad stuff their moms and dads did, you know?
Or maybe they're just eliminating the competition so they can pick up where The Pride left off.

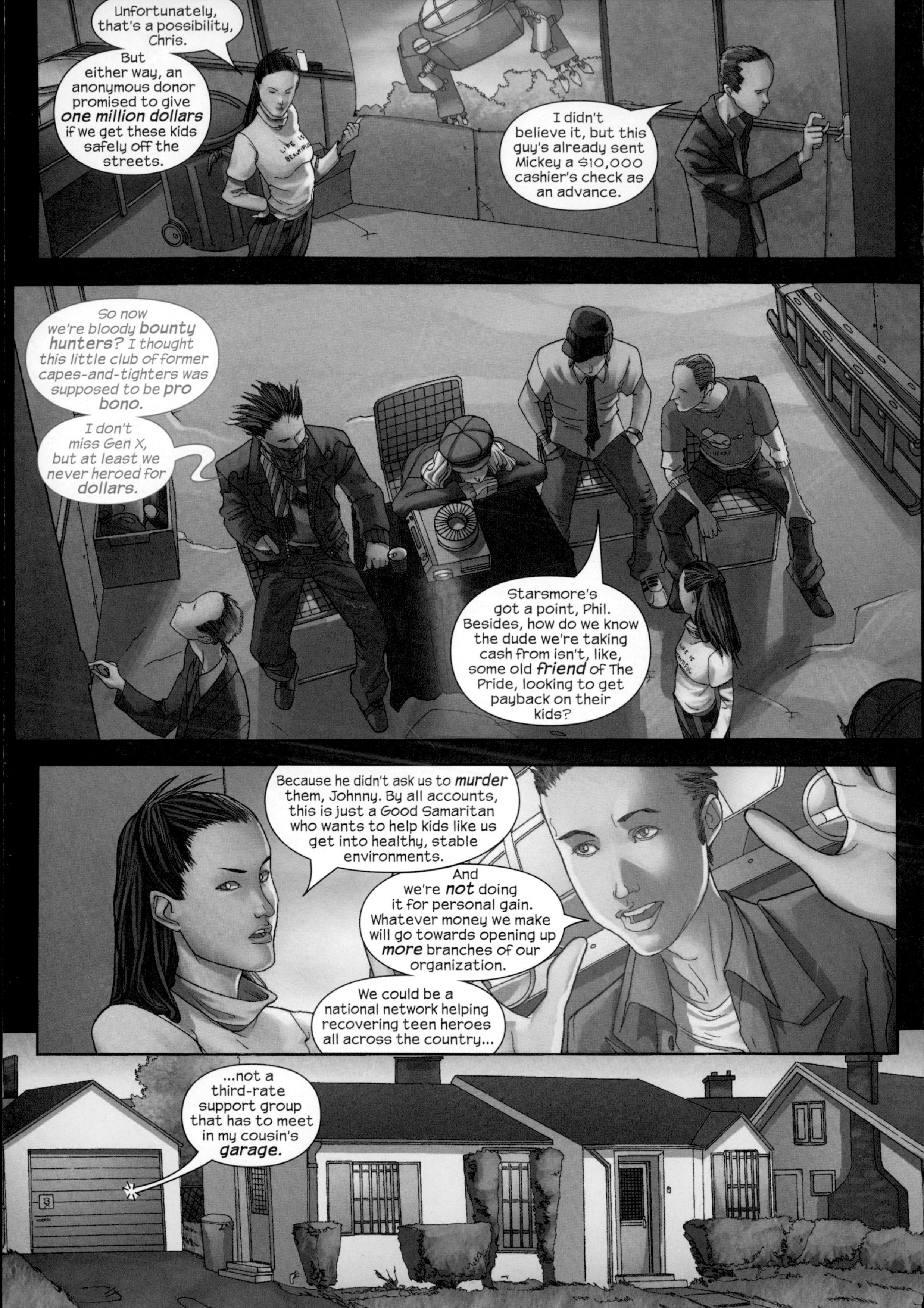
Unfortunately, that's a possibility, Chris.
But either way, an anonymous donor promised to give one million dollars if we get these kids safely off the streets.
I didn't believe it, but this guy's already sent Mickey a $10,000 cashier's check as an advance.
So now we're bloody bounty hunters? I thought this little club of former capes-and-tighters was supposed to be pro bono.
I don't miss Gen X, but at least we never heroed for dollars.
Starsmore's got a point, Phil. Besides, how do we know the dude we're taking cash from isn't, like, some old friend of The Pride, looking to get payback on their kids?
Because he didn't ask us to murder them, Johnny. By all accounts, this is just a Good Samaritan who wants to help kids like us get into healthy, stable environments.
And we're not doing it for personal gain. Whatever money we make will go towards opening up more branches of our organization.
We could be a national network helping recovering teen heroes all across the country...
...not a third-rate support group that has to meet in my cousin's garage.

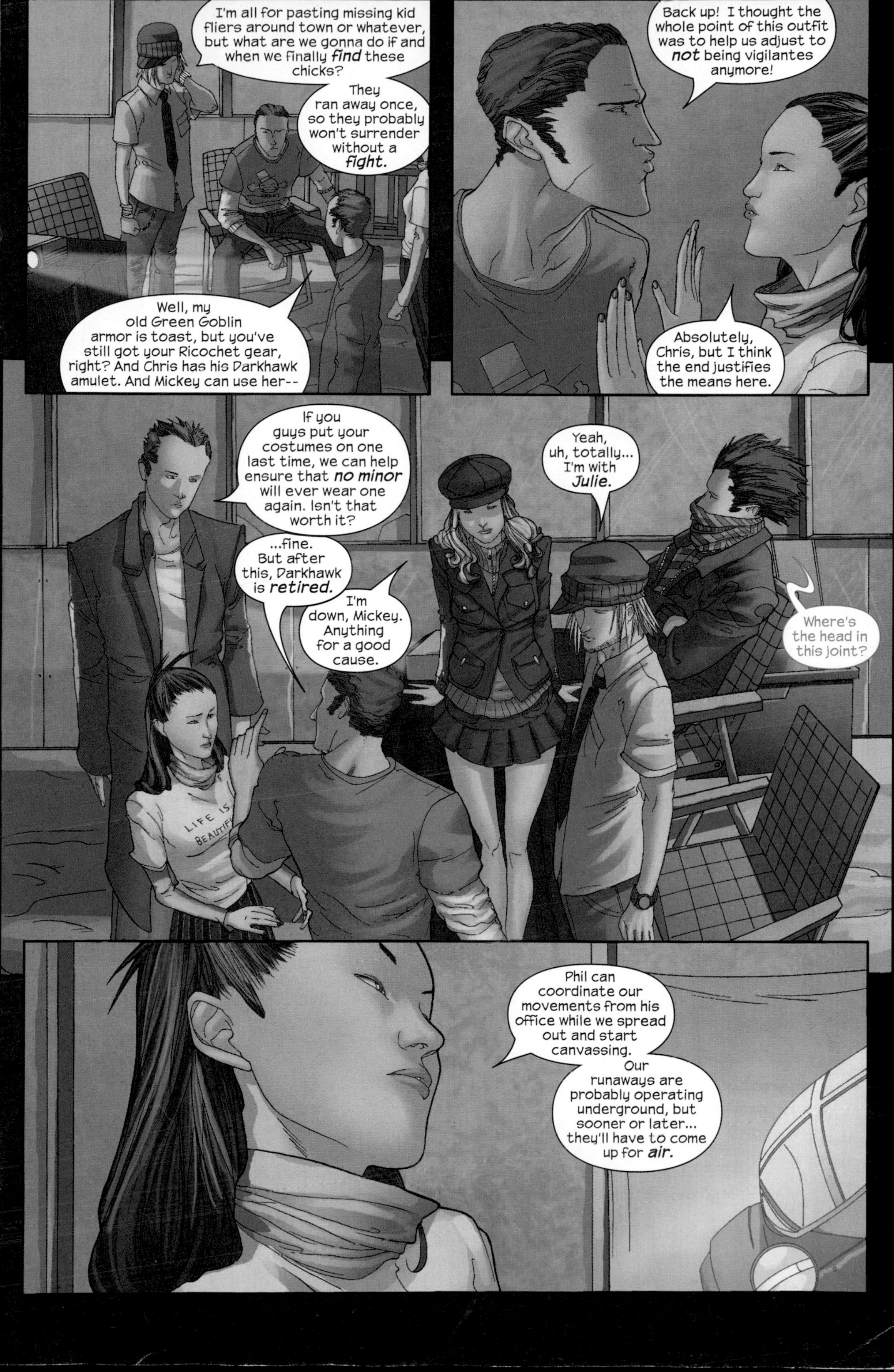
I'm all for pasting missing kid fliers around town or whatever, but what are we gonna do if and when we finally *find* these chicks?
They ran away once, so they probably won't surrender without a *fight.*
Well, my old Green Goblin armor is toast, but you've still got your Ricochet gear, right? And Chris has his Darkhawk amulet. And Mickey can use her--
Back up! I thought the whole point of this outfit was to help us adjust to *not* being vigilantes anymore!
Absolutely, Chris, but I think the end justifies the means here.
If you guys put your costumes on one last time, we can help ensure that *no minor* will ever wear one again. Isn't that worth it?
...fine. But after this, Darkhawk is *retired.*
I'm down, Mickey. Anything for a good cause.
Yeah, uh, totally... I'm with *Julie.*
Where's the head in this joint?
LIFE IS BEAUTIFUL
Phil can coordinate our movements from his office while we spread out and start canvassing.
Our runaways are probably operating underground, but sooner or later... they'll have to come up for *air.*

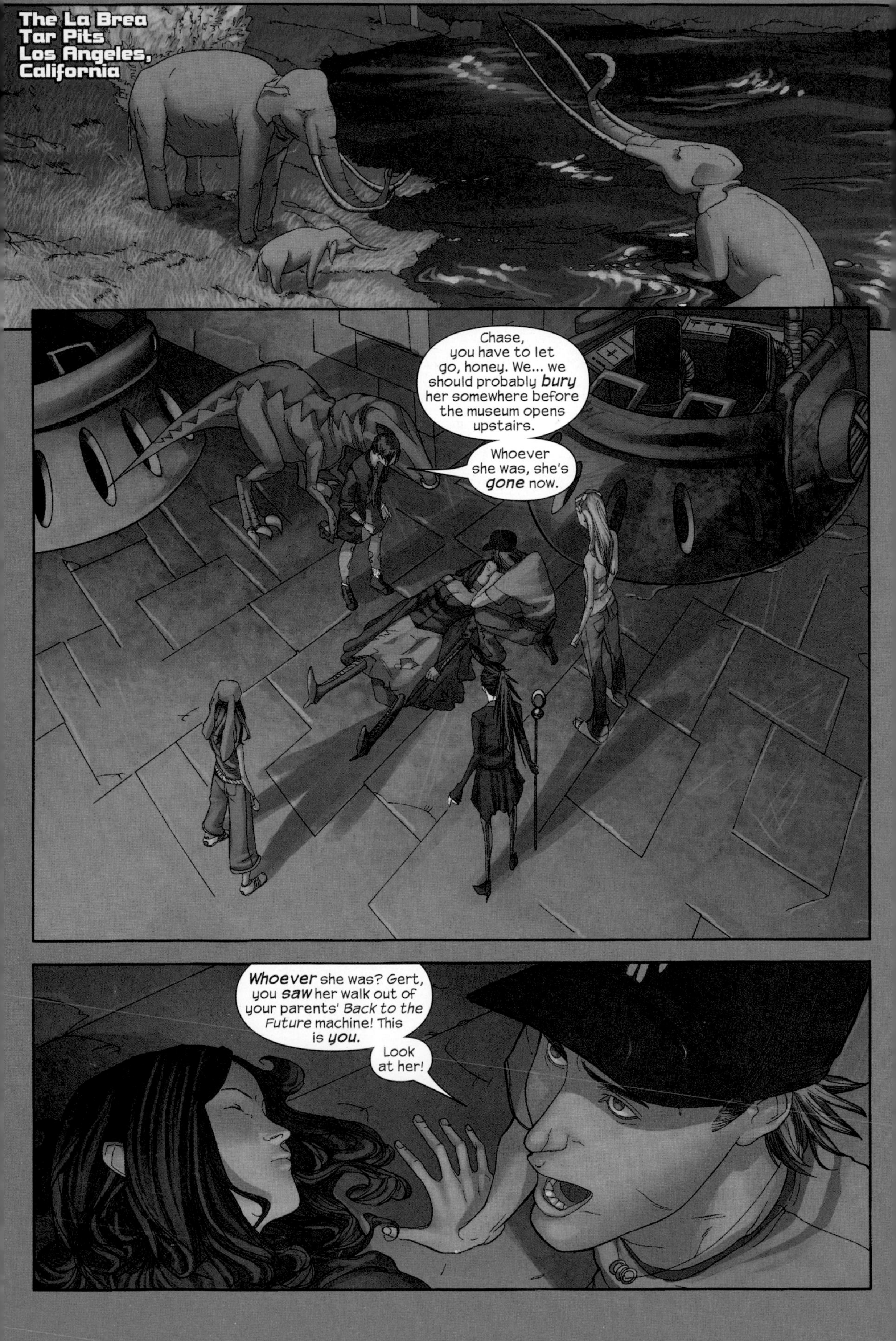
The La Brea Tar Pits Los Angeles, California
Chase, you have to let go, honey. We... we should probably bury her somewhere before the museum opens upstairs.
Whoever she was, she's gone now.
Whoever she was? Gert, you saw her walk out of your parents' Back to the Future machine! This is you.
Look at her!

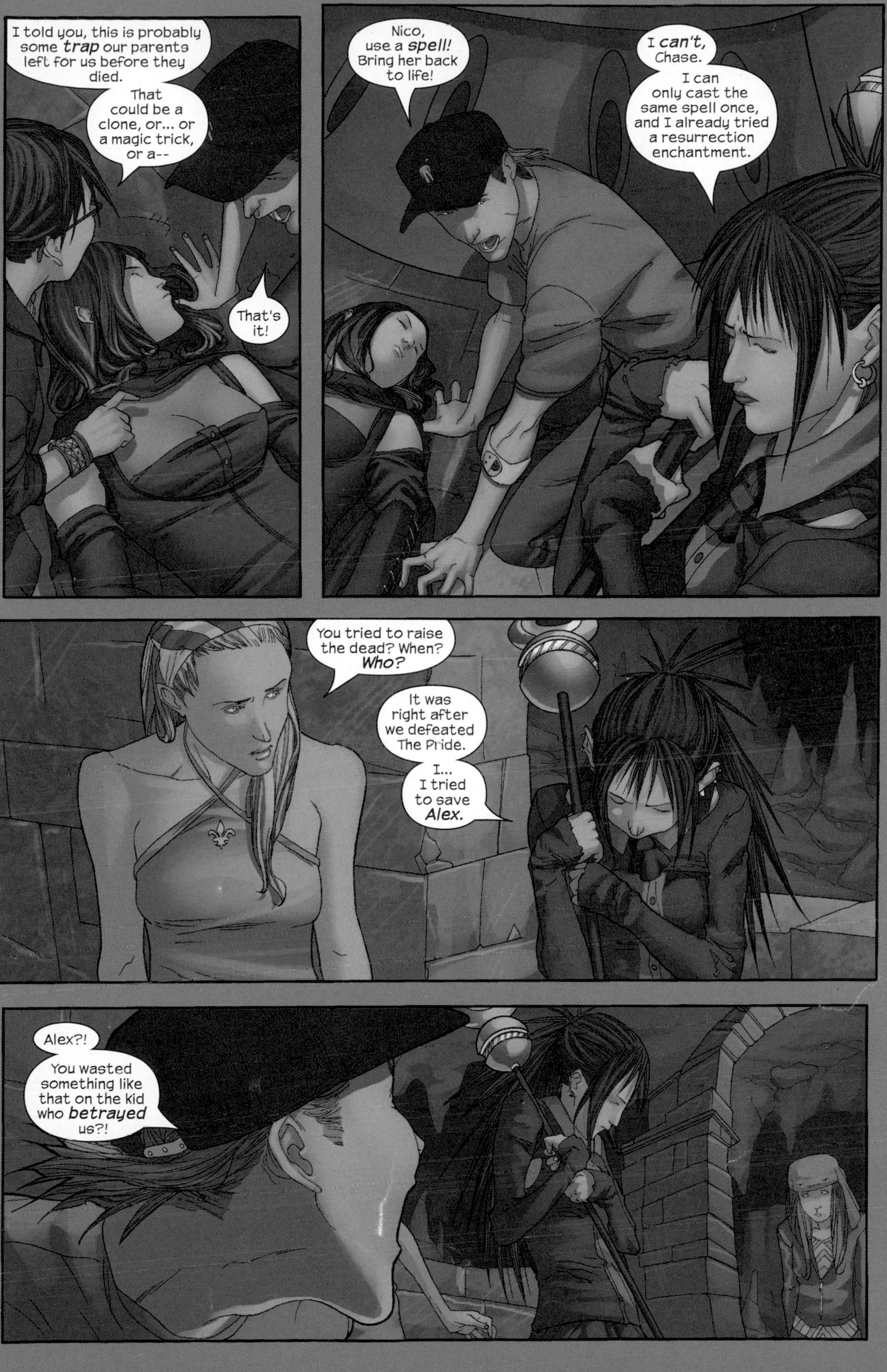
I told you, this is probably some *trap* our parents left for us before they died.
That could be a clone, or... or a magic trick, or a--
That's it!
Nico, use a *spell!* Bring her back to life!
I *can't,* Chase.
I can only cast the same spell once, and I already tried a resurrection enchantment.
You tried to raise the dead? When? ***Who?***
It was right after we defeated The Pride.
I... I tried to save ***Alex.***
Alex?!
You wasted something like that on the kid who ***betrayed*** us?!

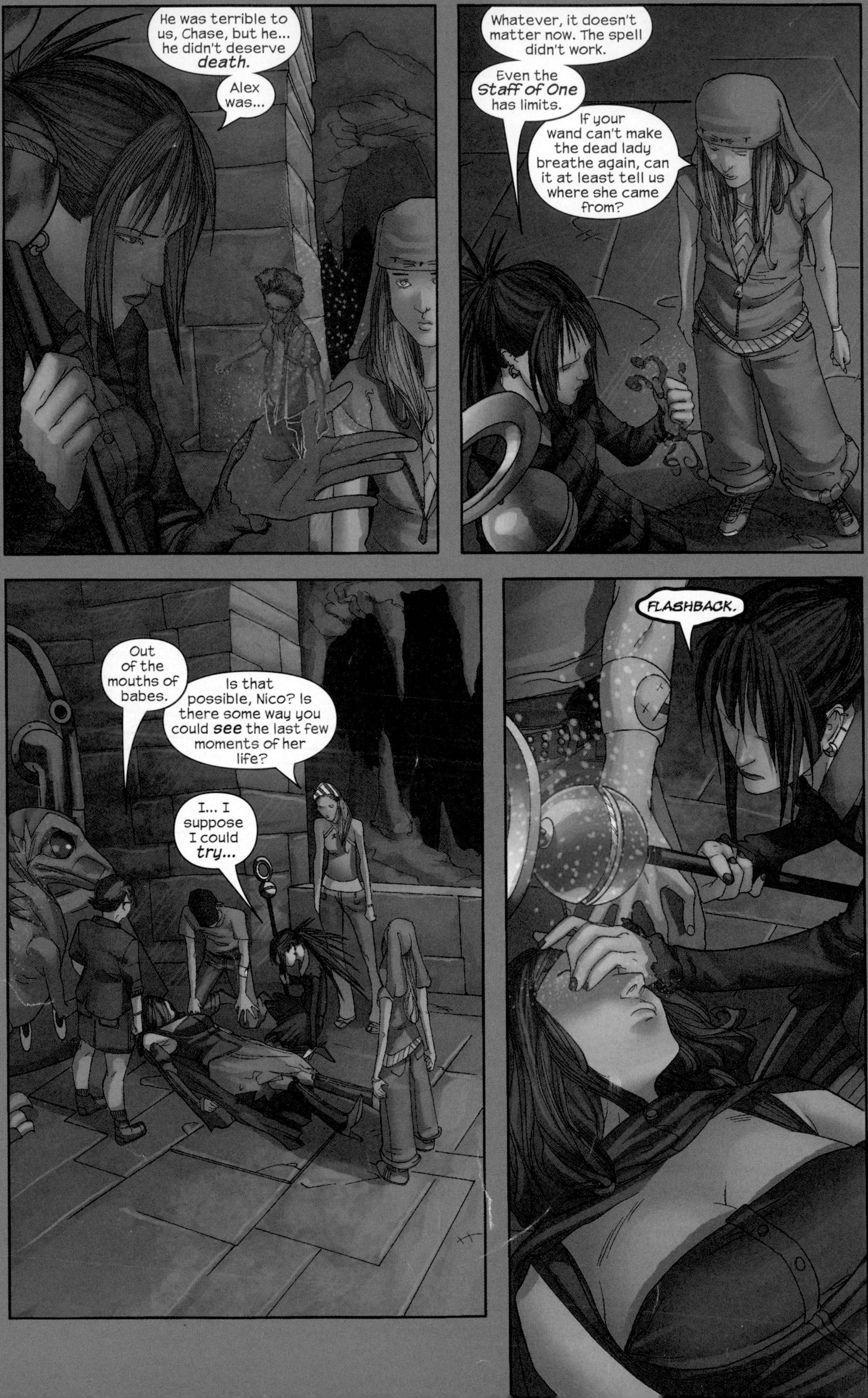

He was terrible to us, Chase, but he... he didn't deserve death.
Alex was...
Whatever, it doesn't matter now. The spell didn't work.
Even the Staff of One has limits.
If your wand can't make the dead lady breathe again, can it at least tell us where she came from?
Out of the mouths of babes.
Is that possible, Nico? Is there some way you could see the last few moments of her life?
I... I suppose I could try...
FLASHBACK.

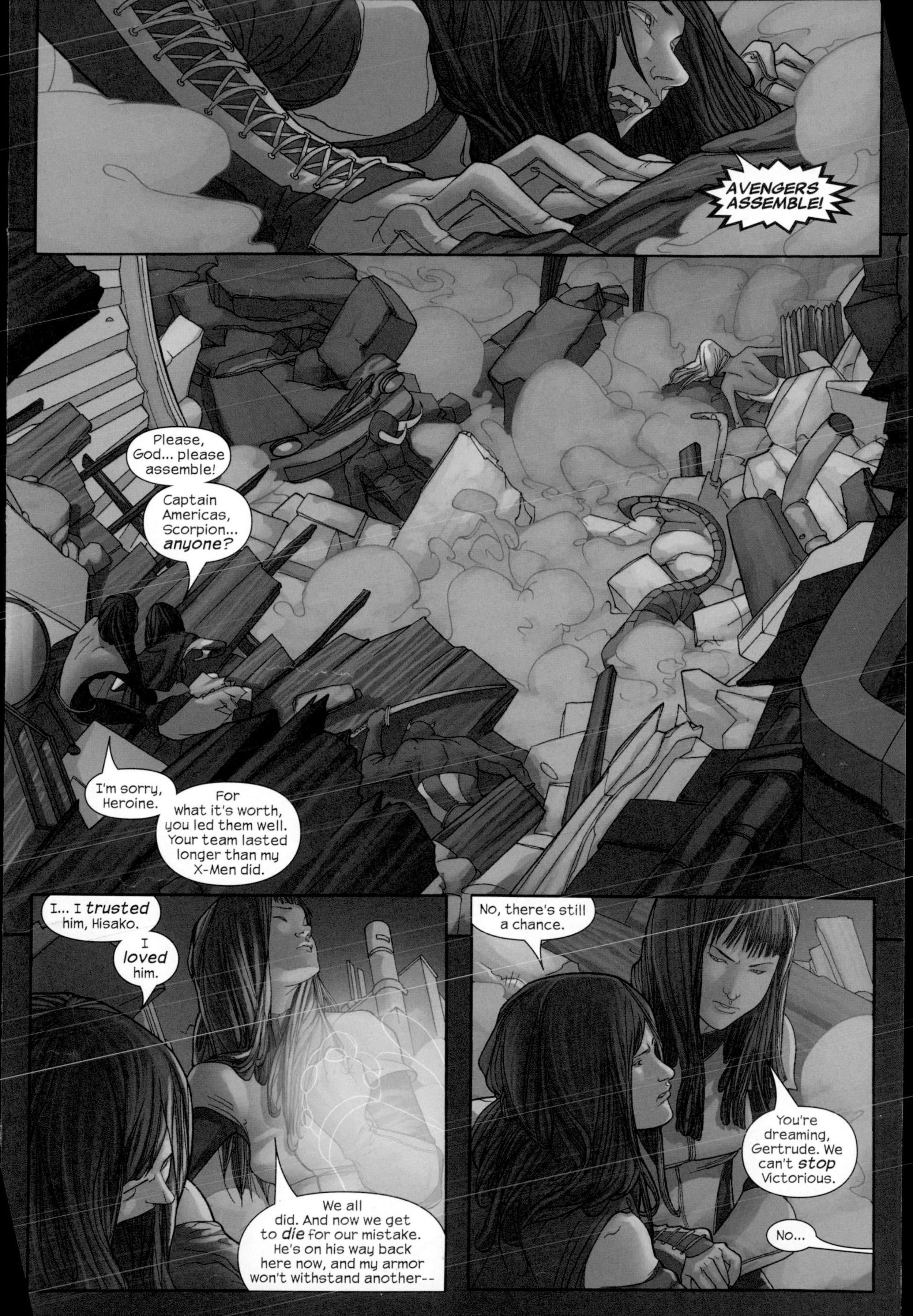
AVENGERS ASSEMBLE!
Please, God... please assemble!
Captain Americas, Scorpion... *anyone*?
I'm sorry, Heroine.
For what it's worth, you led them well. Your team lasted longer than my X-Men did.
I... I *trusted* him, Hisako.
I *loved* him.
We all did. And now we get to *die* for our mistake. He's on his way back here now, and my armor won't withstand another--
No, there's still a chance.
You're dreaming, Gertrude. We can't *stop* Victorious.
No...

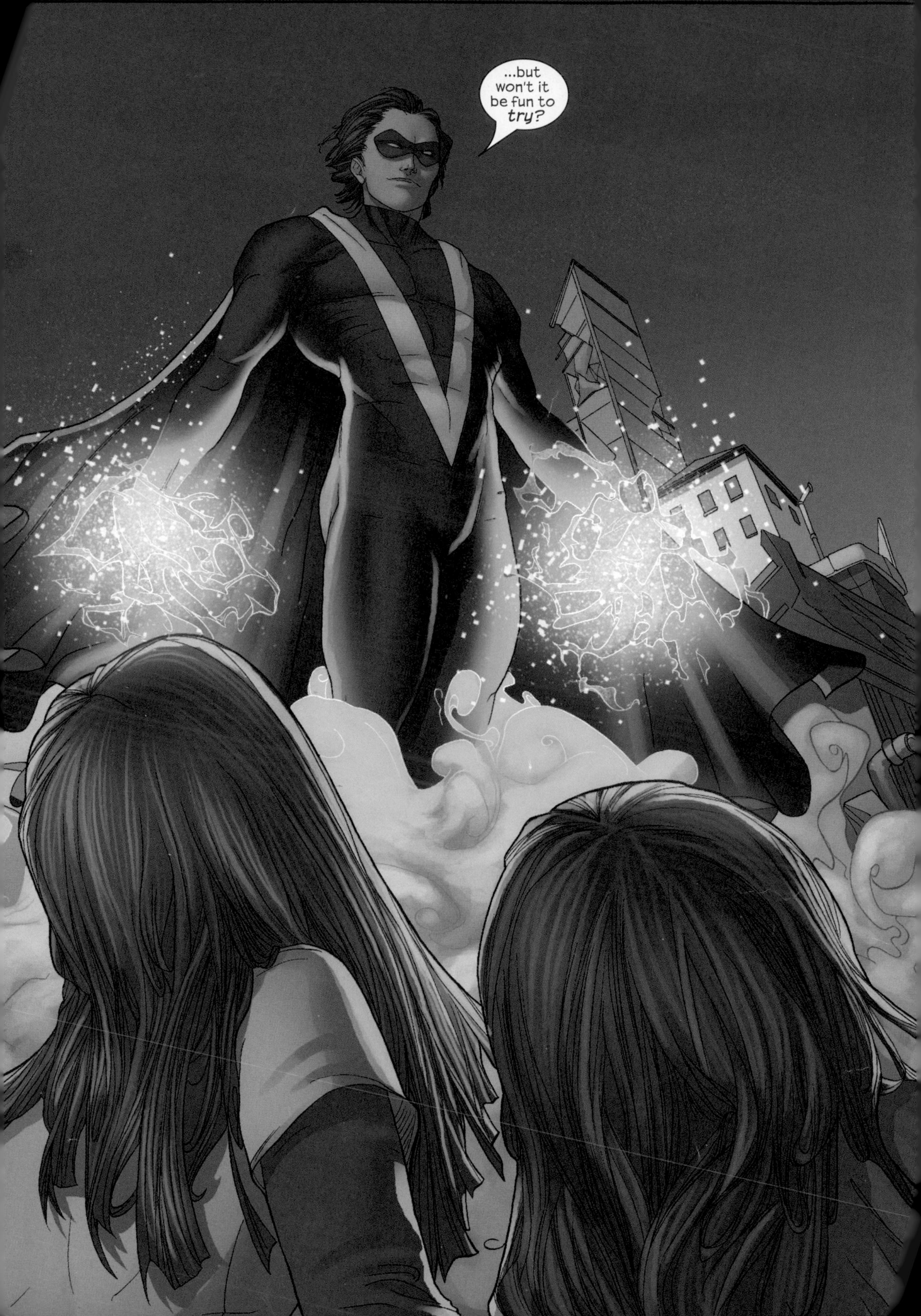
...but won't it be fun to *try*?

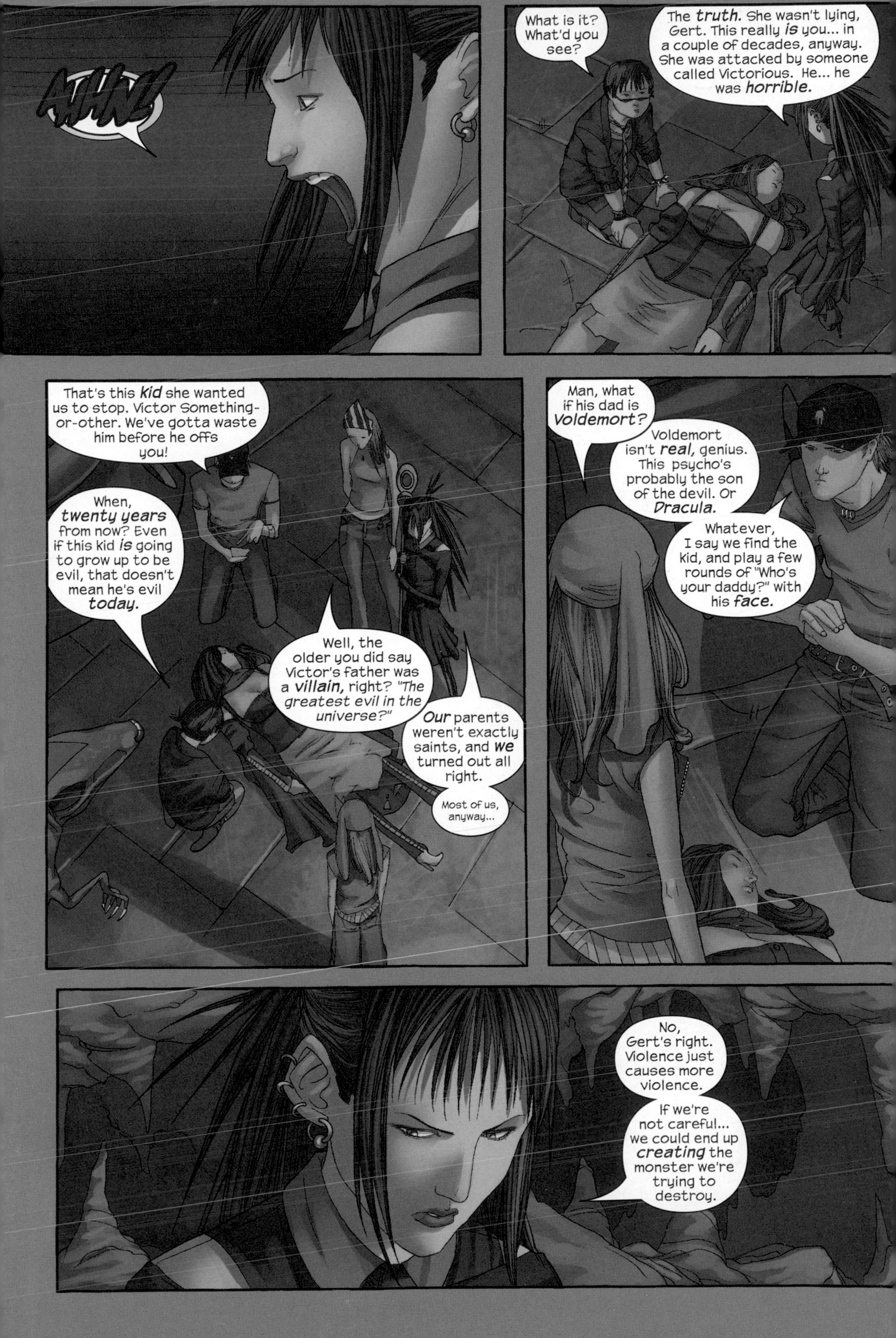

AHHH!
What is it? What'd you see?
The truth. She wasn't lying, Gert. This really is you... in a couple of decades, anyway. She was attacked by someone called Victorious. He... he was horrible.
That's this kid she wanted us to stop. Victor Something-or-other. We've gotta waste him before he offs you!
When, twenty years from now? Even if this kid is going to grow up to be evil, that doesn't mean he's evil today.
Well, the older you did say Victor's father was a villain, right? "The greatest evil in the universe?"
Our parents weren't exactly saints, and we turned out all right.
Most of us, anyway...
Man, what if his dad is Voldemort?
Voldemort isn't real, genius. This psycho's probably the son of the devil. Or Dracula.
Whatever, I say we find the kid, and play a few rounds of "Who's your daddy?" with his face.
No, Gert's right. Violence just causes more violence.
If we're not careful... we could end up creating the monster we're trying to destroy.

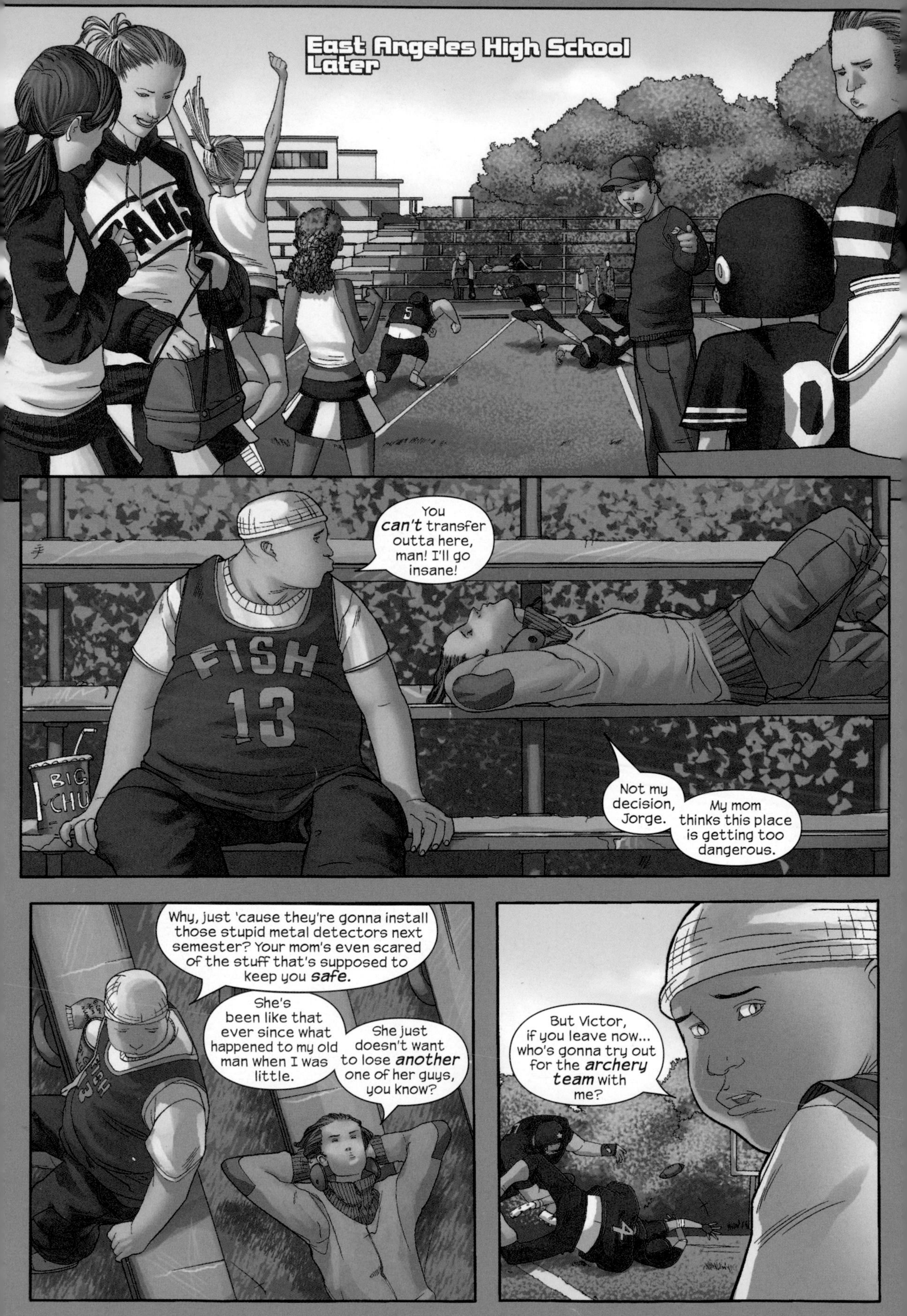
East Angeles High School
Later
EAHS
5
0
FISH
13
BIG
CHU
You can't transfer outta here, man! I'll go insane!
Not my decision, Jorge.
My mom thinks this place is getting too dangerous.
Why, just 'cause they're gonna install those stupid metal detectors next semester? Your mom's even scared of the stuff that's supposed to keep you safe.
She's been like that ever since what happened to my old man when I was little.
She just doesn't want to lose another one of her guys, you know?
But Victor, if you leave now... who's gonna try out for the archery team with me?

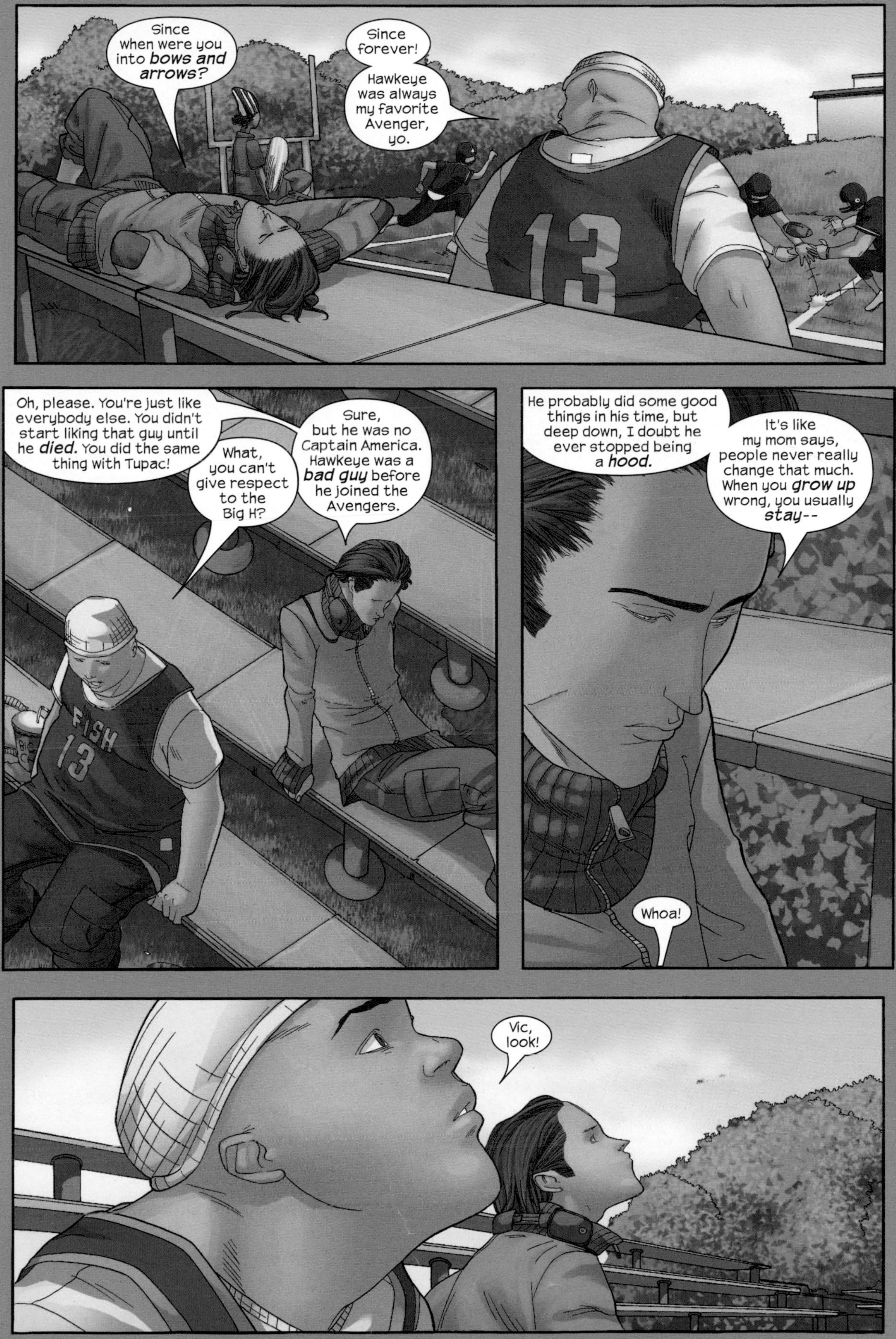

Since when were you into *bows and arrows?*
Since forever!
Hawkeye was always my favorite Avenger, yo.
Oh, please. You're just like everybody else. You didn't start liking that guy until he *died.* You did the same thing with Tupac!
What, you can't give respect to the Big H?
Sure, but he was no Captain America. Hawkeye was a *bad guy* before he joined the Avengers.
He probably did some good things in his time, but deep down, I doubt he ever stopped being a *hood.*
It's like my mom says, people never really change that much. When you *grow up* wrong, you usually *stay*--
Whoa!
FISH
13
Vic, look!

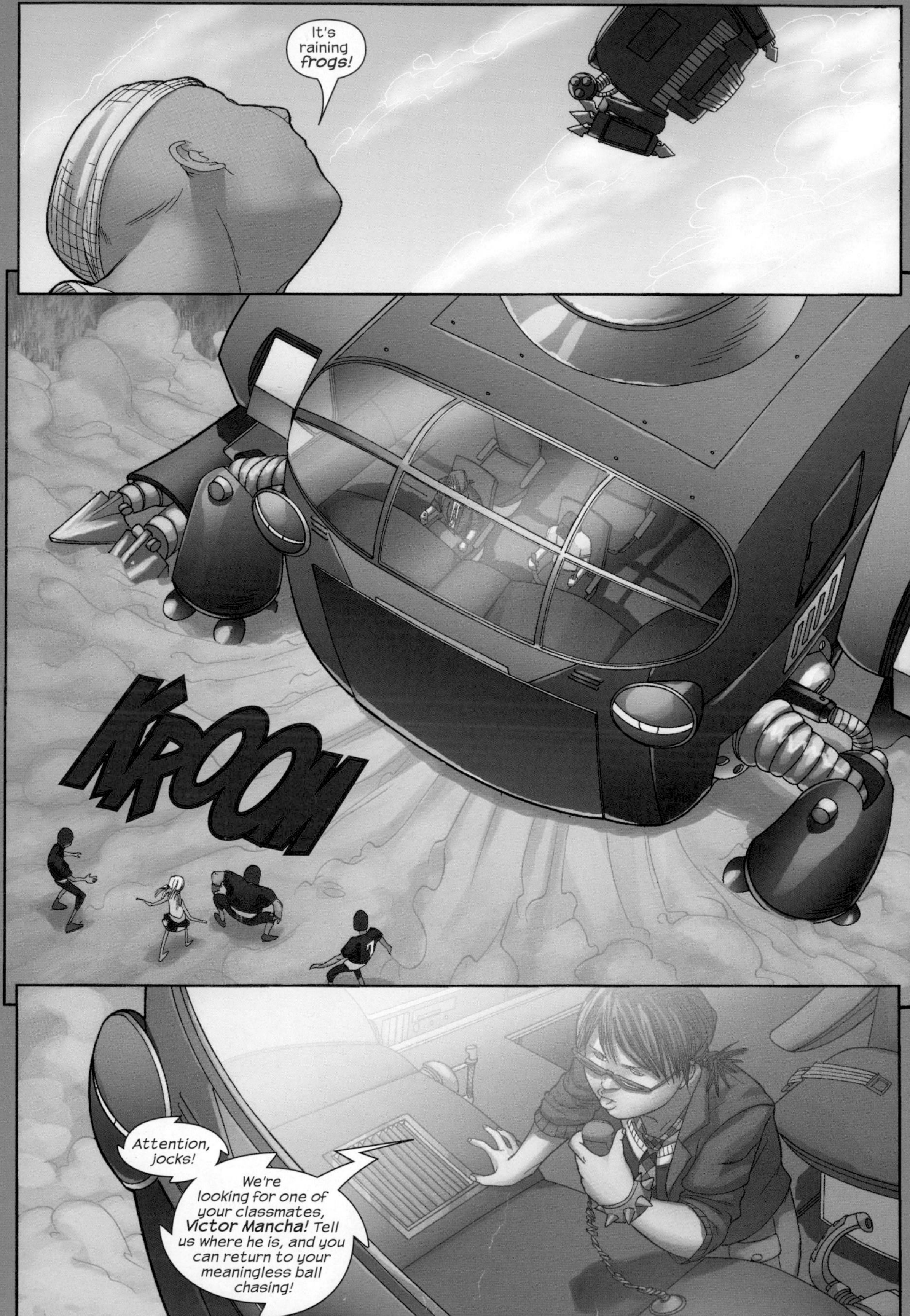
It's raining frogs!
KROOM
Attention, jocks!
We're looking for one of your classmates, Victor Mancha! Tell us where he is, and you can return to your meaningless ball chasing!

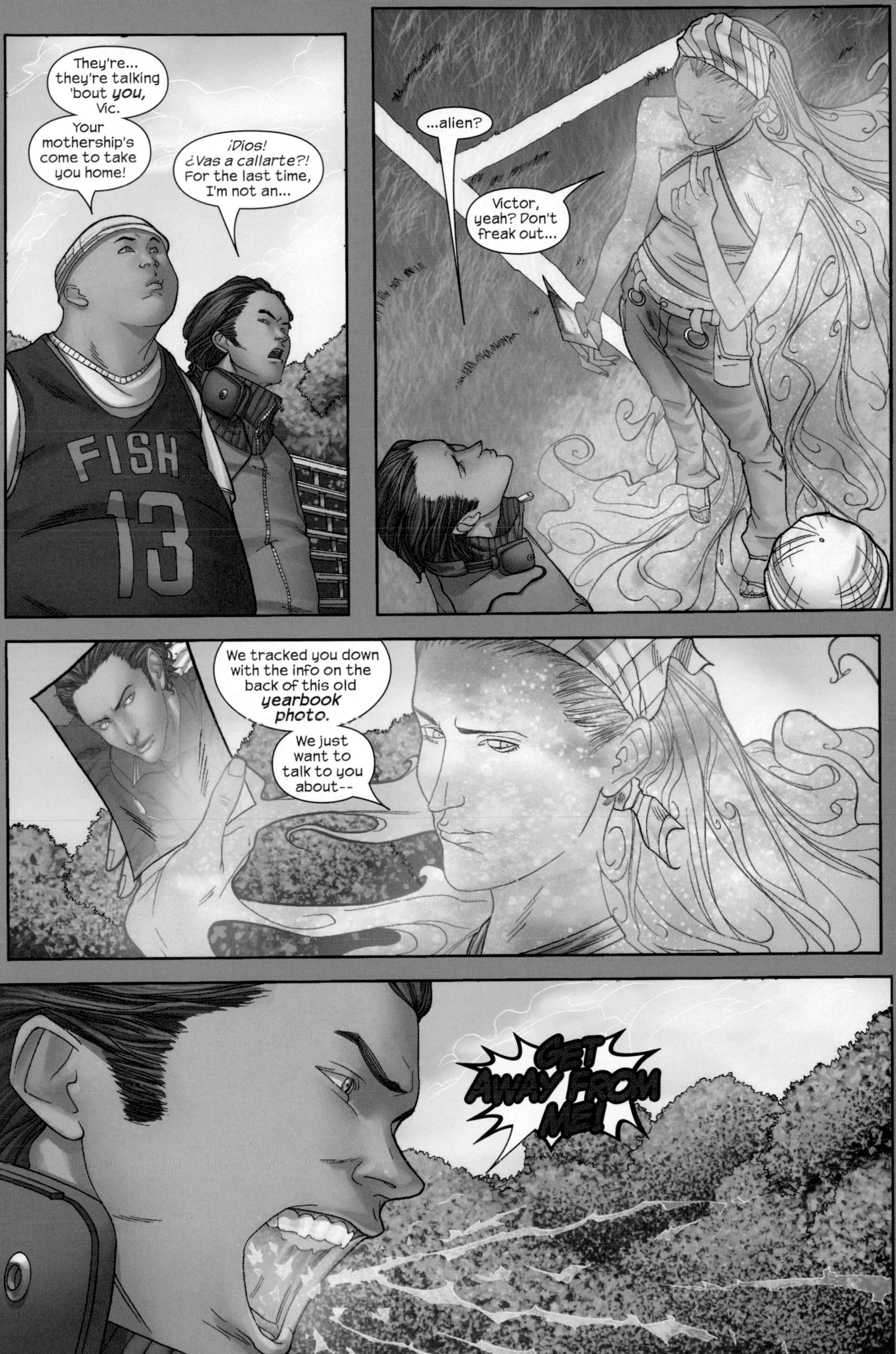

They're... they're talking 'bout *you,* Vic.
Your mothership's come to take you home!
¡Dios! ¿Vas a callarte?! For the last time, I'm not an...
...alien?
Victor, yeah? Don't freak out...
We tracked you down with the info on the back of this old ***yearbook photo.***
We just want to talk to you about--
GET AWAY FROM ME!
FISH
13

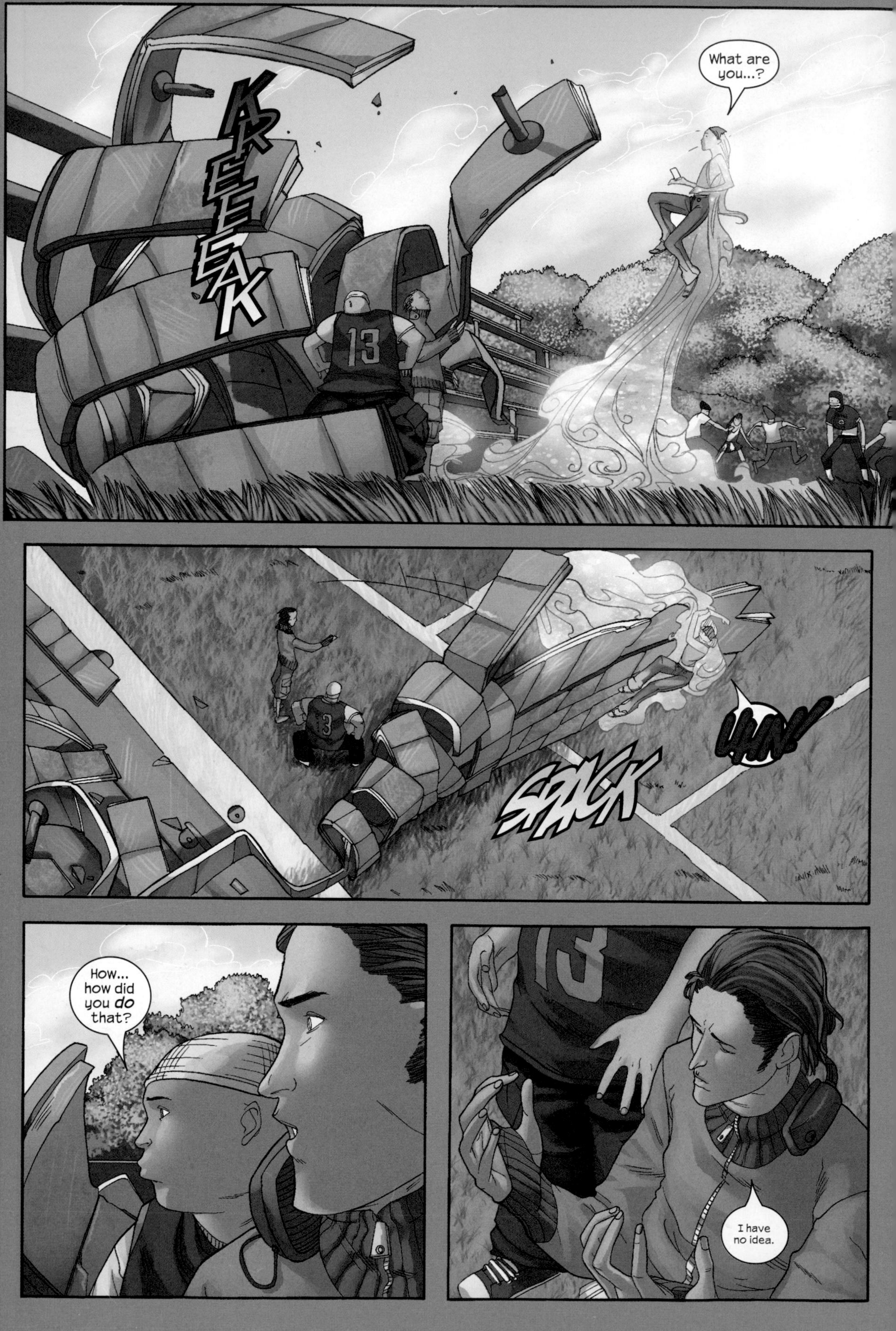
What are you...?
KREEEAK
SPACK
UHN!
How... how did you *do* that?
I have no idea.

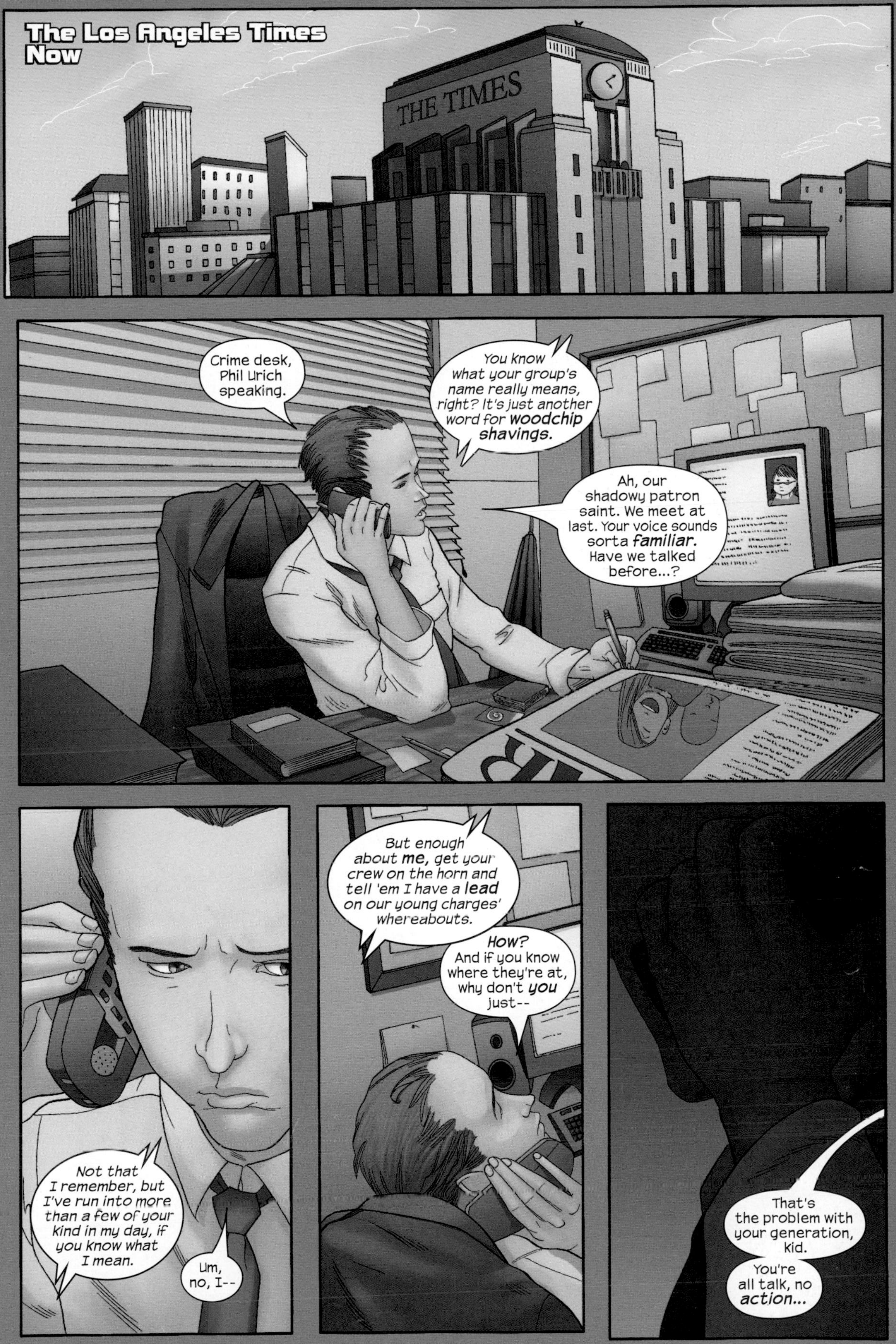
The Los Angeles Times
Now
THE TIMES
Crime desk, Phil Urich speaking.
You know what your group's name really means, right? It's just another word for woodchip shavings.
Ah, our shadowy patron saint. We meet at last. Your voice sounds sorta familiar. Have we talked before...?
Not that I remember, but I've run into more than a few of your kind in my day, if you know what I mean.
Um, no, I--
But enough about me, get your crew on the horn and tell 'em I have a lead on our young charges' whereabouts.
How? And if you know where they're at, why don't you just--
That's the problem with your generation, kid.
You're all talk, no action...

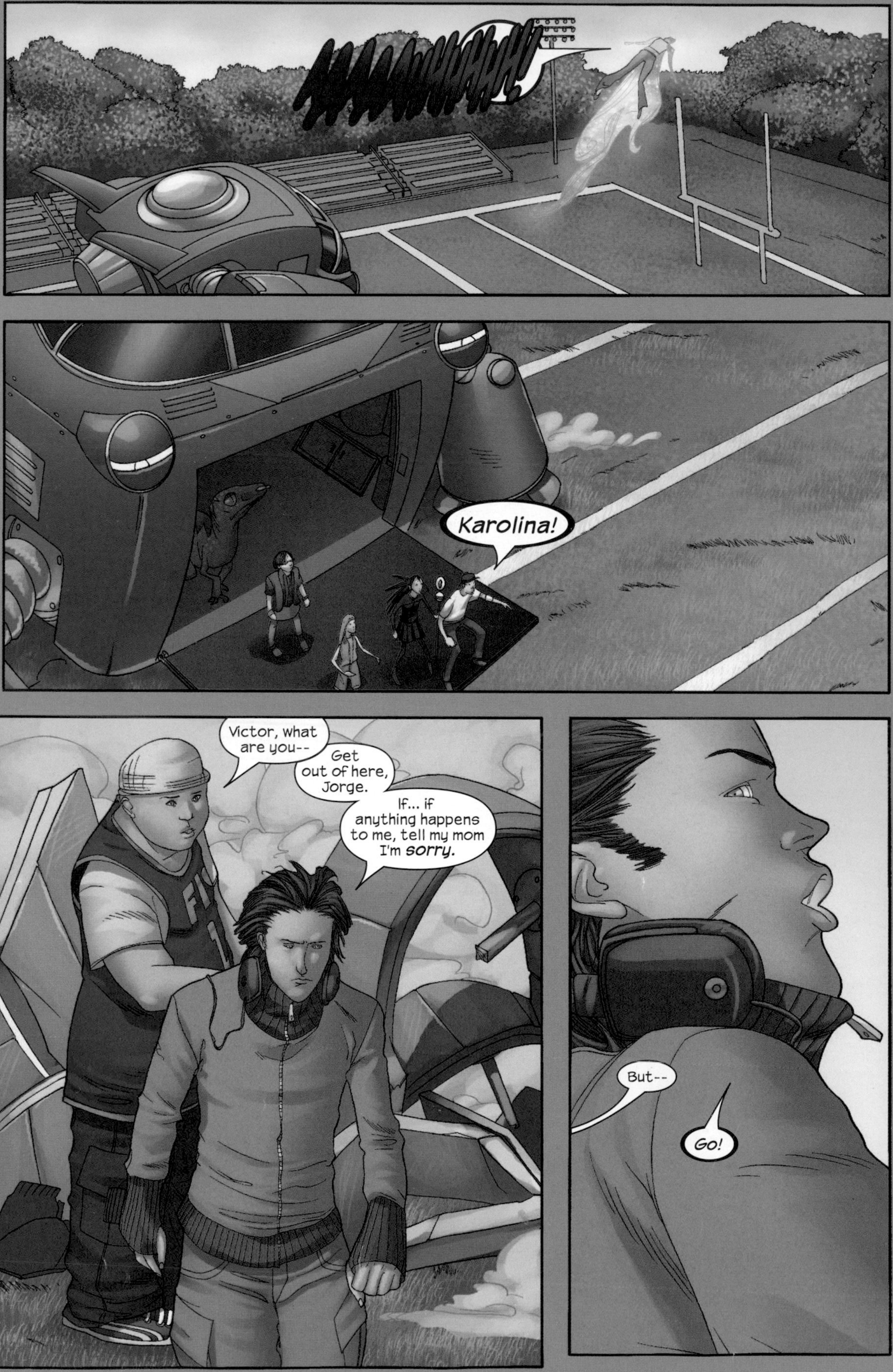
AAAAAHHHHHH!
Karolina!
Victor, what are you--
Get out of here, Jorge.
If... if anything happens to me, tell my mom I'm *sorry.*
But--
Go!

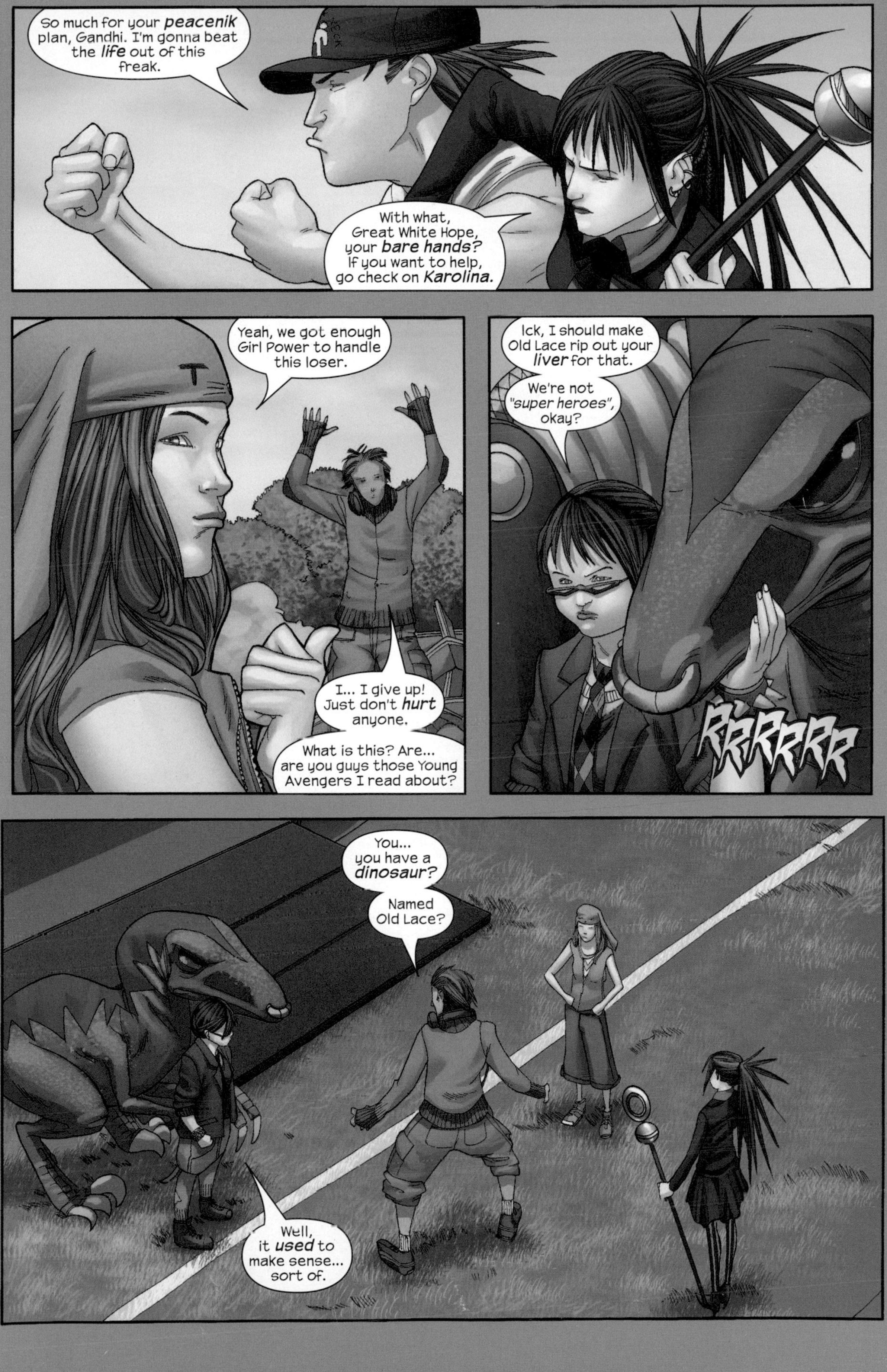
So much for your *peacenik* plan, Gandhi. I'm gonna beat the *life* out of this freak.
With what, Great White Hope, your *bare hands?* If you want to help, go check on *Karolina.*
Yeah, we got enough Girl Power to handle this loser.
I... I give up! Just don't *hurt* anyone.
What is this? Are... are you guys those Young Avengers I read about?
Ick, I should make Old Lace rip out your *liver* for that.
We're not *"super heroes"*, okay?
RRRRRR
You... you have a *dinosaur?*
Named Old Lace?
Well, it *used* to make sense... sort of.

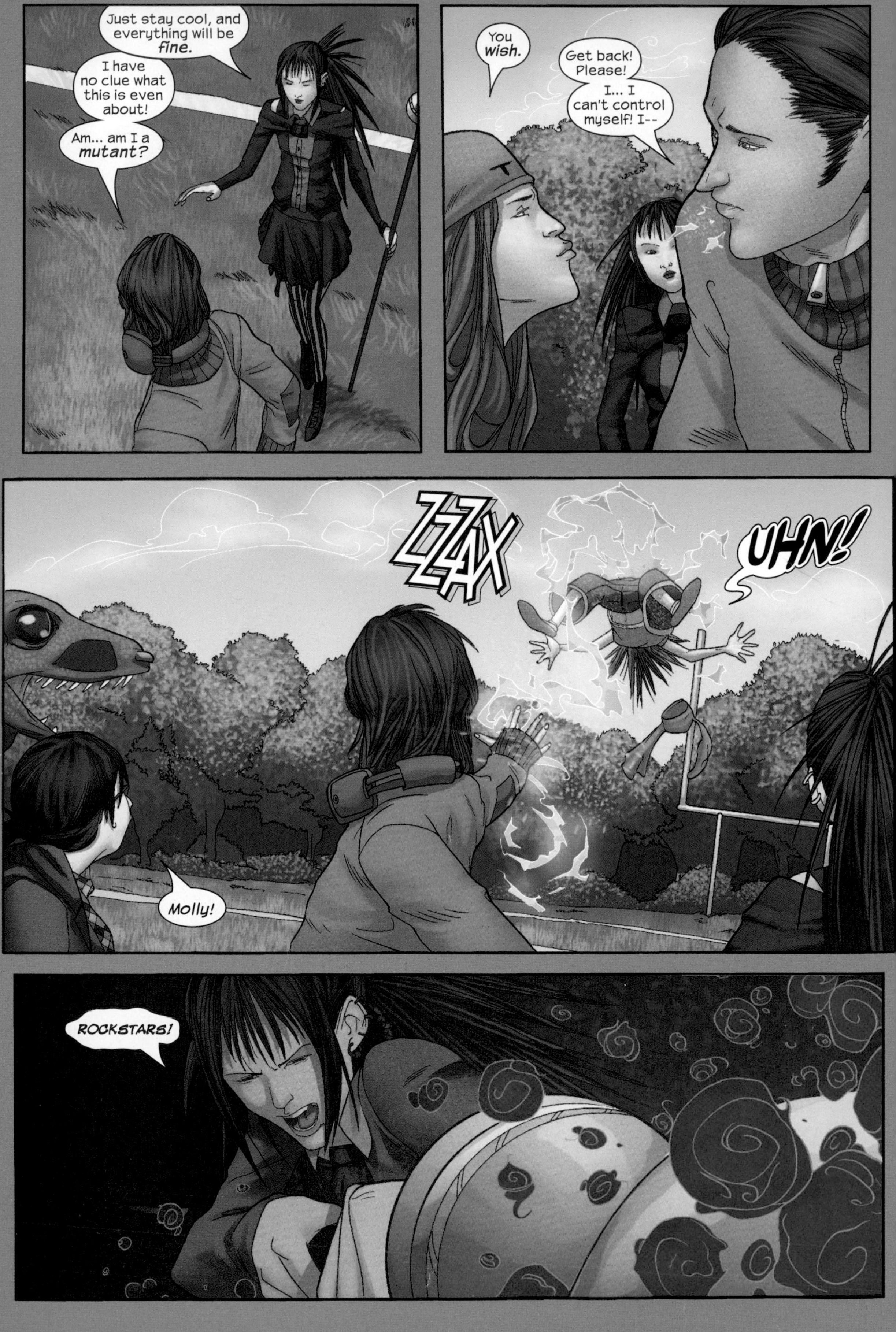

Just stay cool, and everything will be *fine*.
I have no clue what this is even about!
Am... am I a *mutant?*
You *wish.*
Get back! Please!
I... I can't control myself! I--
ZZZAX
UHN!
Molly!
ROCKSTARS!

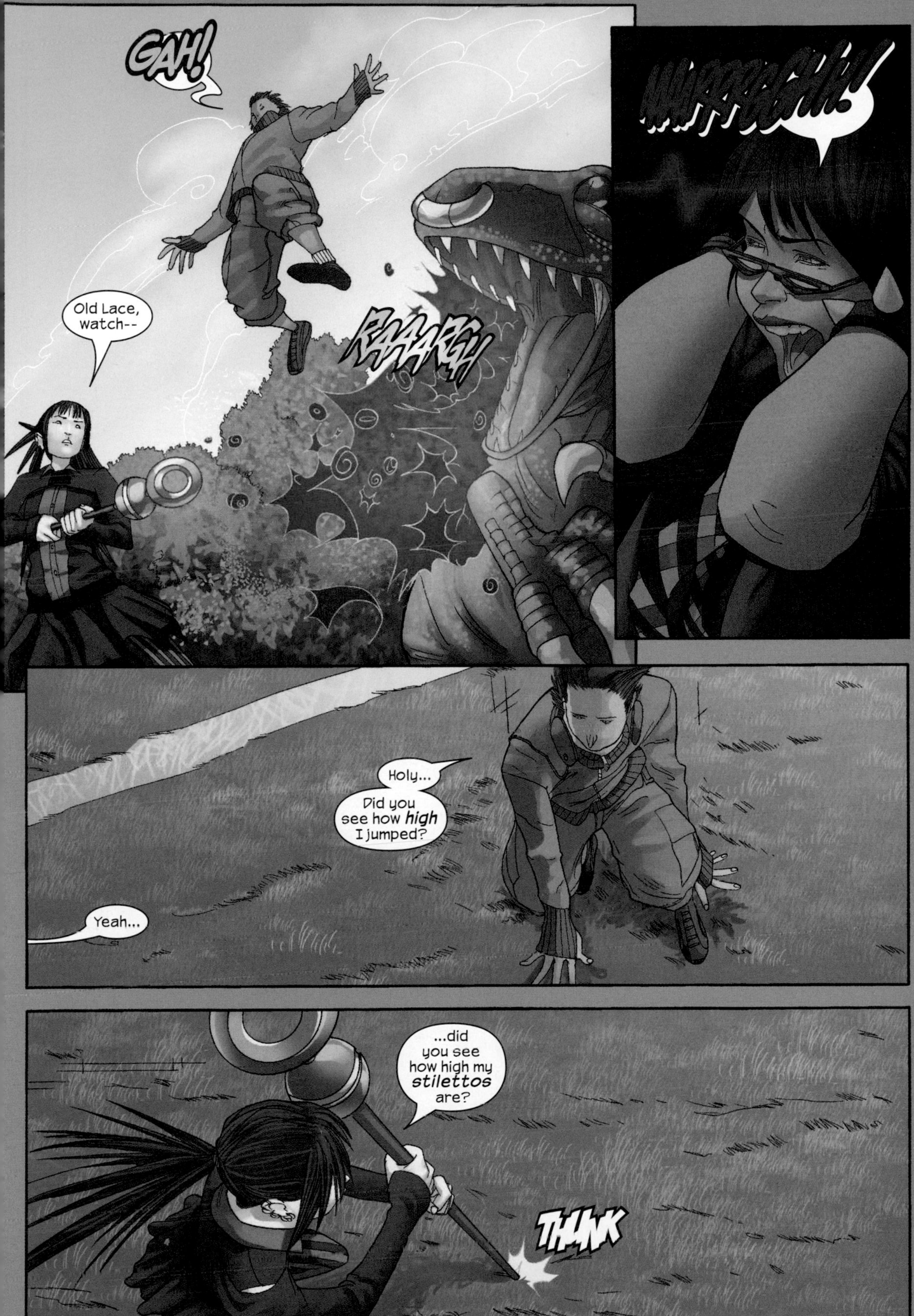
GAH!
Old Lace, watch--
RAAARGH
Holy... Did you see how *high* I jumped?
Yeah...
...did you see how high my *stilettos* are?
THUNK

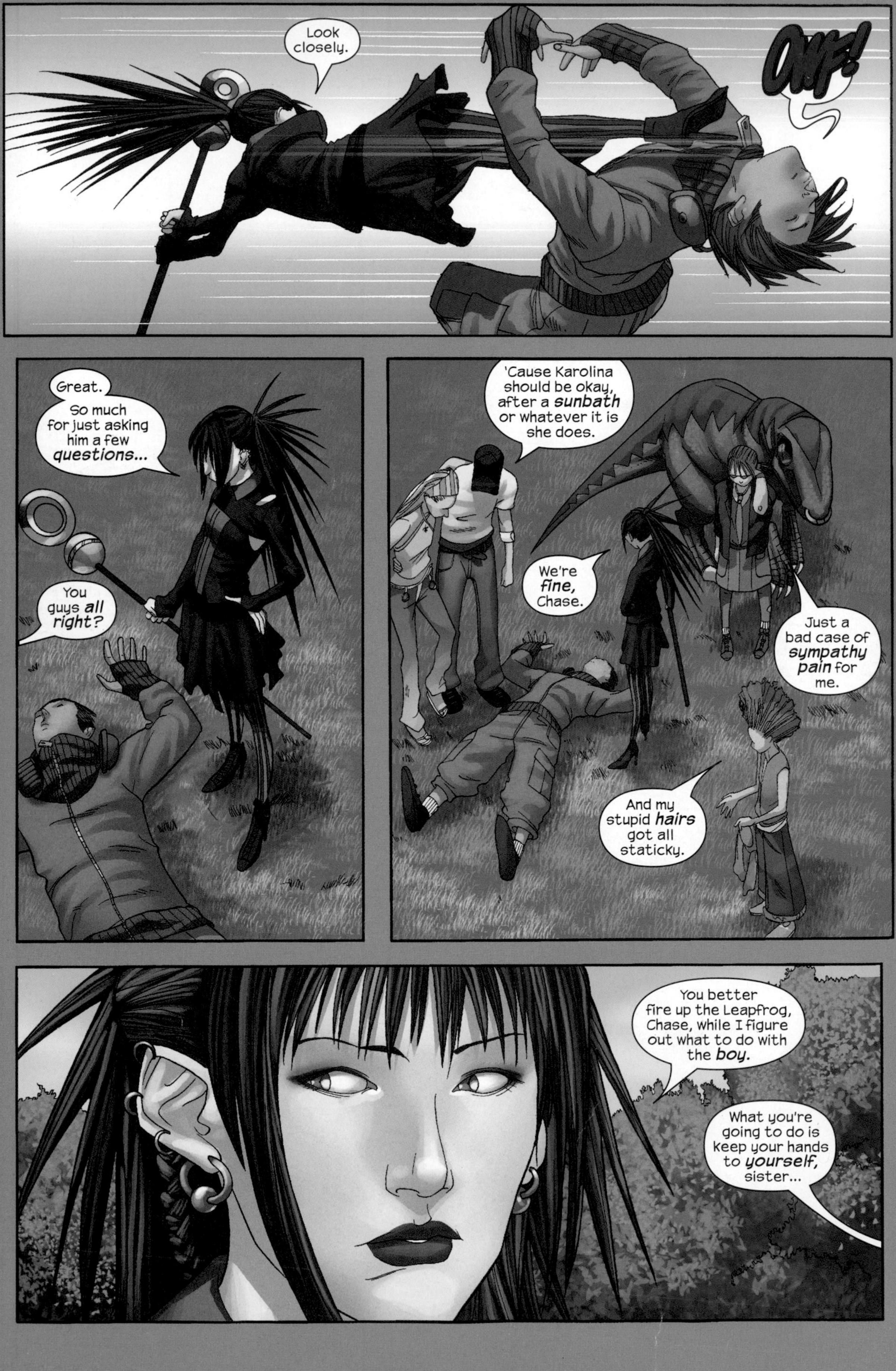

Look closely.
OMF!
Great.
So much for just asking him a few questions...
You guys all right?
'Cause Karolina should be okay, after a sunbath or whatever it is she does.
We're fine, Chase.
Just a bad case of sympathy pain for me.
And my stupid hairs got all staticky.
You better fire up the Leapfrog, Chase, while I figure out what to do with the boy.
What you're going to do is keep your hands to yourself, sister...

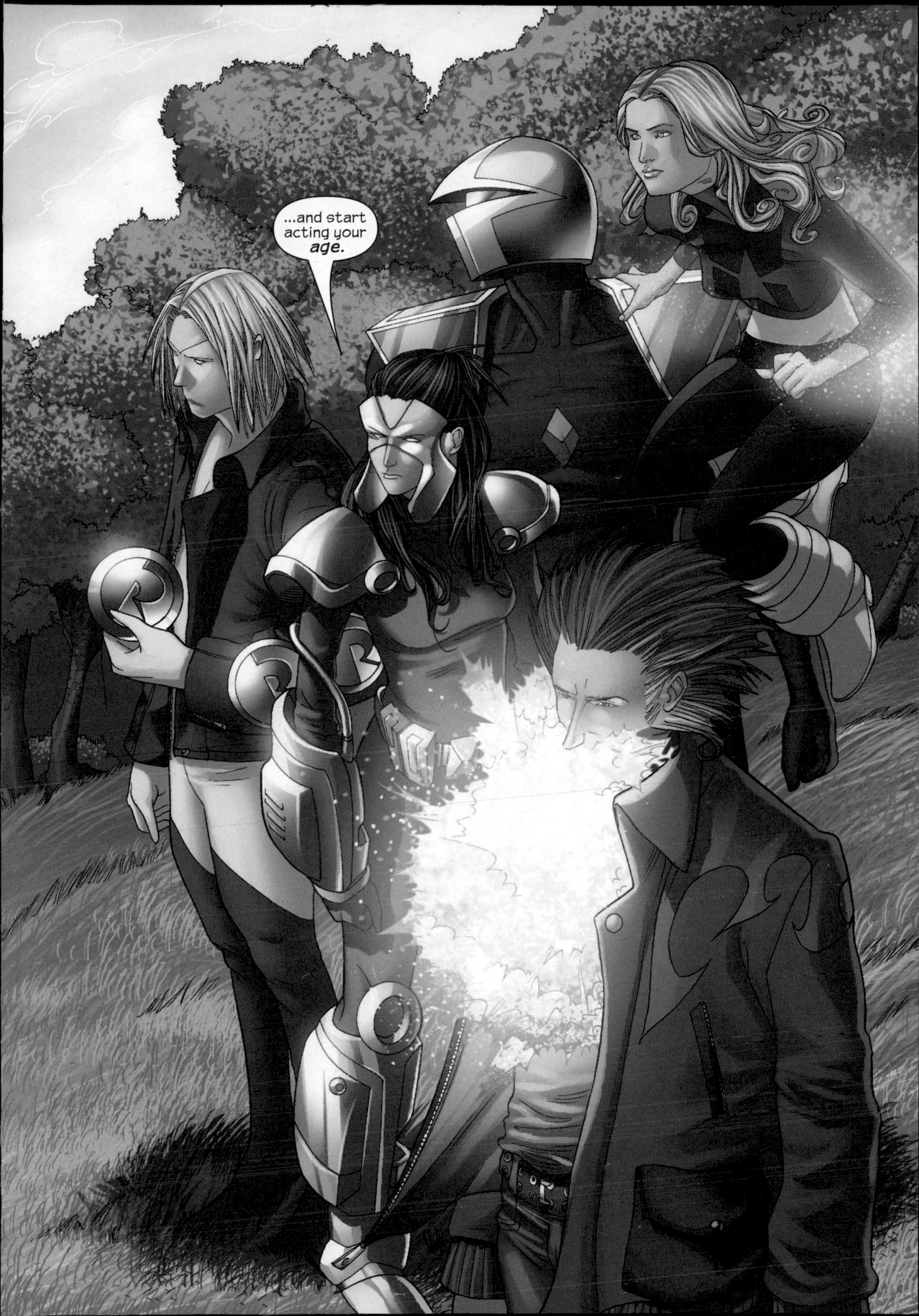
...and start acting your *age.*

3

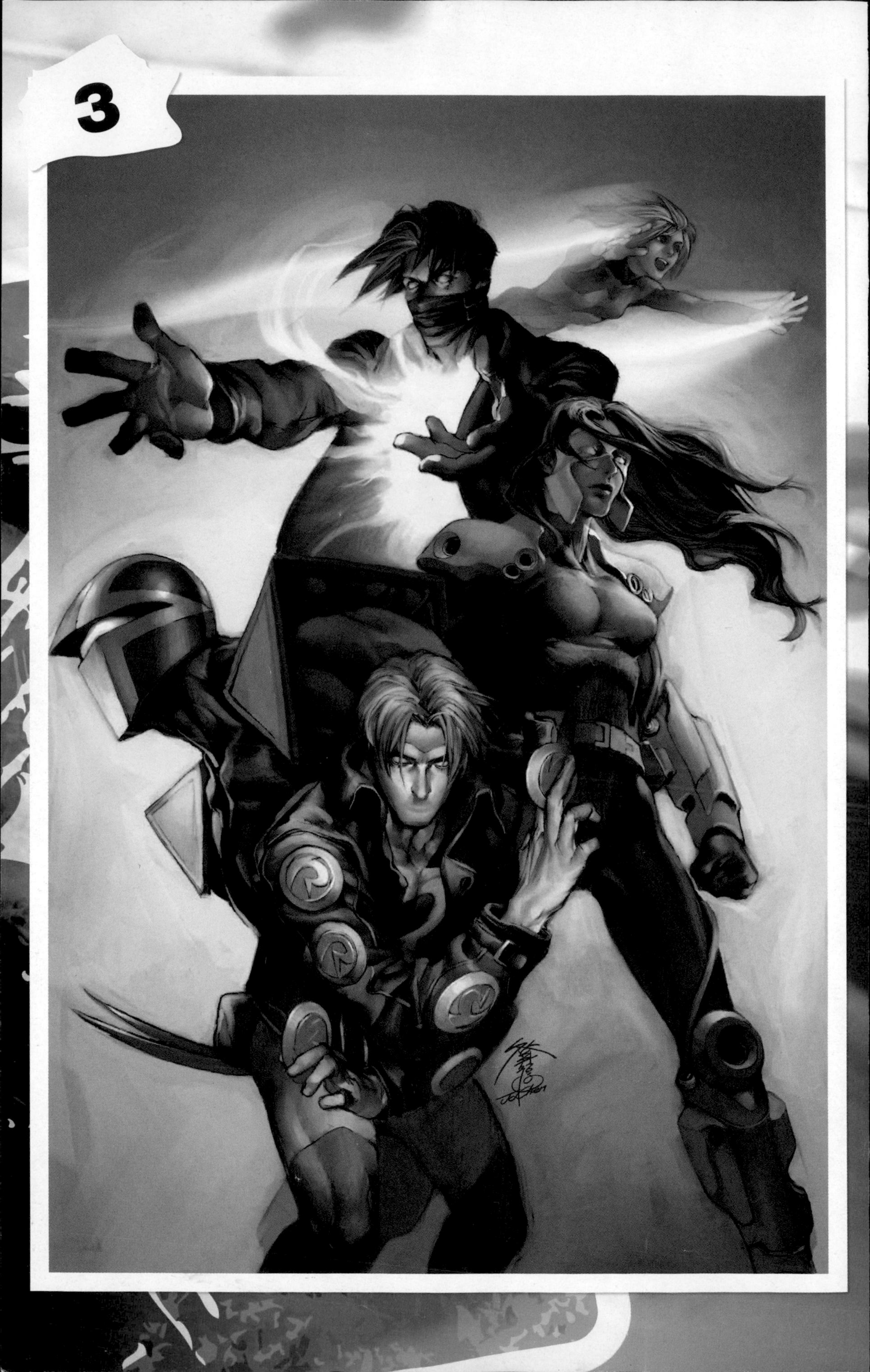

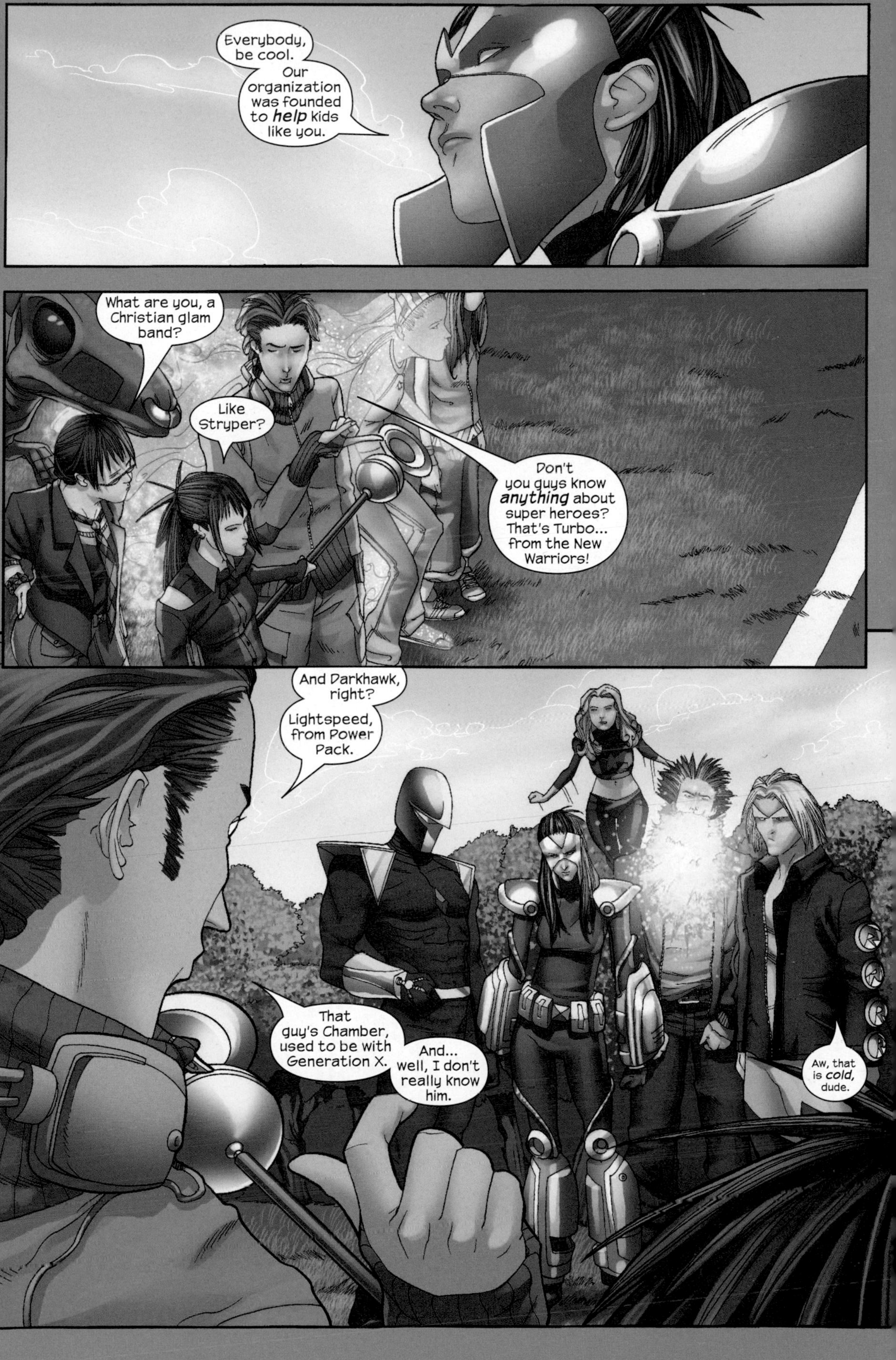
Everybody, be cool.
Our organization was founded to *help* kids like you.
What are you, a Christian glam band?
Like Stryper?
Don't you guys know *anything* about super heroes? That's Turbo... from the New Warriors!
And Darkhawk, right?
Lightspeed, from Power Pack.
That guy's Chamber, used to be with Generation X.
And... well, I don't really know him.
Aw, that is *cold,* dude.

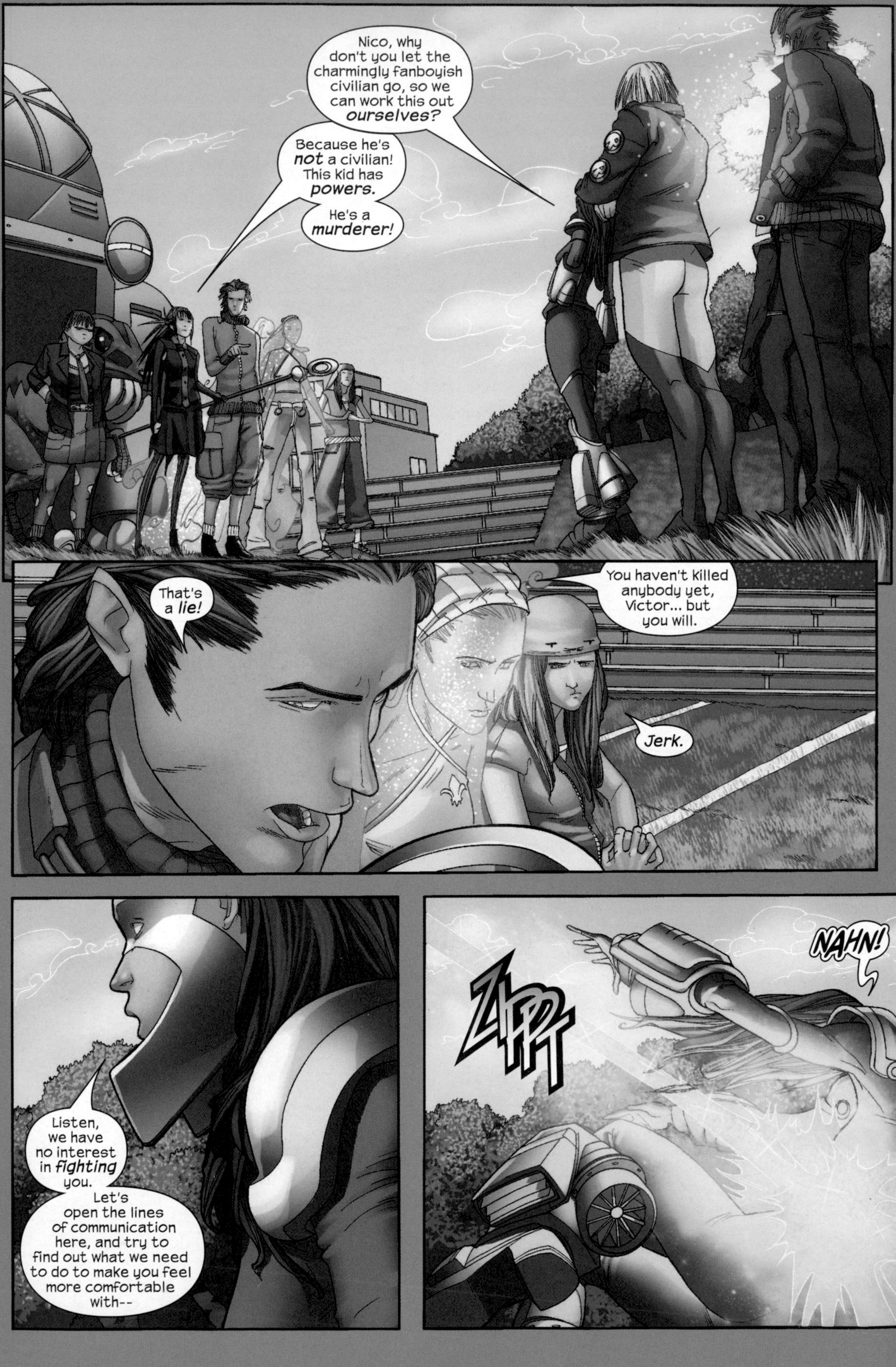
Nico, why don't you let the charmingly fanboyish civilian go, so we can work this out ourselves?
Because he's not a civilian! This kid has powers.
He's a murderer!
That's a lie!
You haven't killed anybody yet, Victor... but you will.
Jerk.
Listen, we have no interest in fighting you.
Let's open the lines of communication here, and try to find out what we need to do to make you feel more comfortable with--
ZAPT
NAHN!

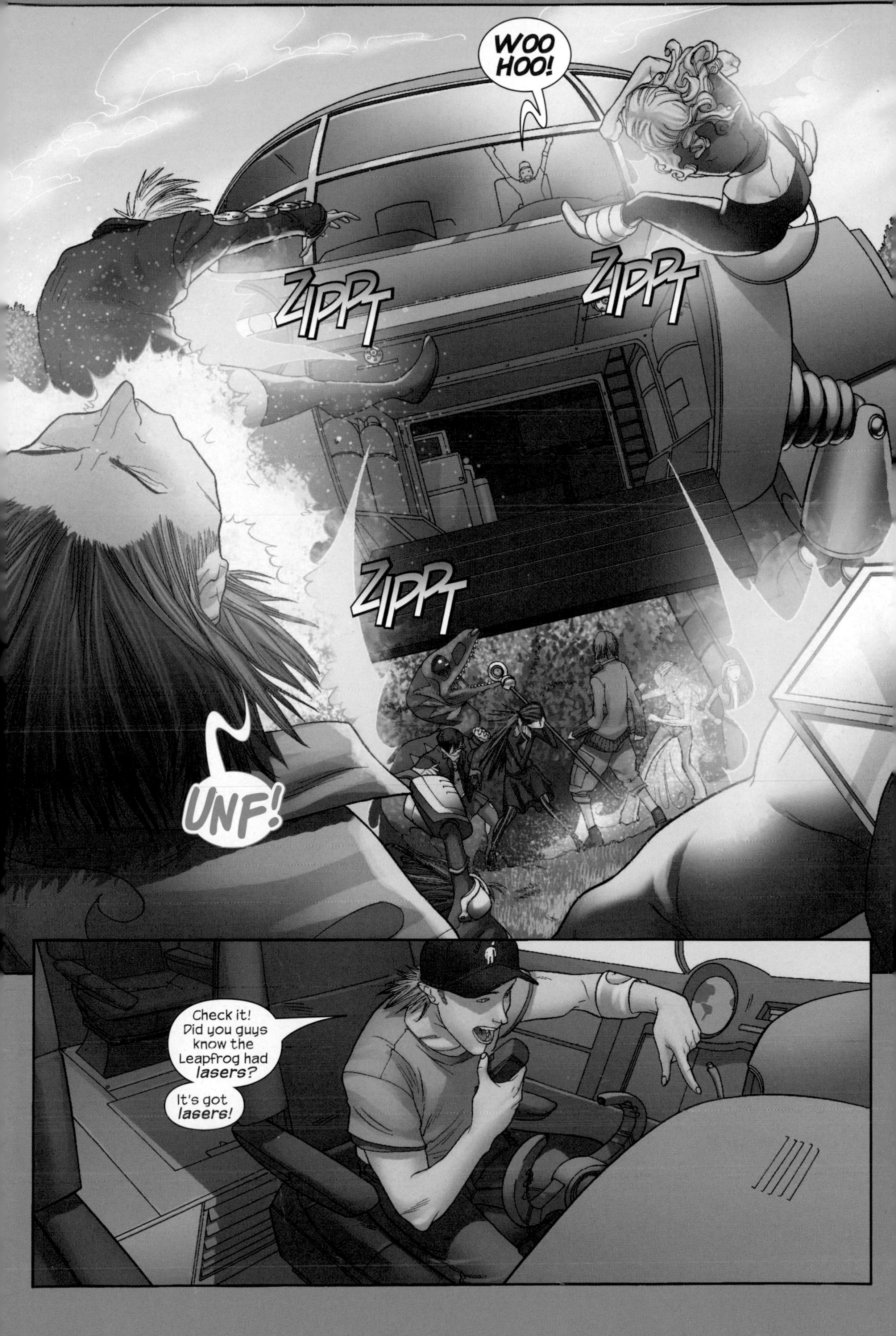
WOO HOO!
ZIPPT
ZIPPT
ZIPPT
UNF!
Check it! Did you guys know the Leapfrog had *lasers?*
It's got *lasers!*

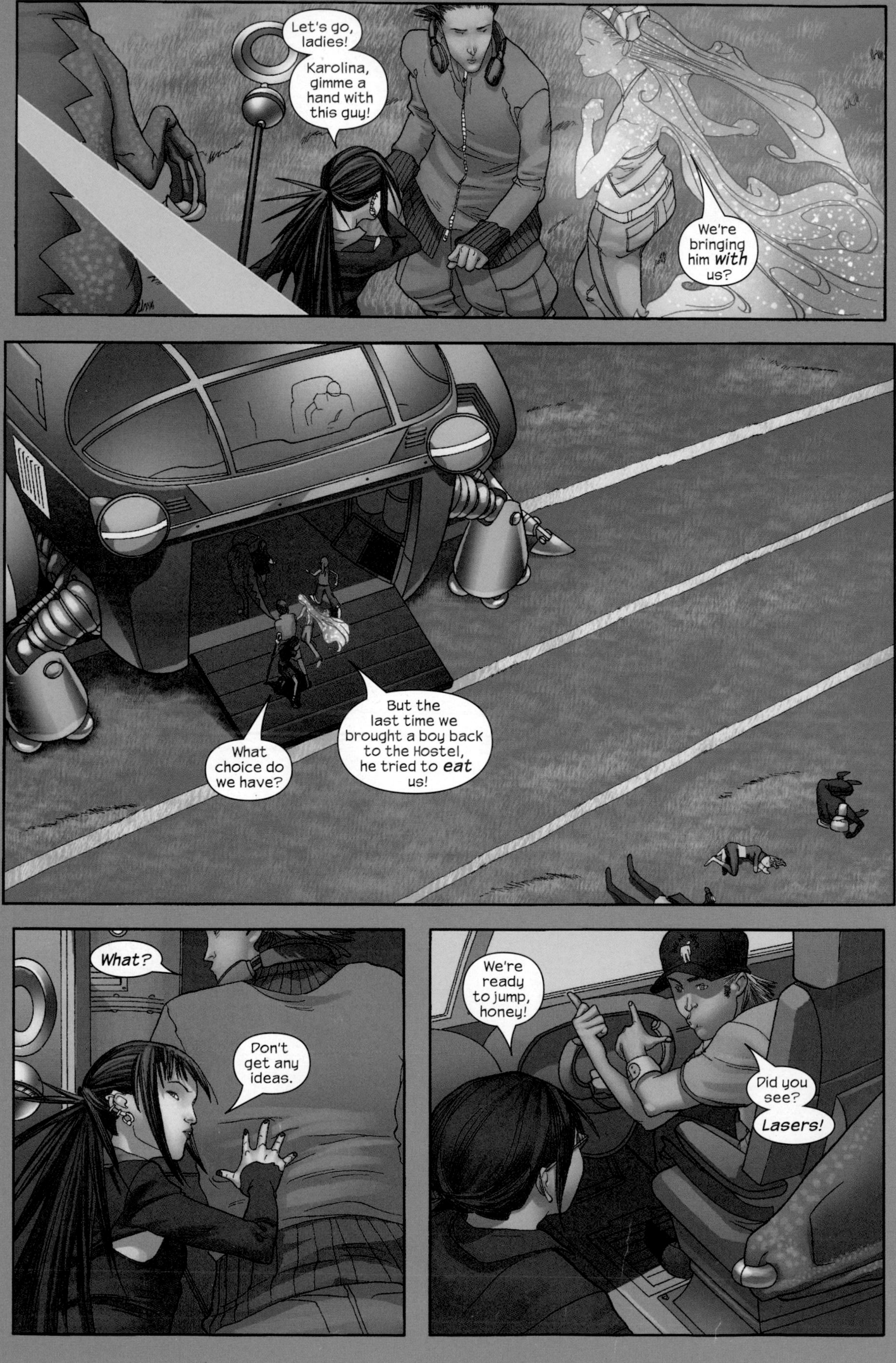
Let's go, ladies!
Karolina, gimme a hand with this guy!
We're bringing him with us?
What choice do we have?
But the last time we brought a boy back to the Hostel, he tried to eat us!
What?
Don't get any ideas.
We're ready to jump, honey!
Did you see?
Lasers!

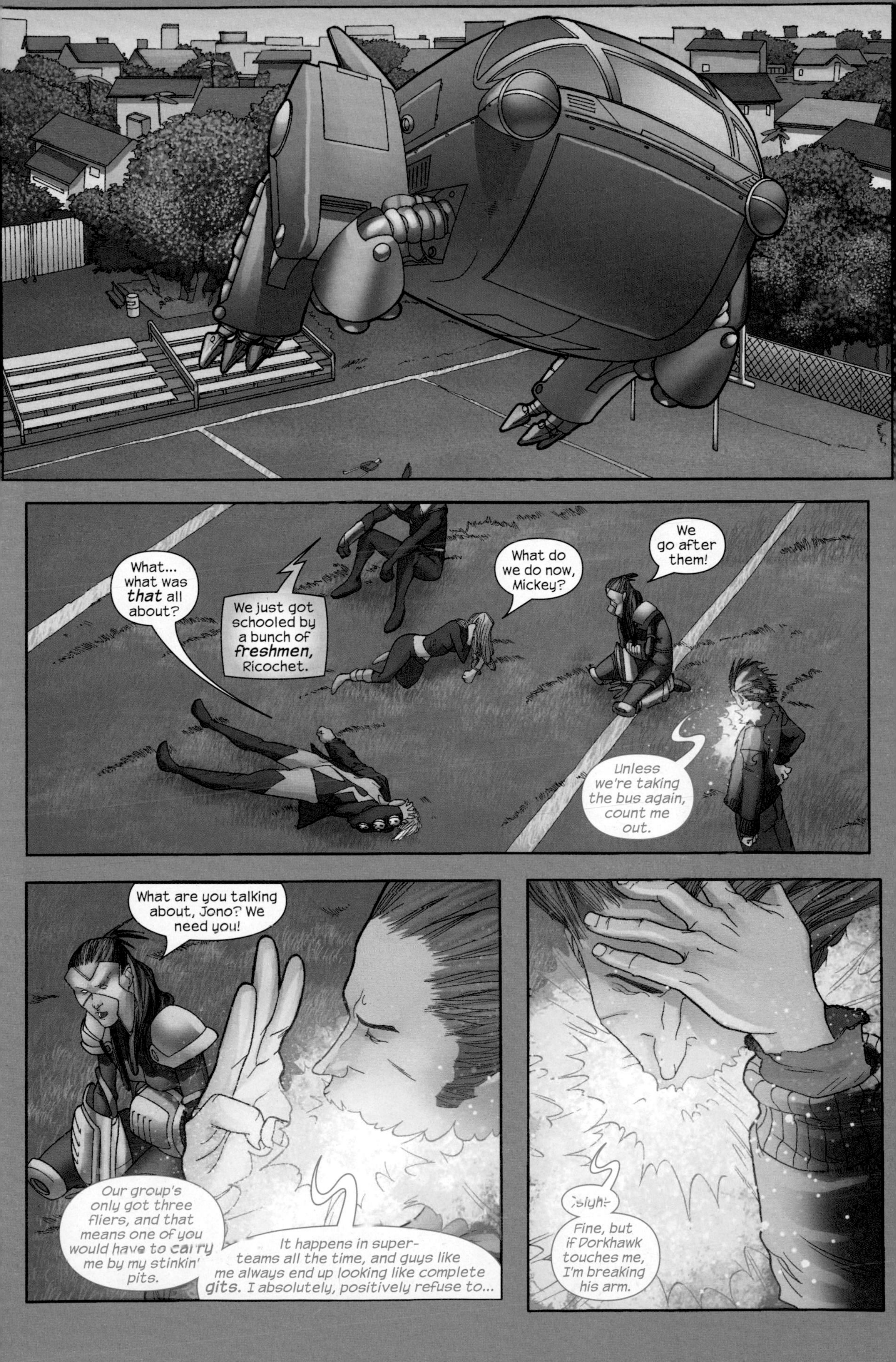
What... what was that all about?
We just got schooled by a bunch of freshmen, Ricochet.
What do we do now, Mickey?
We go after them!
Unless we're taking the bus again, count me out.
What are you talking about, Jono? We need you!
Our group's only got three fliers, and that means one of you would have to carry me by my stinkin' pits.
It happens in super-teams all the time, and guys like me always end up looking like complete gits. I absolutely, positively refuse to...
sigh
Fine, but if Dorkhawk touches me, I'm breaking his arm.

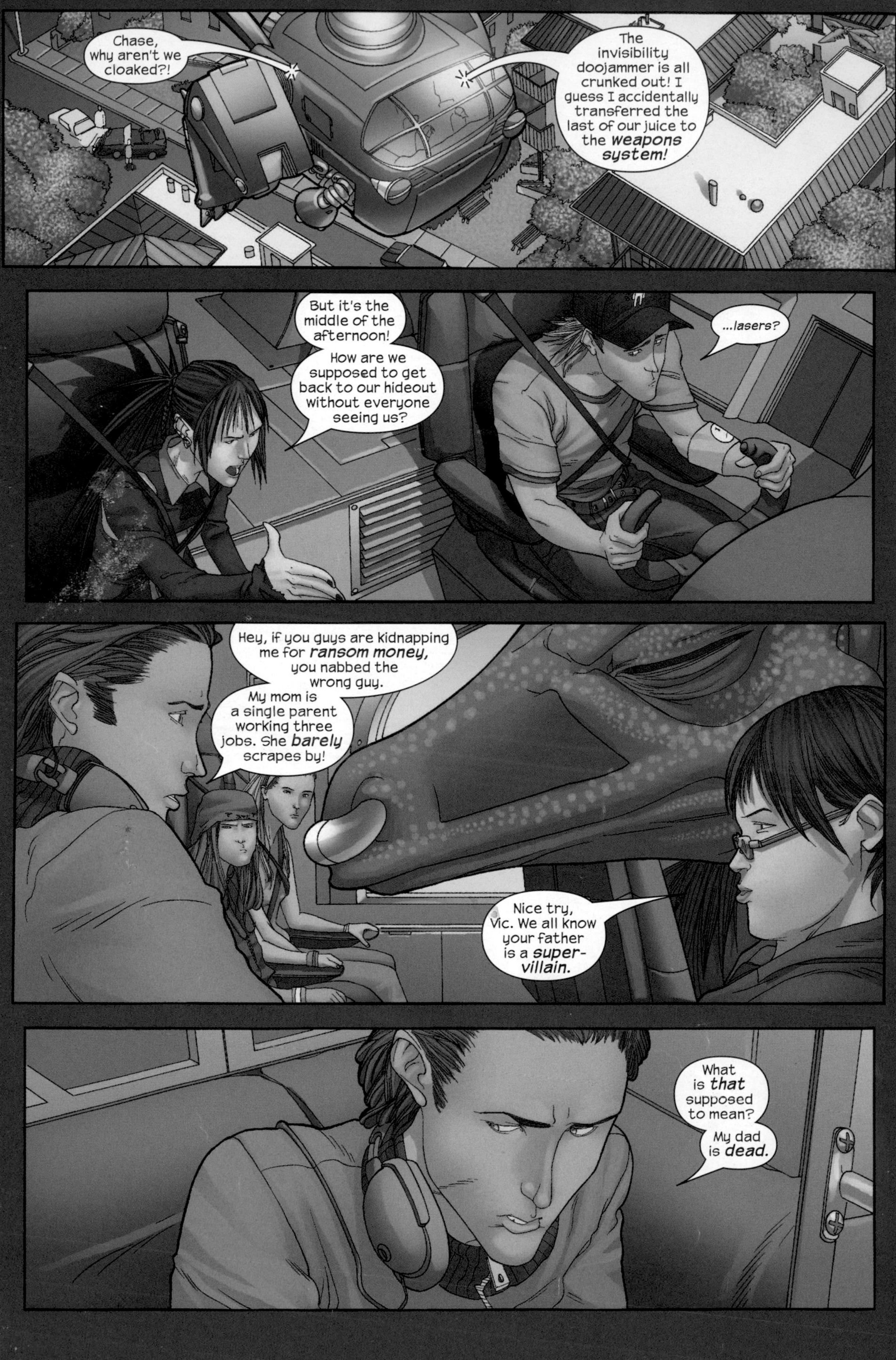
Chase, why aren't we cloaked?!
The invisibility doojammer is all crunked out! I guess I accidentally transferred the last of our juice to the *weapons system!*
But it's the middle of the afternoon!
How are we supposed to get back to our hideout without everyone seeing us?
...lasers?
Hey, if you guys are kidnapping me for *ransom money,* you nabbed the wrong guy.
My mom is a single parent working three jobs. She *barely* scrapes by!
Nice try, Vic. We all know your father is a *super-villain.*
What is *that* supposed to mean?
My dad is *dead.*

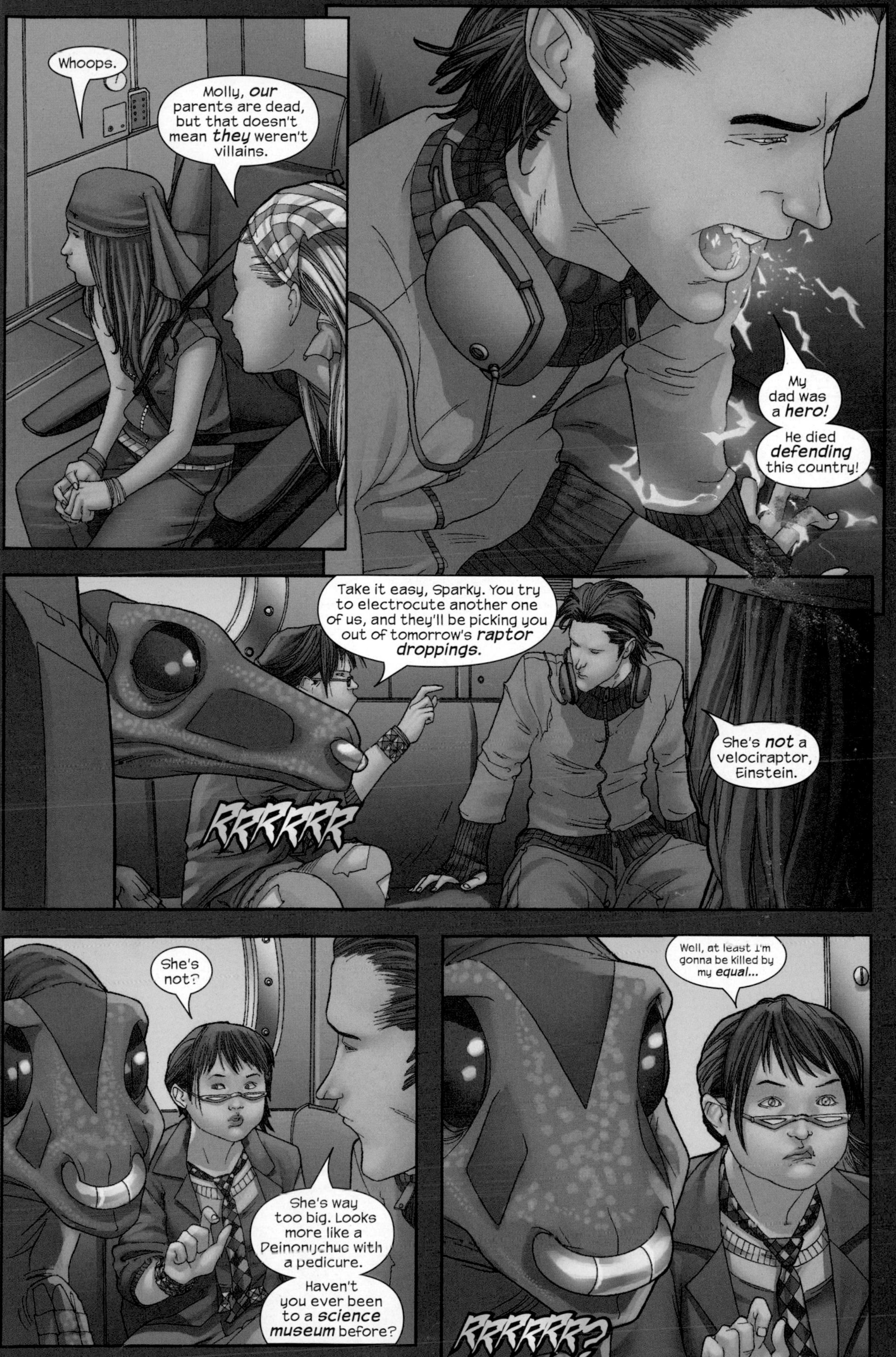
Whoops.
Molly, our parents are dead, but that doesn't mean they weren't villains.
My dad was a hero!
He died defending this country!
Take it easy, Sparky. You try to electrocute another one of us, and they'll be picking you out of tomorrow's raptor droppings.
RRRRRR
She's not a velociraptor, Einstein.
She's not?
She's way too big. Looks more like a Deinonychus with a pedicure.
Haven't you ever been to a science museum before?
Well, at least I'm gonna be killed by my equal...
RRRRRR?

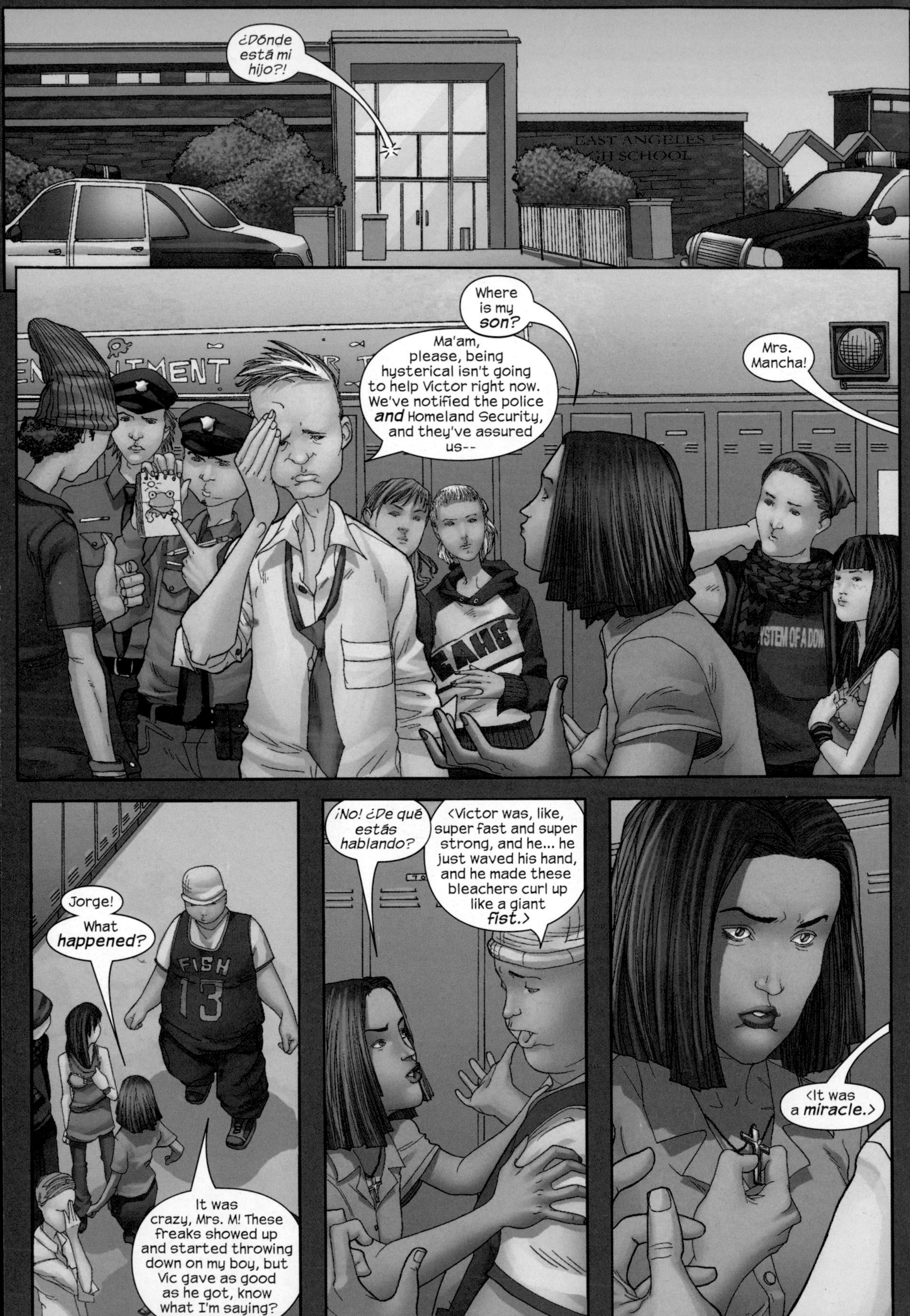
¿Dónde está mi hijo?!
EAST ANGELES HIGH SCHOOL
Where is my son?
Ma'am, please, being hysterical isn't going to help Victor right now. We've notified the police and Homeland Security, and they've assured us--
Mrs. Mancha!
Jorge! What happened?
It was crazy, Mrs. M! These freaks showed up and started throwing down on my boy, but Vic gave as good as he got, know what I'm saying?
¡No! ¿De qué estás hablando?
<Victor was, like, super fast and super strong, and he... he just waved his hand, and he made these bleachers curl up like a giant fist.>
<It was a miracle.>

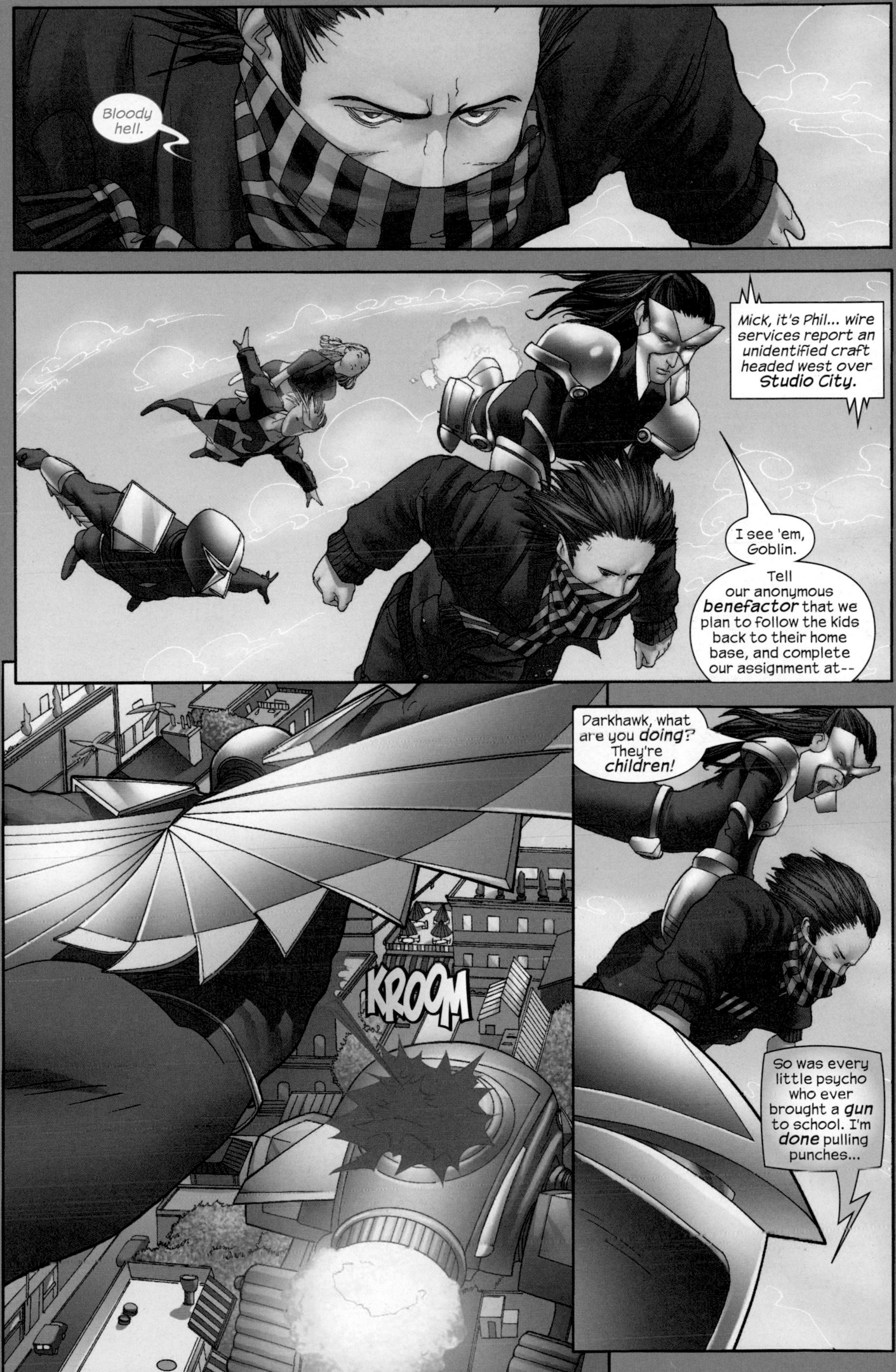
Bloody hell.
Mick, it's Phil... wire services report an unidentified craft headed west over Studio City.
I see 'em, Goblin.
Tell our anonymous benefactor that we plan to follow the kids back to their home base, and complete our assignment at--
Darkhawk, what are you doing? They're children!
KROOM
So was every little psycho who ever brought a gun to school. I'm done pulling punches...

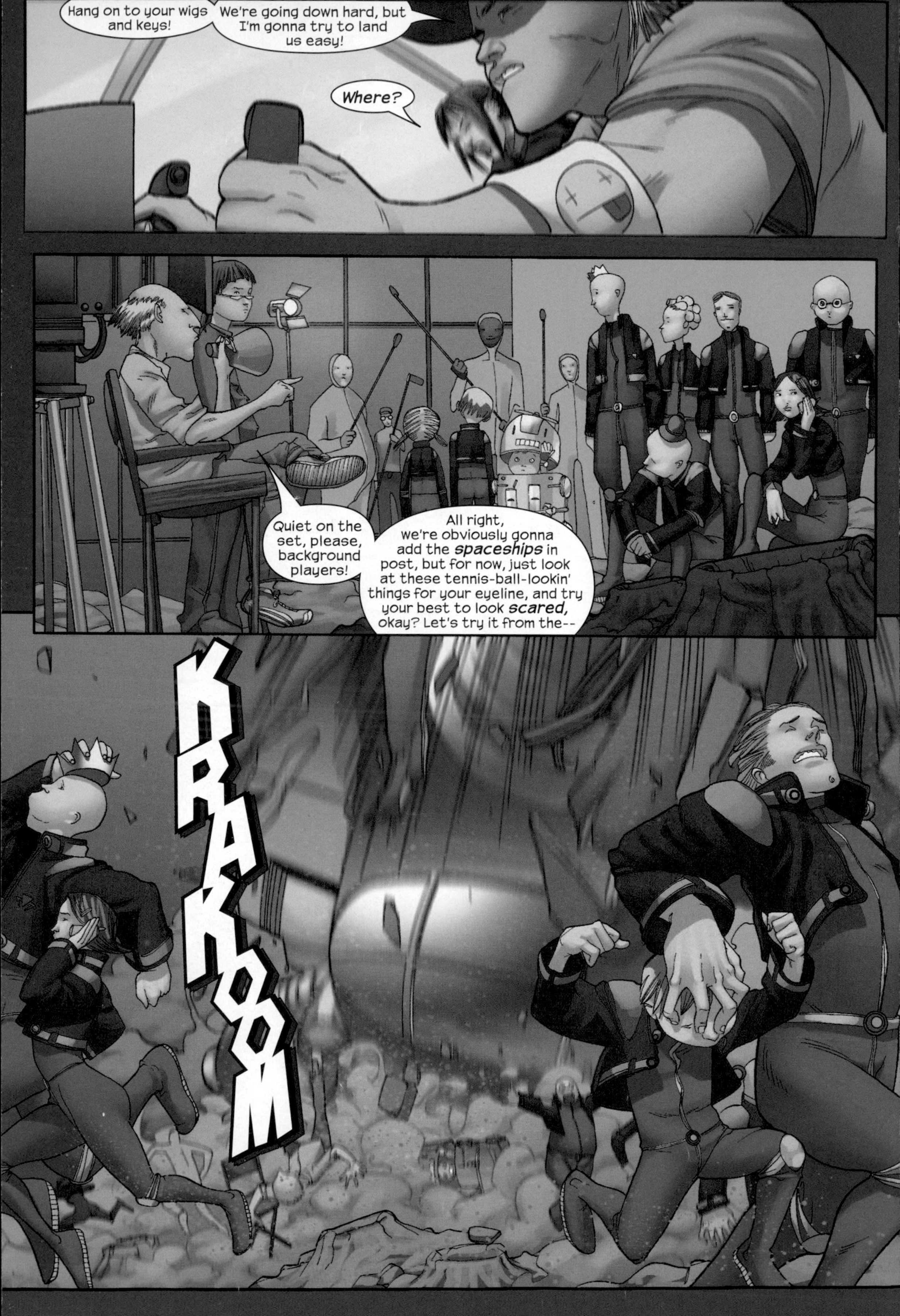

Hang on to your wigs and keys!
We're going down hard, but I'm gonna try to land us easy!
Where?
Quiet on the set, please, background players!
All right, we're obviously gonna add the *spaceships* in post, but for now, just look at these tennis-ball-lookin' things for your eyeline, and try your best to look *scared,* okay? Let's try it from the--
KRAKOOM

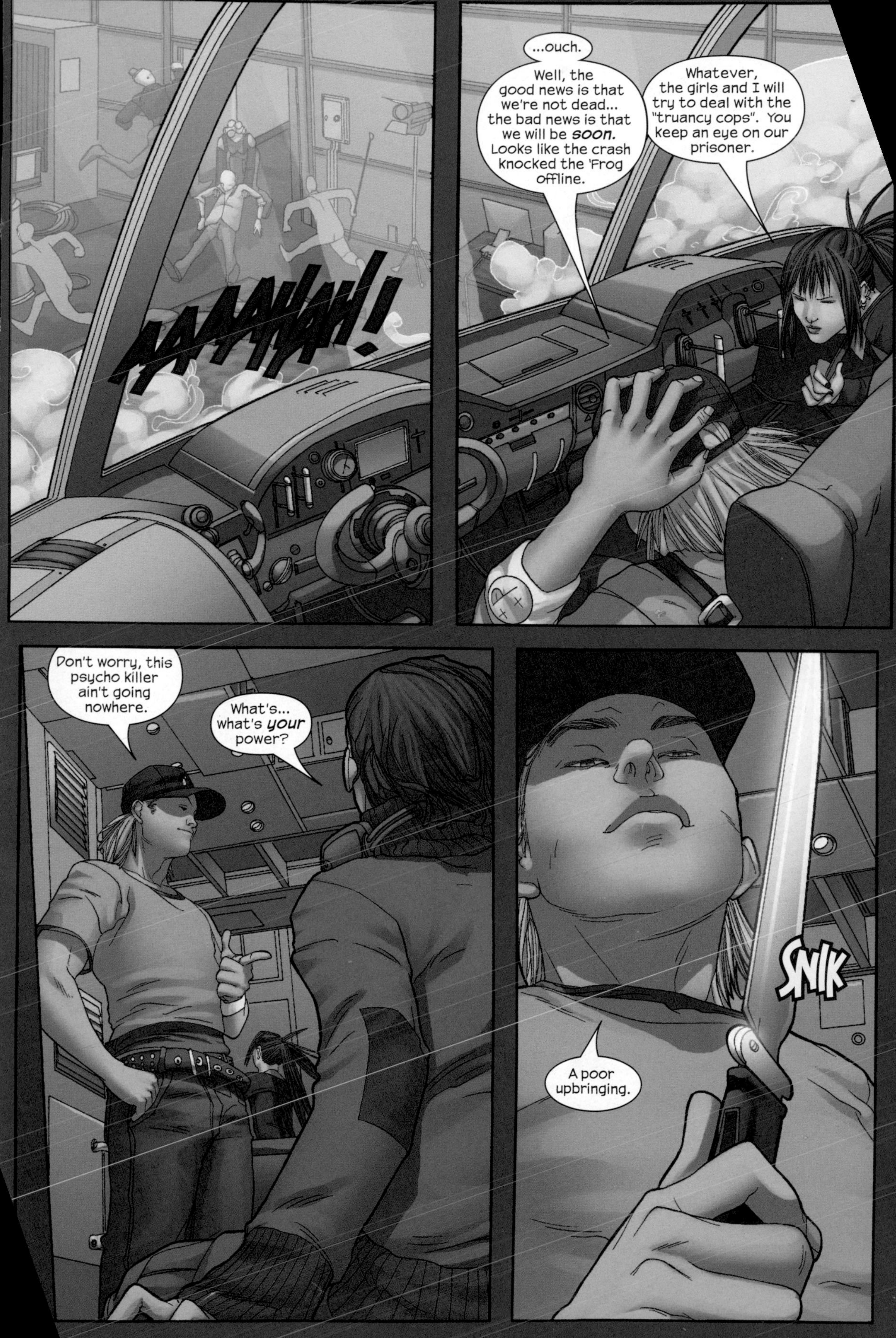
AAAAHHH!
...ouch.
Well, the good news is that we're not dead... the bad news is that we will be *soon.* Looks like the crash knocked the 'Frog offline.
Whatever, the girls and I will try to deal with the "truancy cops". You keep an eye on our prisoner.
Don't worry, this psycho killer ain't going nowhere.
What's... what's *your* power?
SNIK
A poor upbringing.

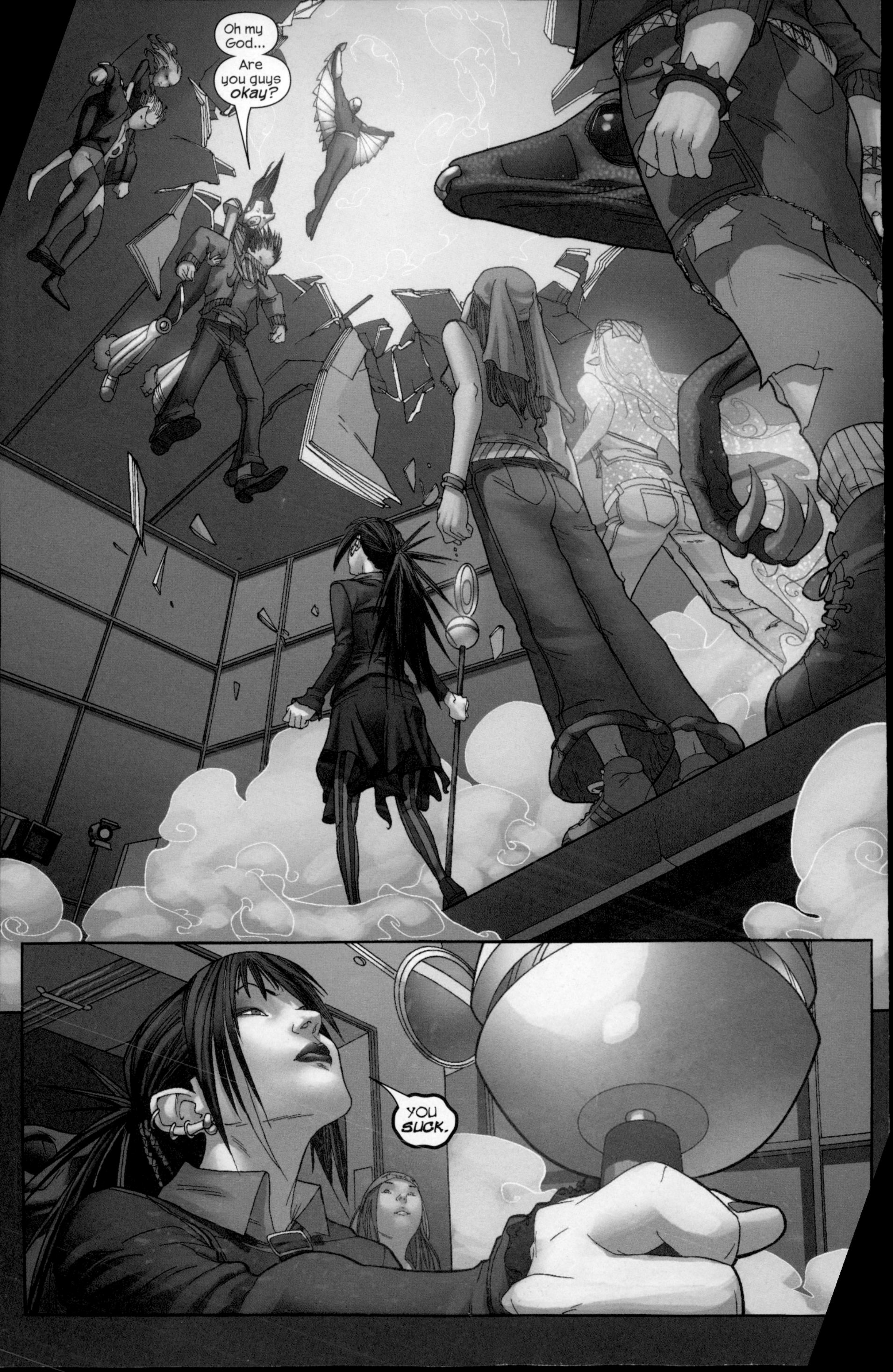
Oh my God...
Are you guys okay?
YOU SUCK.

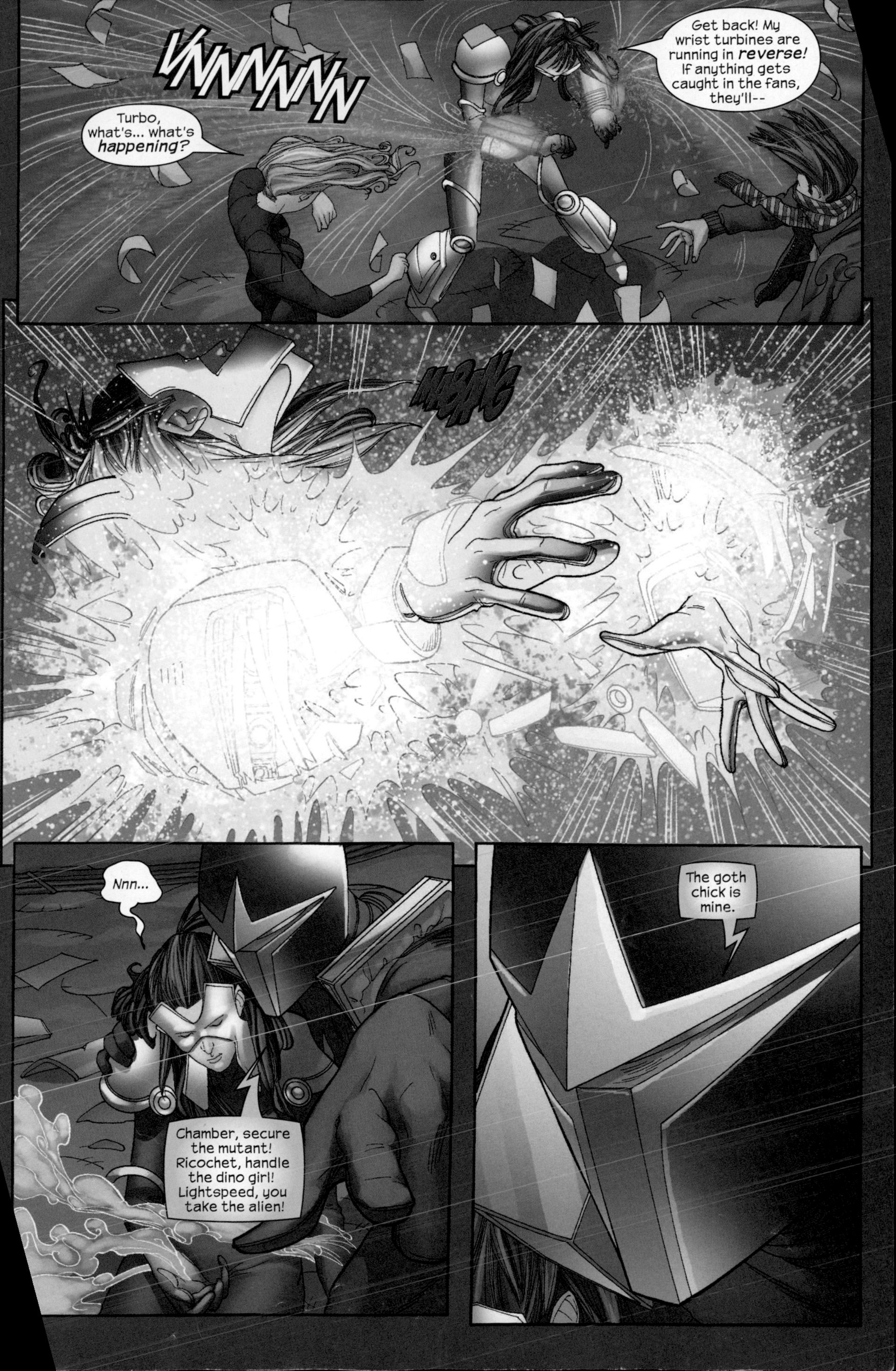
VNNNNNNN
Turbo, what's... what's *happening?*
Get back! My wrist turbines are running in ***reverse!*** If anything gets caught in the fans, they'll--
Nnn...
Chamber, secure the mutant! Ricochet, handle the dino girl! Lightspeed, you take the alien!
The goth chick is mine.

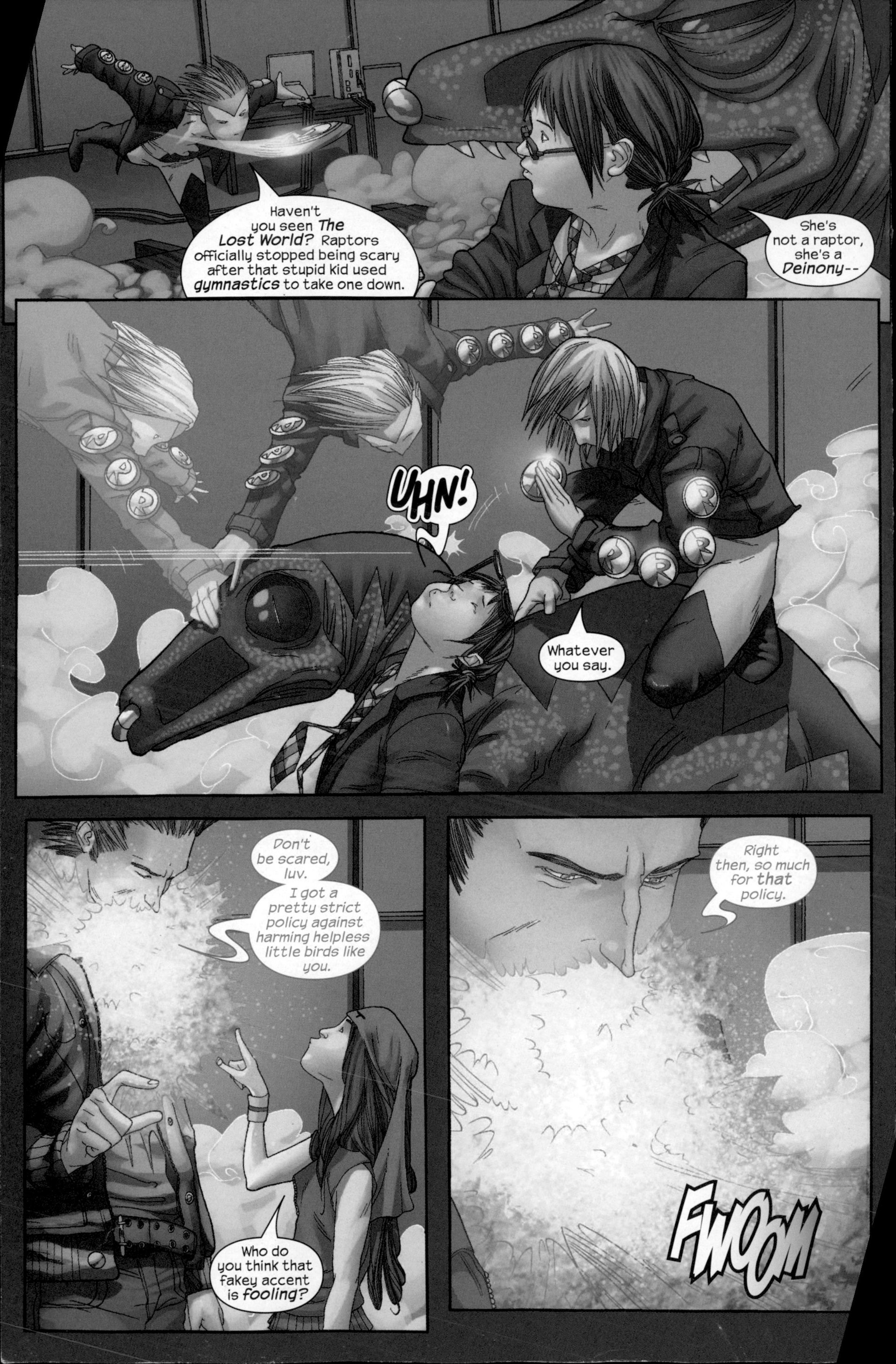
Haven't you seen The Lost World? Raptors officially stopped being scary after that stupid kid used gymnastics to take one down.
She's not a raptor, she's a Deinony--
UHN!
Whatever you say.
Don't be scared, luv.
I got a pretty strict policy against harming helpless little birds like you.
Who do you think that fakey accent is fooling?
Right then, so much for that policy.
FWOOM

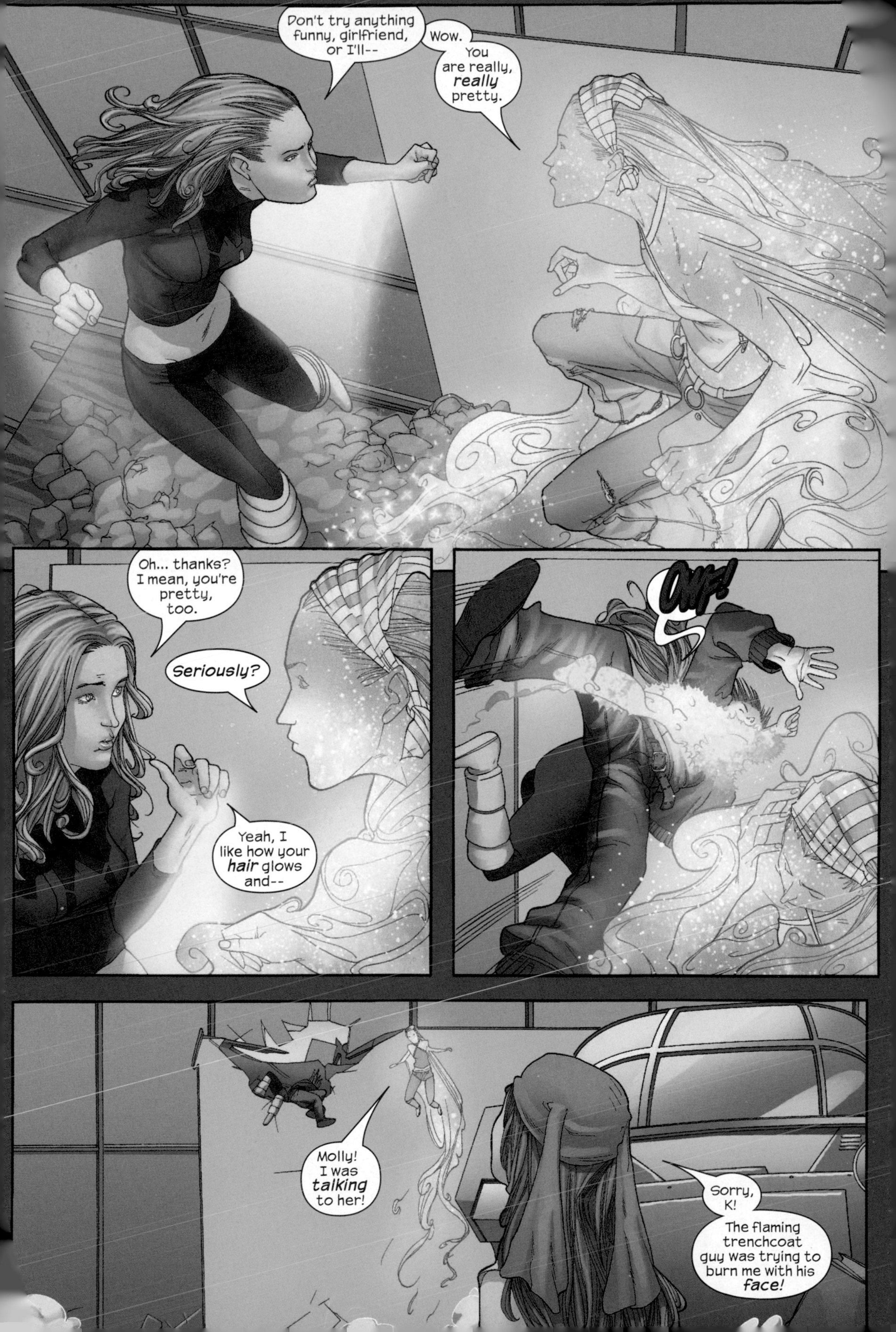

Don't try anything funny, girlfriend, or I'll--
Wow.
You are really, *really* pretty.
Oh... thanks? I mean, you're pretty, too.
Seriously?
Yeah, I like how your *hair* glows and--
OOF!
Molly! I was *talking* to her!
Sorry, K!
The flaming trenchcoat guy was trying to burn me with his *face!*

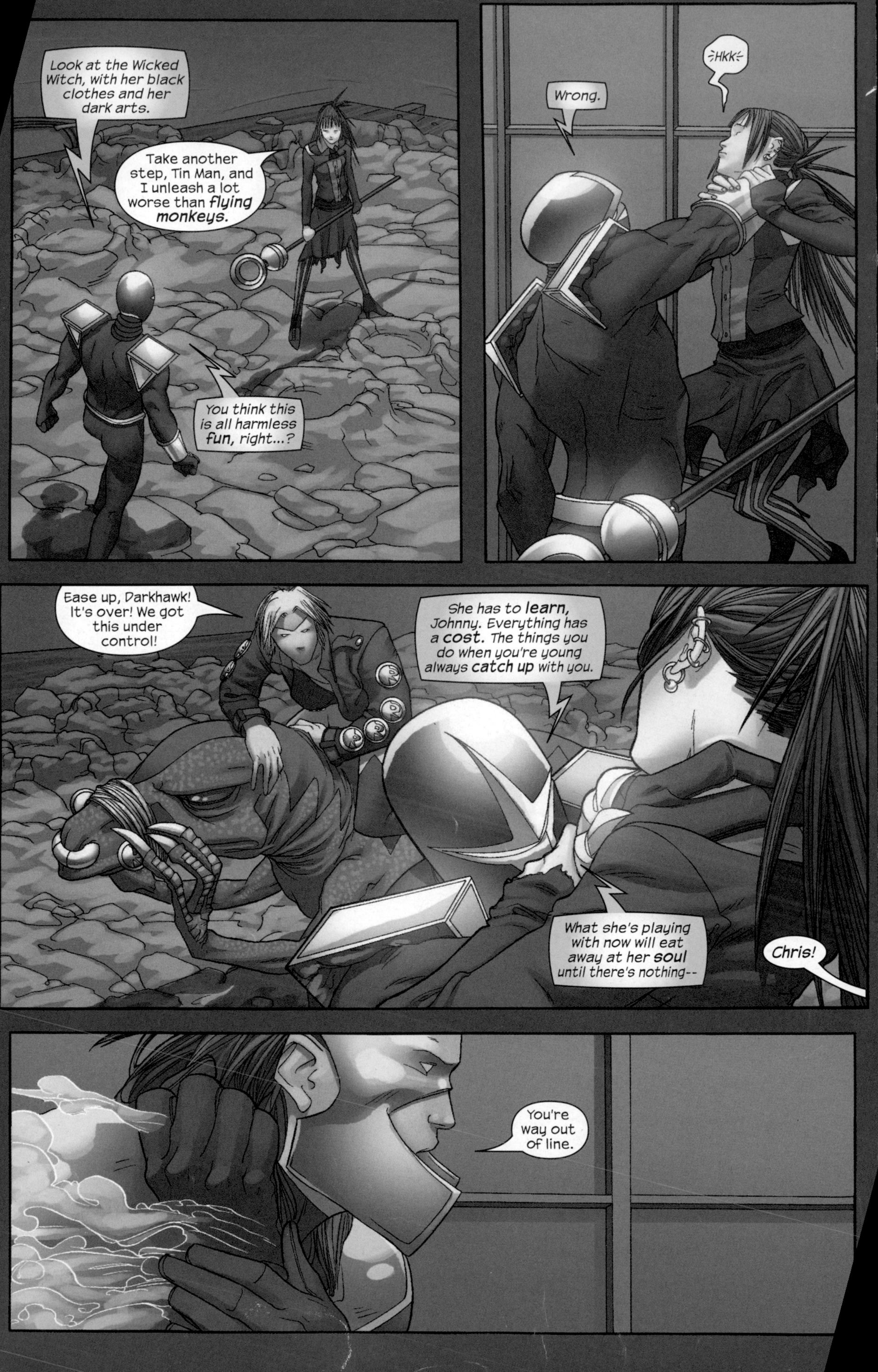
Look at the Wicked Witch, with her black clothes and her dark arts.
Take another step, Tin Man, and I unleash a lot worse than **flying monkeys.**
You think this is all harmless **fun**, right...?
Wrong.
HKK
Ease up, Darkhawk! It's over! We got this under control!
She has to **learn,** Johnny. Everything has a **cost.** The things you do when you're young always **catch up** with you.
What she's playing with now will eat away at her **soul** until there's nothing--
Chris!
You're way out of line.

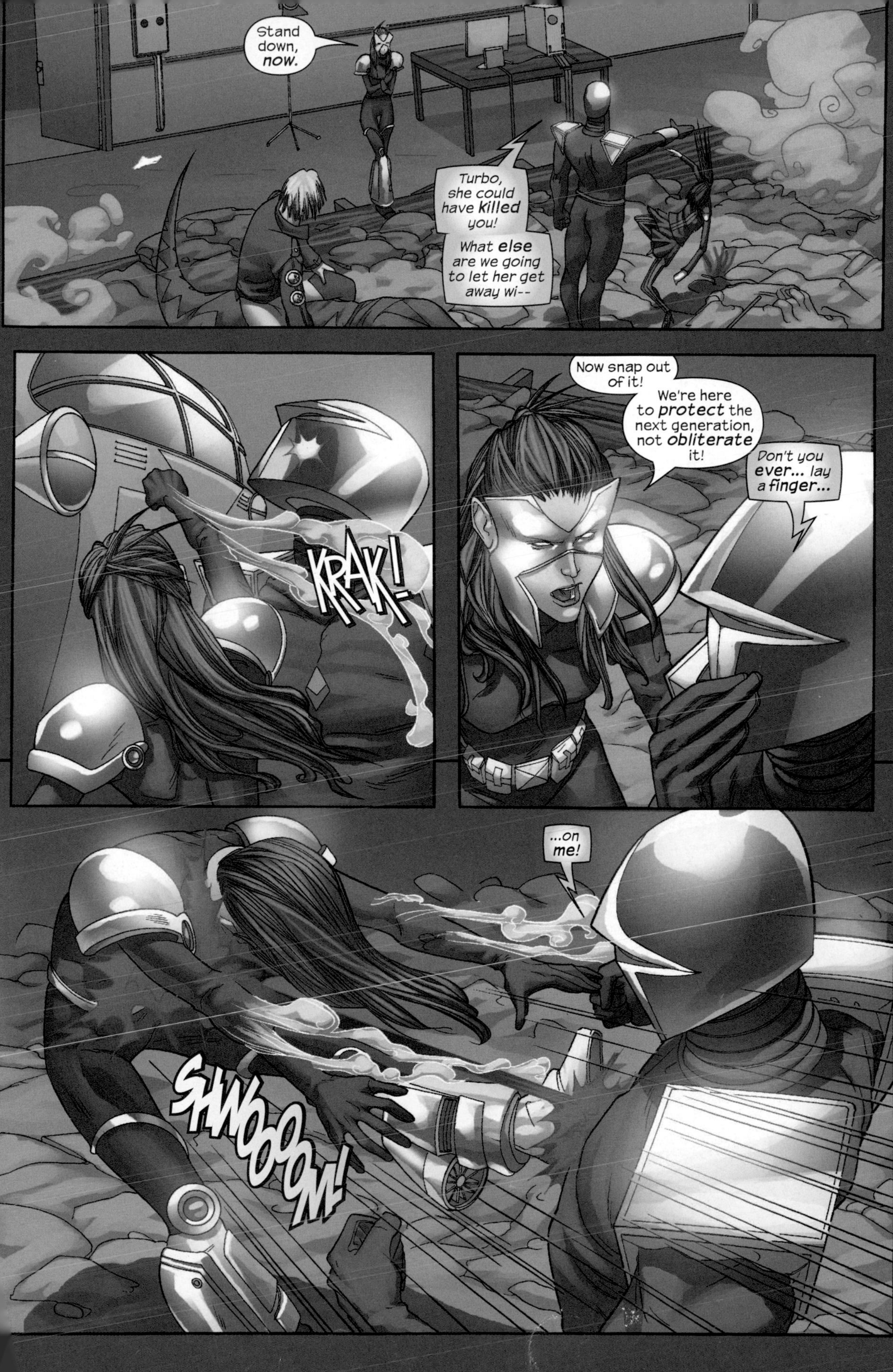
Stand down, **now.**
Turbo, she could have **killed** you!
What **else** are we going to let her get away wi--
KRAK!
Now snap out of it!
We're here to **protect** the next generation, not **obliterate** it!
Don't you **ever...** lay a **finger...**
...on **me!**
SHWOOOOM!

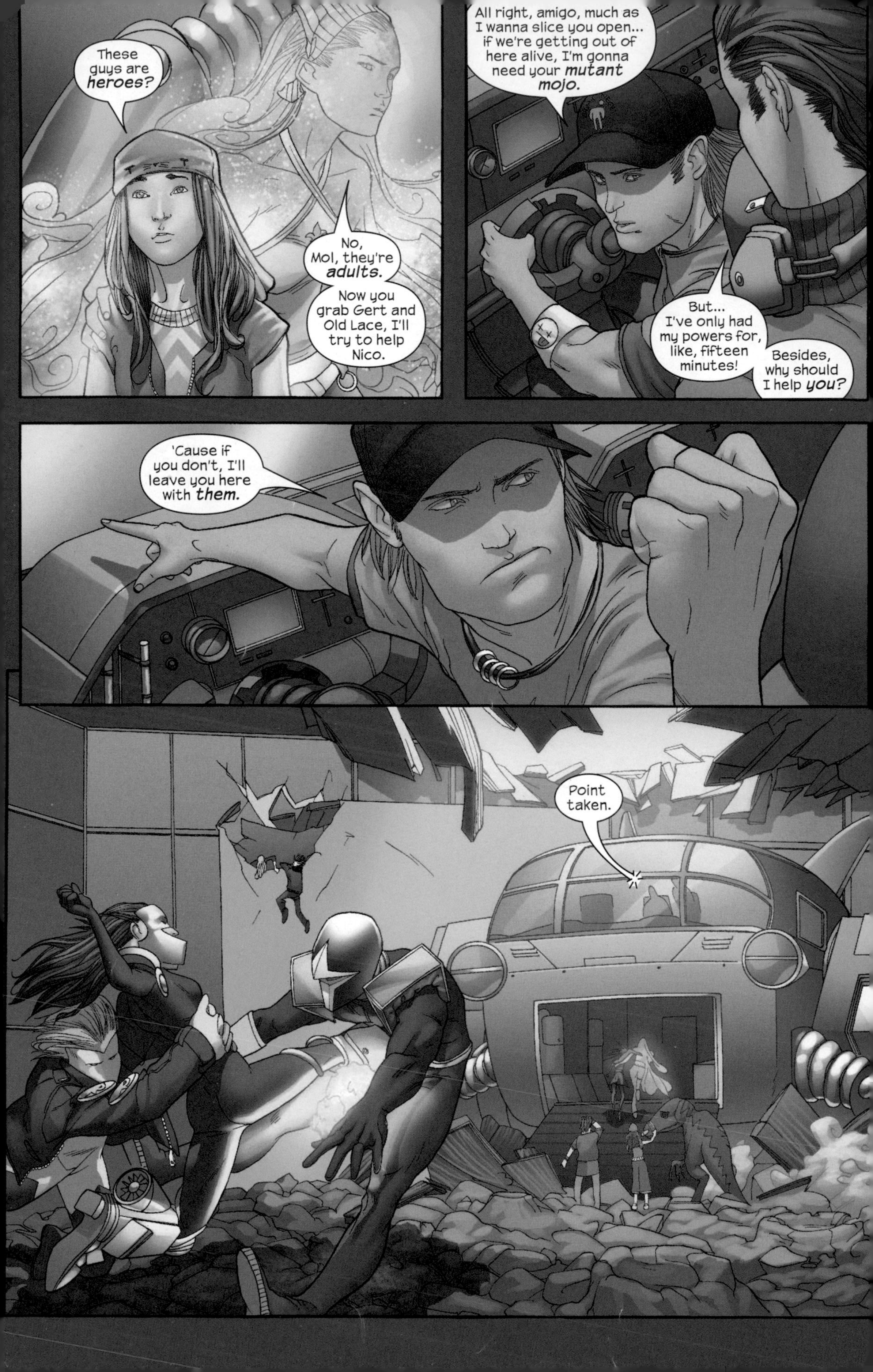
These guys are heroes?
No, Mol, they're adults.
Now you grab Gert and Old Lace, I'll try to help Nico.
All right, amigo, much as I wanna slice you open... if we're getting out of here alive, I'm gonna need your mutant mojo.
But... I've only had my powers for, like, fifteen minutes!
Besides, why should I help you?
'Cause if you don't, I'll leave you here with them.
Point taken.

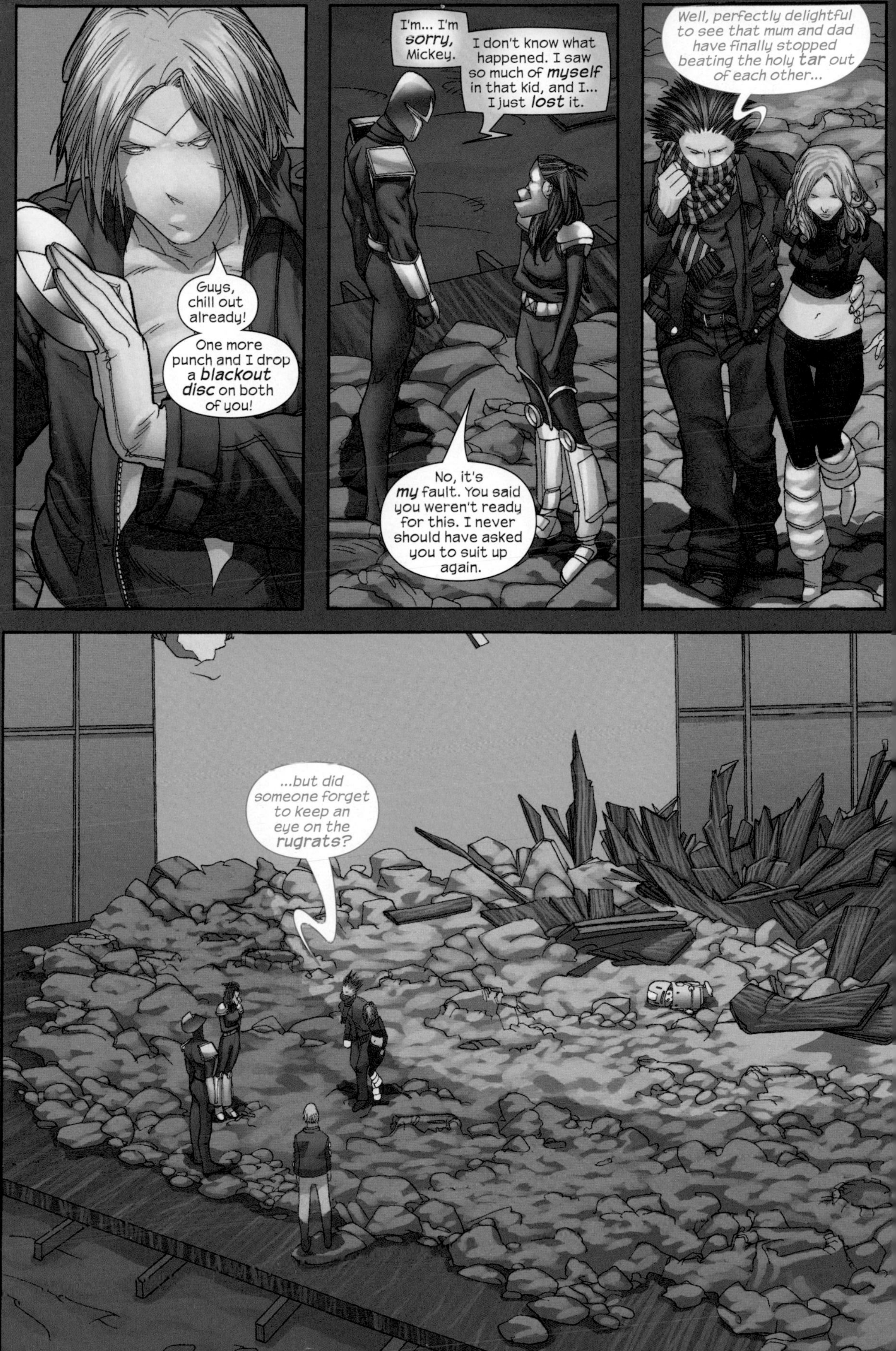
Guys, chill out already!
One more punch and I drop a blackout disc on both of you!
I'm... I'm sorry, Mickey.
I don't know what happened. I saw so much of myself in that kid, and I... I just lost it.
No, it's my fault. You said you weren't ready for this. I never should have asked you to suit up again.
Well, perfectly delightful to see that mum and dad have finally stopped beating the holy tar out of each other...
...but did someone forget to keep an eye on the rugrats?

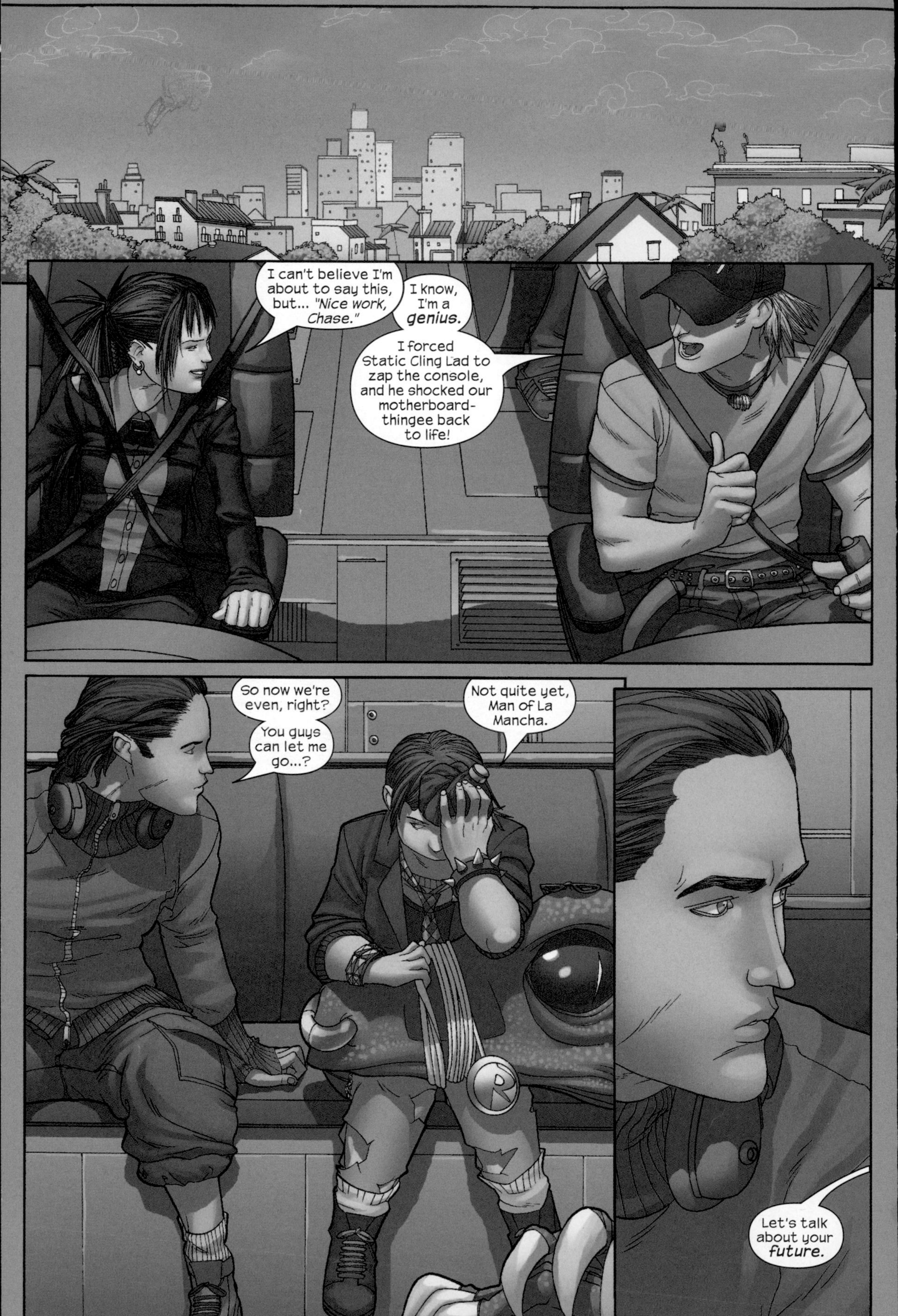
I can't believe I'm about to say this, but... "Nice work, Chase."
I know, I'm a genius.
I forced Static Cling Lad to zap the console, and he shocked our motherboard-thingee back to life!
So now we're even, right?
You guys can let me go...?
Not quite yet, Man of La Mancha.
Let's talk about your future.

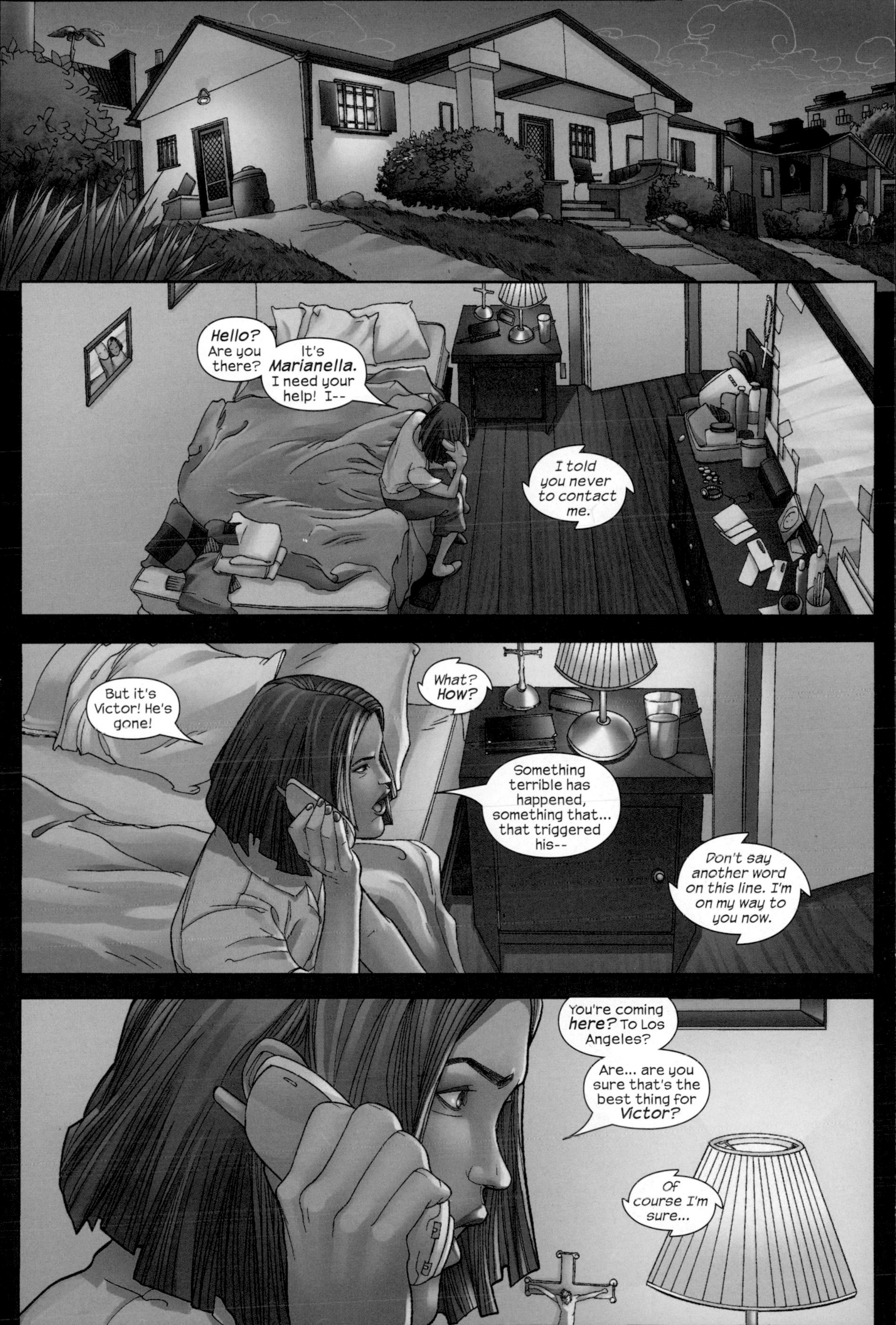

Hello? Are you there?
It's Marianella. I need your help! I--
I told you never to contact me.
But it's Victor! He's gone!
What? How?
Something terrible has happened, something that... that triggered his--
Don't say another word on this line. I'm on my way to you now.
You're coming here? To Los Angeles?
Are... are you sure that's the best thing for Victor?
Of course I'm sure...

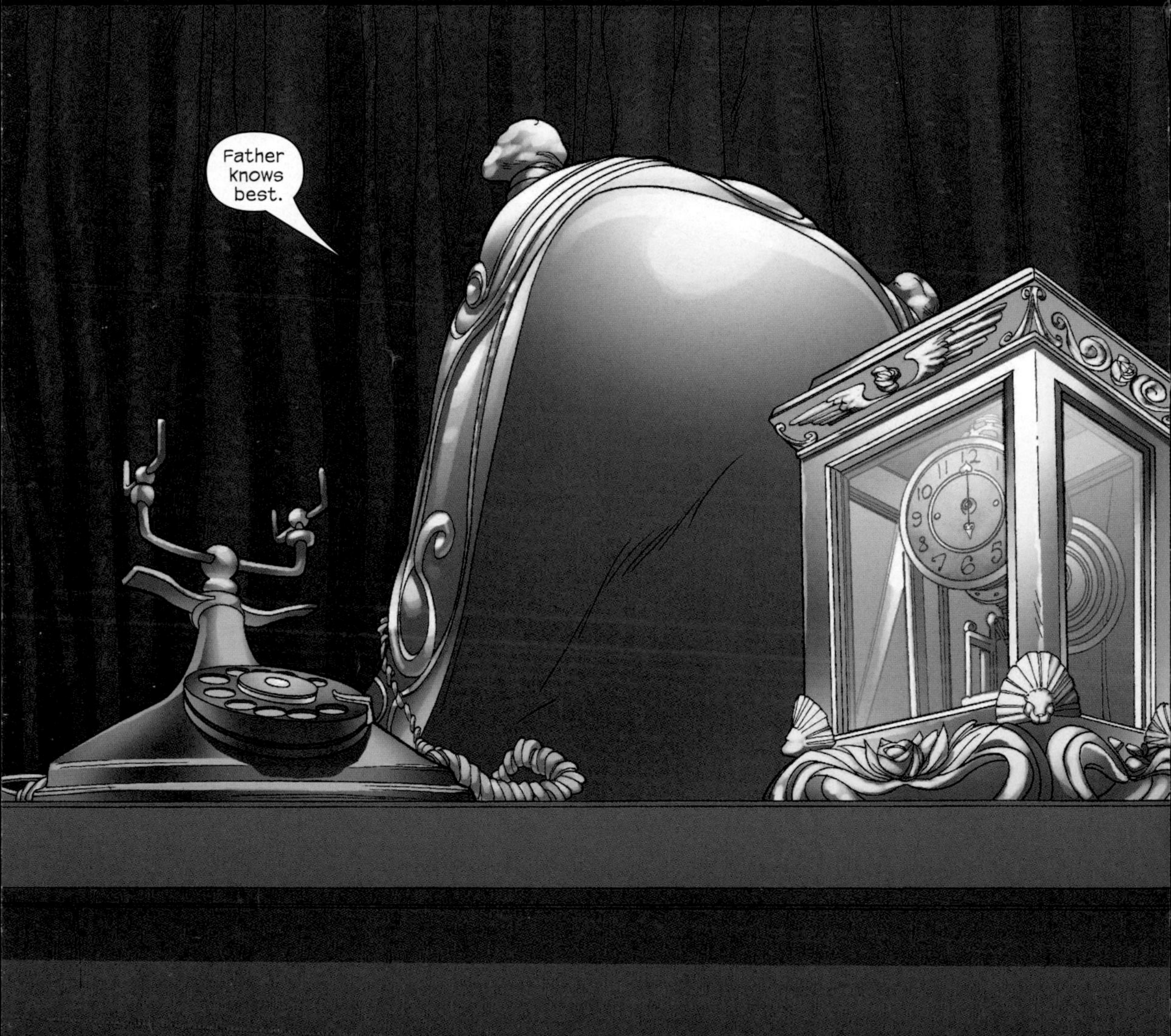
Father knows best.

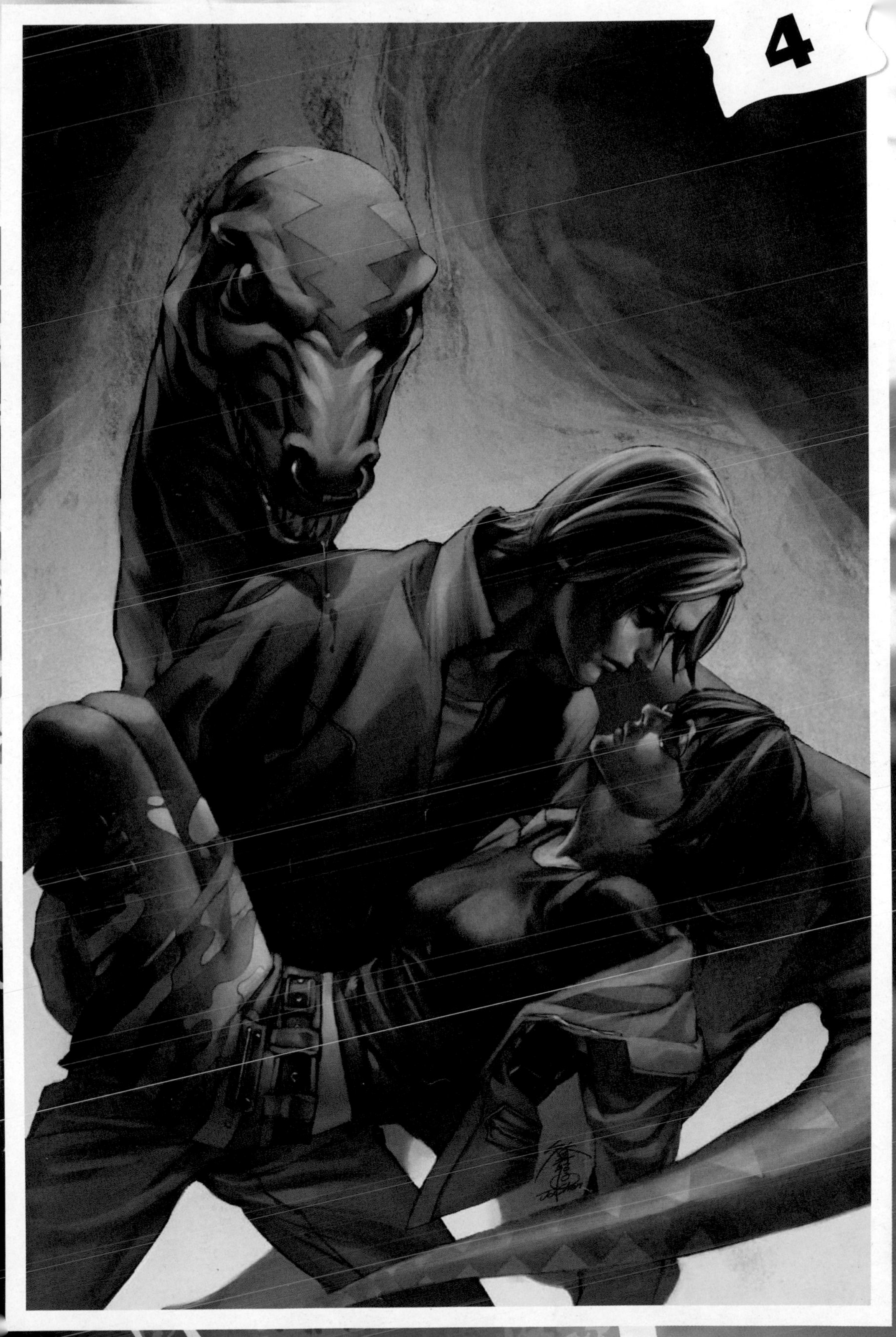
4

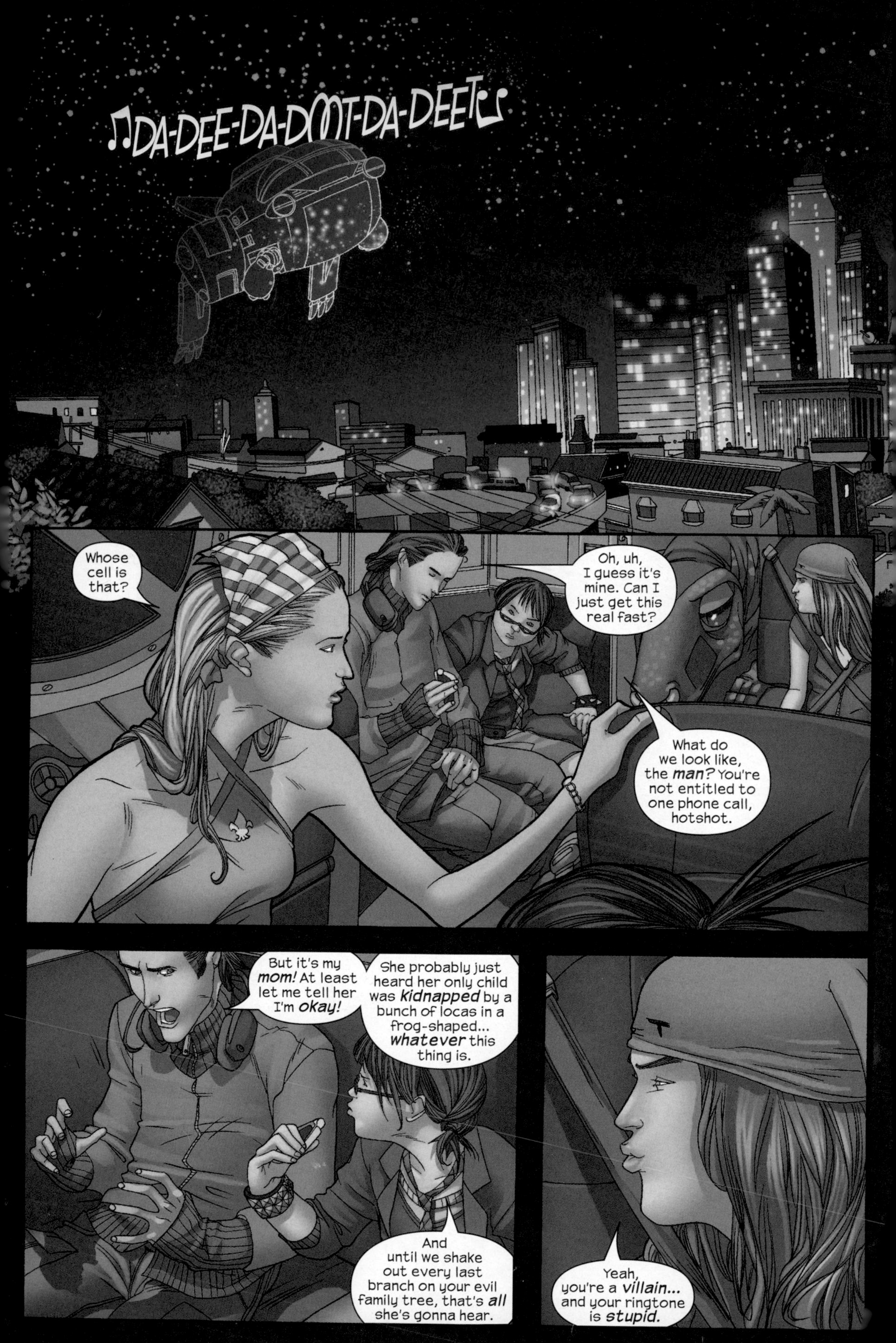
♫DA-DEE-DA-DOOT-DA-DEET♫
Whose cell is that?
Oh, uh, I guess it's mine. Can I just get this real fast?
What do we look like, the man? You're not entitled to one phone call, hotshot.
But it's my mom! At least let me tell her I'm okay!
She probably just heard her only child was kidnapped by a bunch of locas in a frog-shaped... whatever this thing is.
And until we shake out every last branch on your evil family tree, that's all she's gonna hear.
Yeah, you're a villain... and your ringtone is stupid.

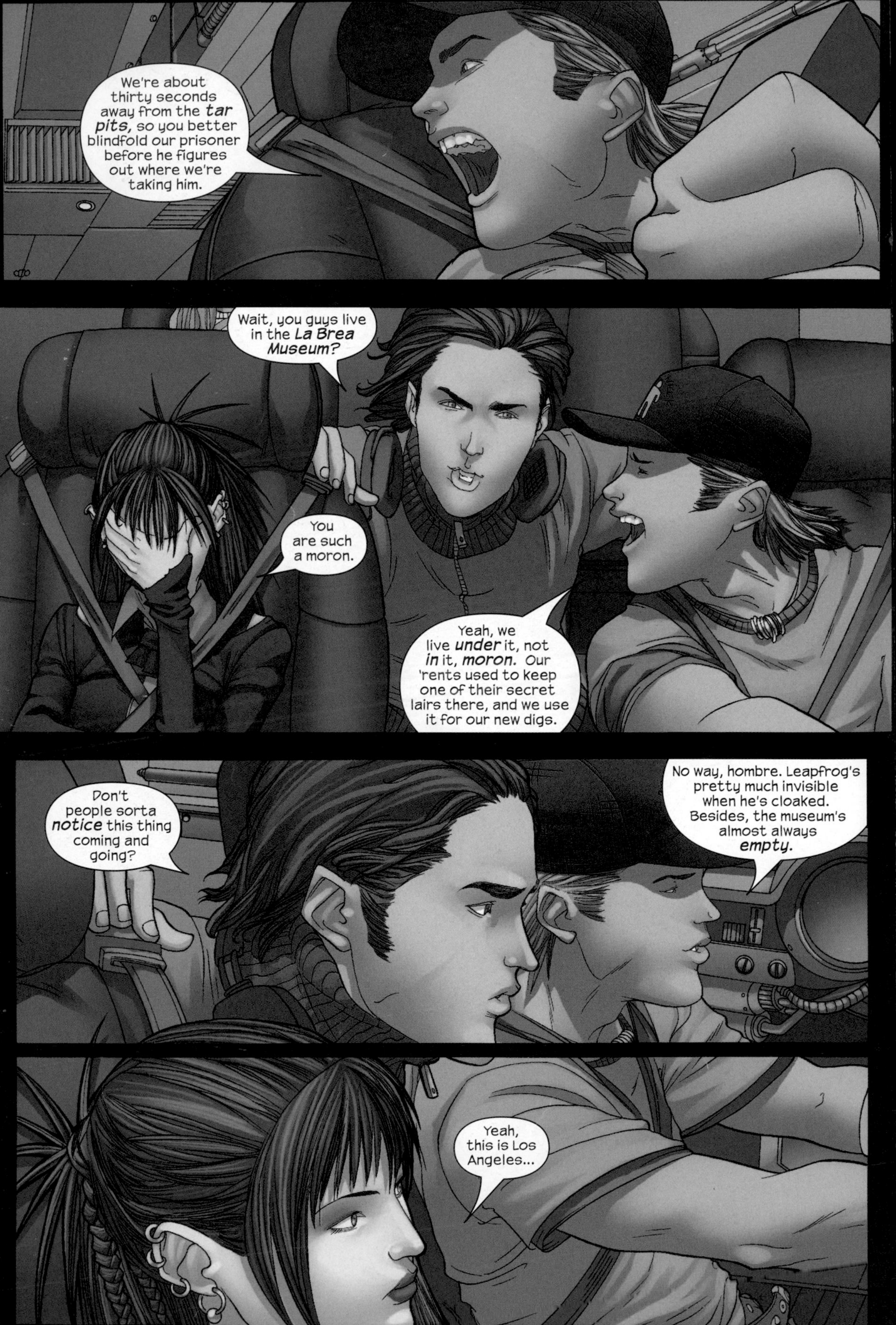

We're about thirty seconds away from the *tar pits,* so you better blindfold our prisoner before he figures out where we're taking him.
Wait, you guys live in the *La Brea Museum*?
You are such a moron.
Yeah, we live *under* it, not *in* it, *moron.* Our 'rents used to keep one of their secret lairs there, and we use it for our new digs.
Don't people sorta *notice* this thing coming and going?
No way, hombre. Leapfrog's pretty much invisible when he's cloaked. Besides, the museum's almost always *empty.*
Yeah, this is Los Angeles...

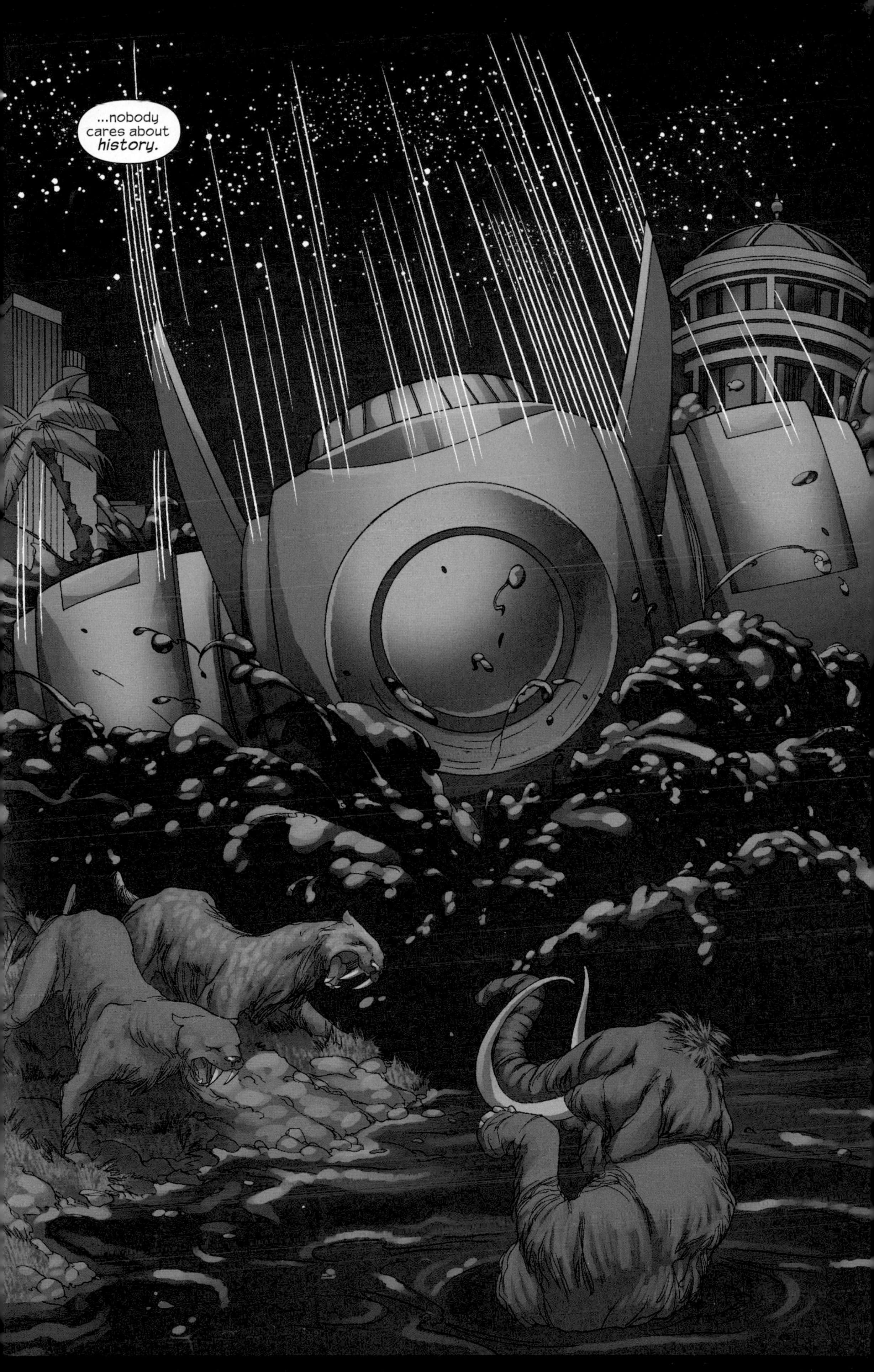
...nobody cares about history.

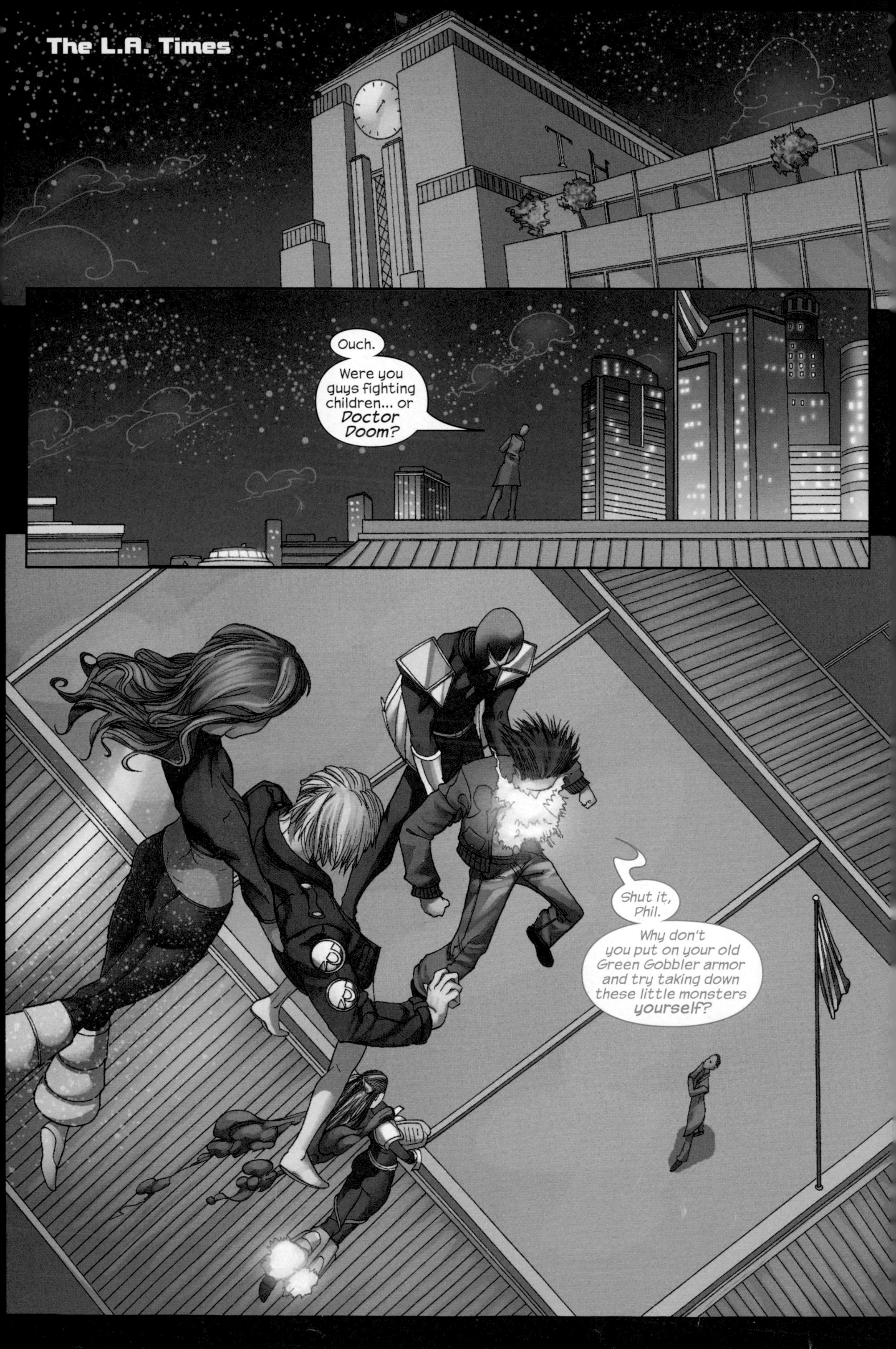
The L.A. Times
Ouch.
Were you guys fighting children... or Doctor Doom?
Shut it, Phil.
Why don't you put on your old Green Gobbler armor and try taking down these little monsters yourself?

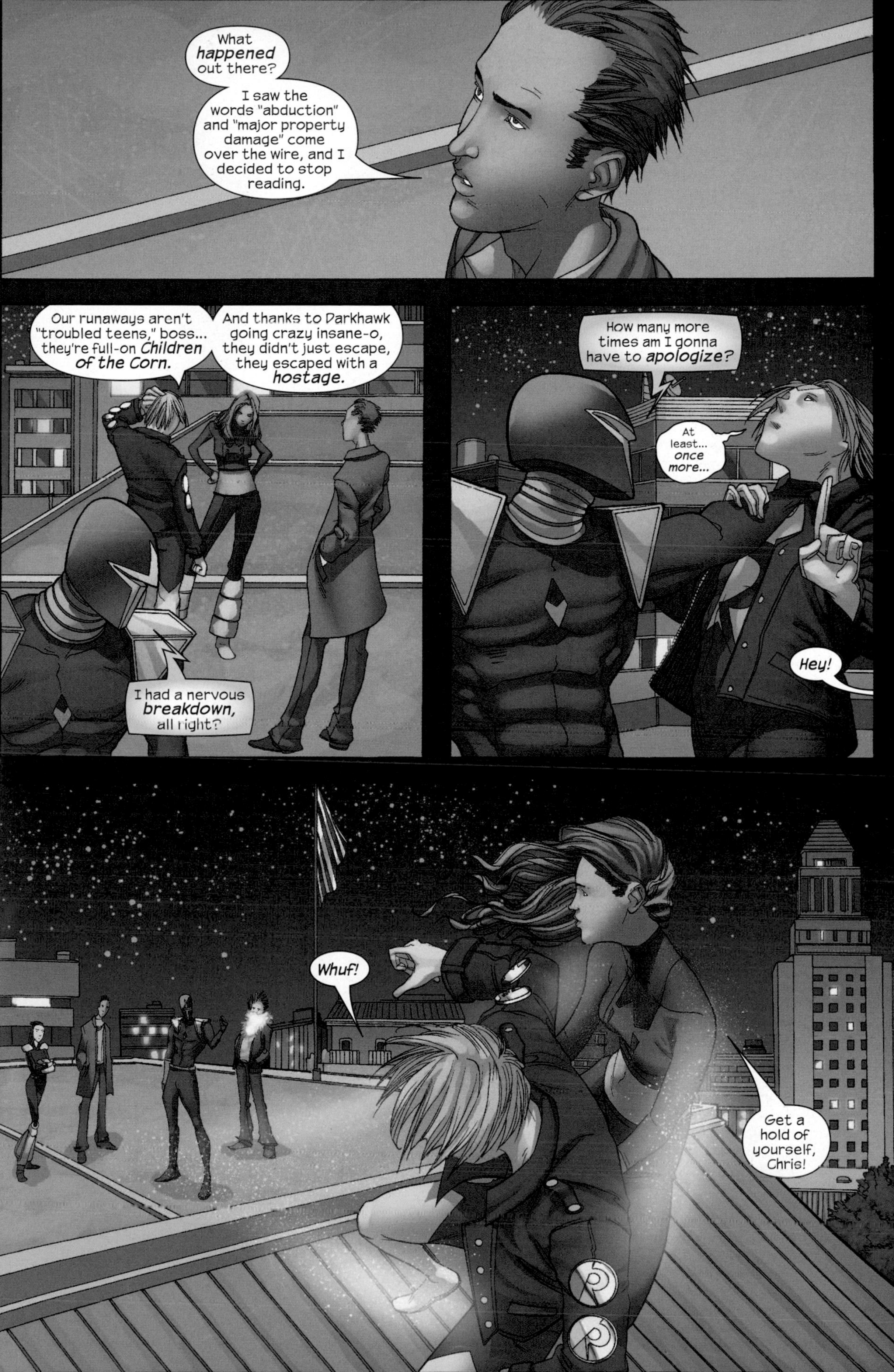
What *happened* out there?
I saw the words "abduction" and "major property damage" come over the wire, and I decided to stop reading.
Our runaways aren't "troubled teens," boss... they're full-on *Children of the Corn.*
And thanks to Darkhawk going crazy insane-o, they didn't just escape, they escaped with a *hostage.*
I had a nervous *breakdown,* all right?
How many more times am I gonna have to *apologize?*
At least... *once more...*
Hey!
Whuf!
Get a hold of yourself, Chris!

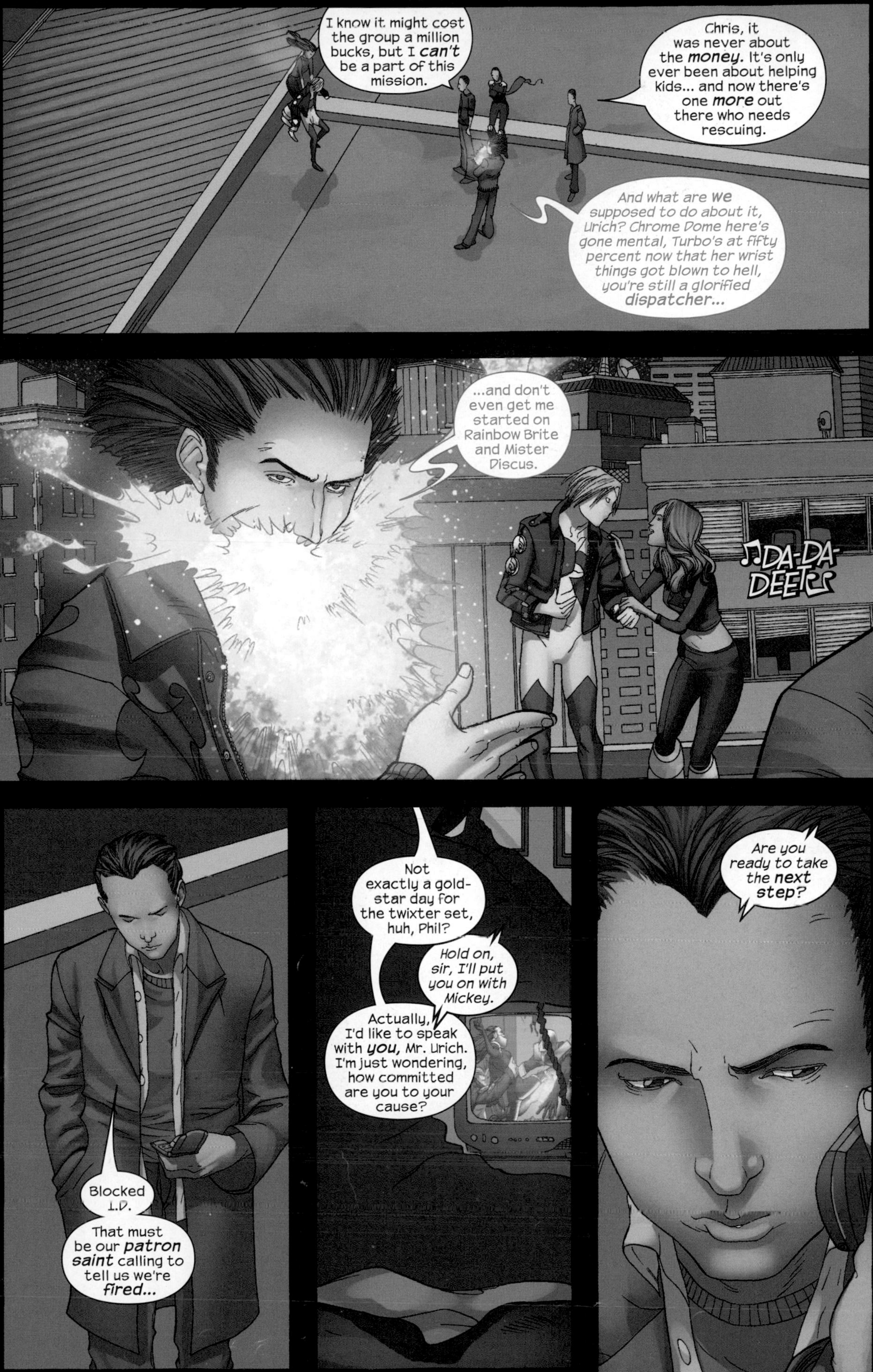
I know it might cost the group a million bucks, but I *can't* be a part of this mission.
Chris, it was never about the *money.* It's only ever been about helping kids... and now there's one *more* out there who needs rescuing.
And what are *we* supposed to do about it, Urich? Chrome Dome here's gone mental, Turbo's at fifty percent now that her wrist things got blown to hell, you're still a glorified *dispatcher...*
...and don't even get me started on Rainbow Brite and Mister Discus.
DA-DA-DEET
Blocked I.D.
That must be our *patron saint* calling to tell us we're *fired...*
Not exactly a gold-star day for the twixter set, huh, Phil?
Hold on, sir, I'll put you on with Mickey.
Actually, I'd like to speak with *you,* Mr. Urich. I'm just wondering, how committed are you to your cause?
Are you ready to take the *next step?*

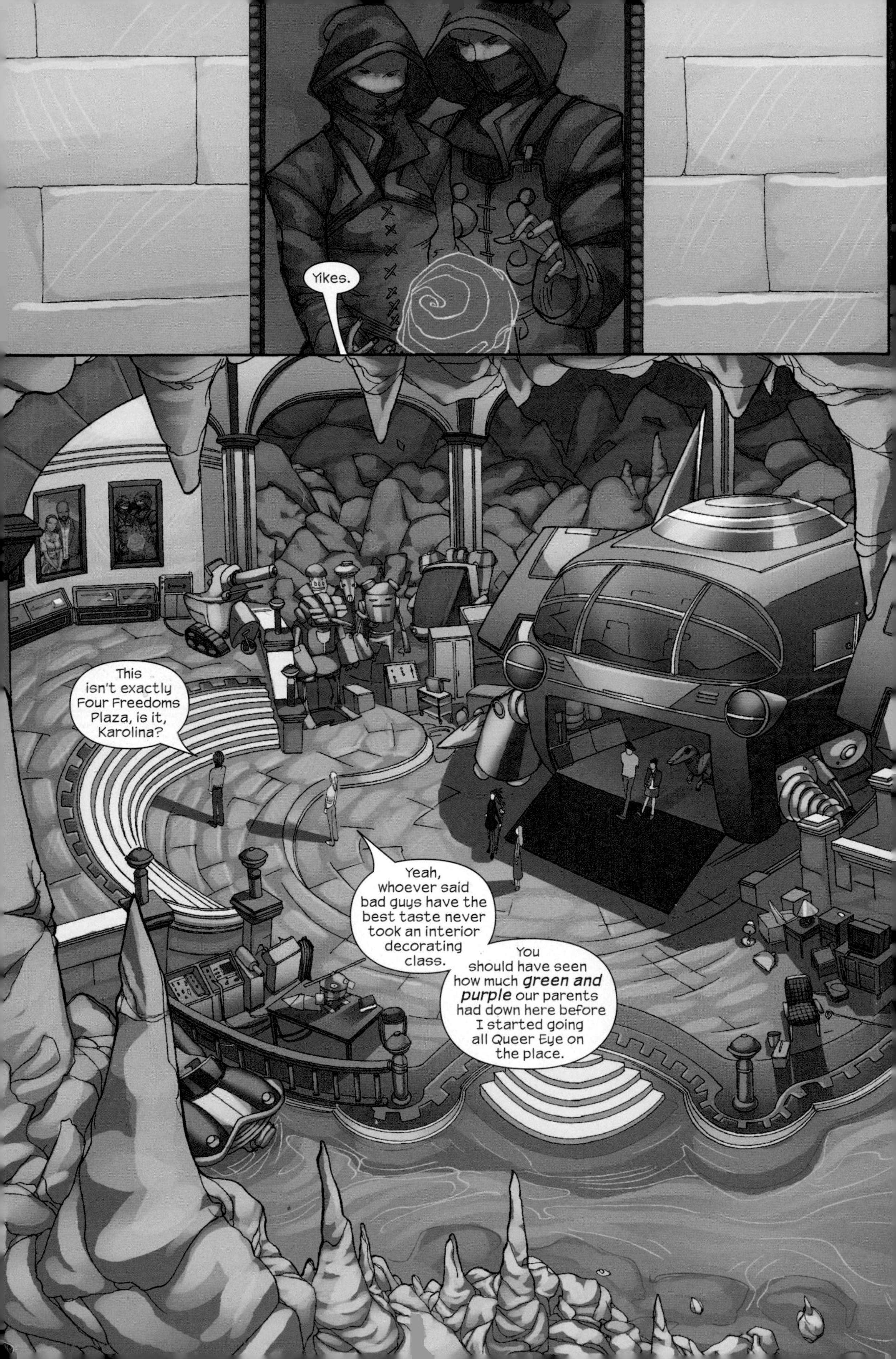
Yikes.
This isn't exactly Four Freedoms Plaza, is it, Karolina?
Yeah, whoever said bad guys have the best taste never took an interior decorating class.
You should have seen how much *green and purple* our parents had down here before I started going all Queer Eye on the place.

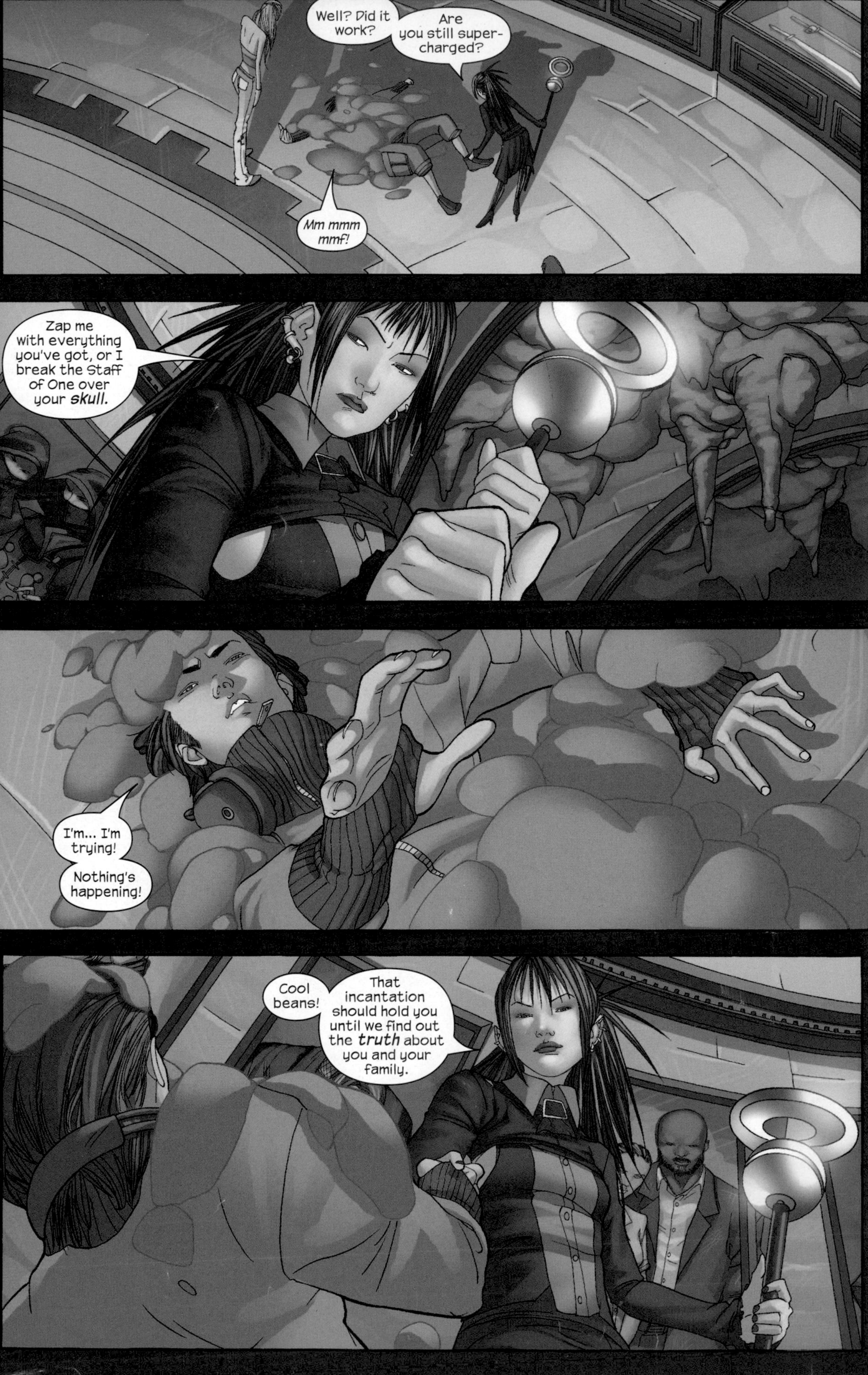

Well? Did it work?
Are you still super-charged?
Mm mmm mmf!
Zap me with everything you've got, or I break the Staff of One over your *skull.*
I'm... I'm trying!
Nothing's happening!
Cool beans!
That incantation should hold you until we find out the *truth* about you and your family.

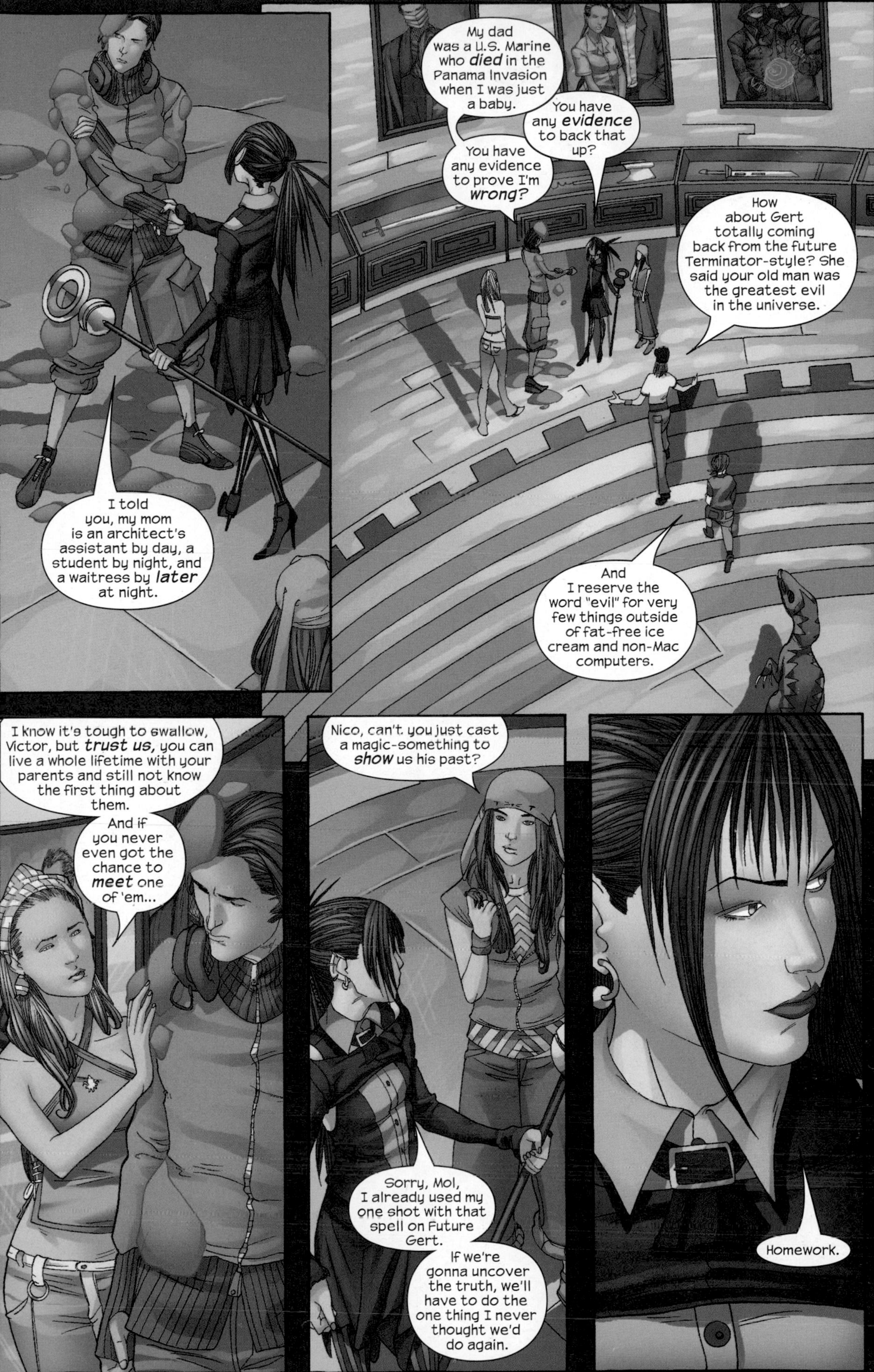
I told you, my mom is an architect's assistant by day, a student by night, and a waitress by *later* at night.
My dad was a U.S. Marine who *died* in the Panama Invasion when I was just a baby.
You have any *evidence* to back that up?
You have any evidence to prove I'm *wrong?*
How about Gert totally coming back from the future Terminator-style? She said your old man was the greatest evil in the universe.
And I reserve the word "evil" for very few things outside of fat-free ice cream and non-Mac computers.
I know it's tough to swallow, Victor, but *trust us,* you can live a whole lifetime with your parents and still not know the first thing about them.
And if you never even got the chance to *meet* one of 'em...
Nico, can't you just cast a magic-something to *show* us his past?
Sorry, Mol, I already used my one shot with that spell on Future Gert.
If we're gonna uncover the truth, we'll have to do the one thing I never thought we'd do again.
Homework.

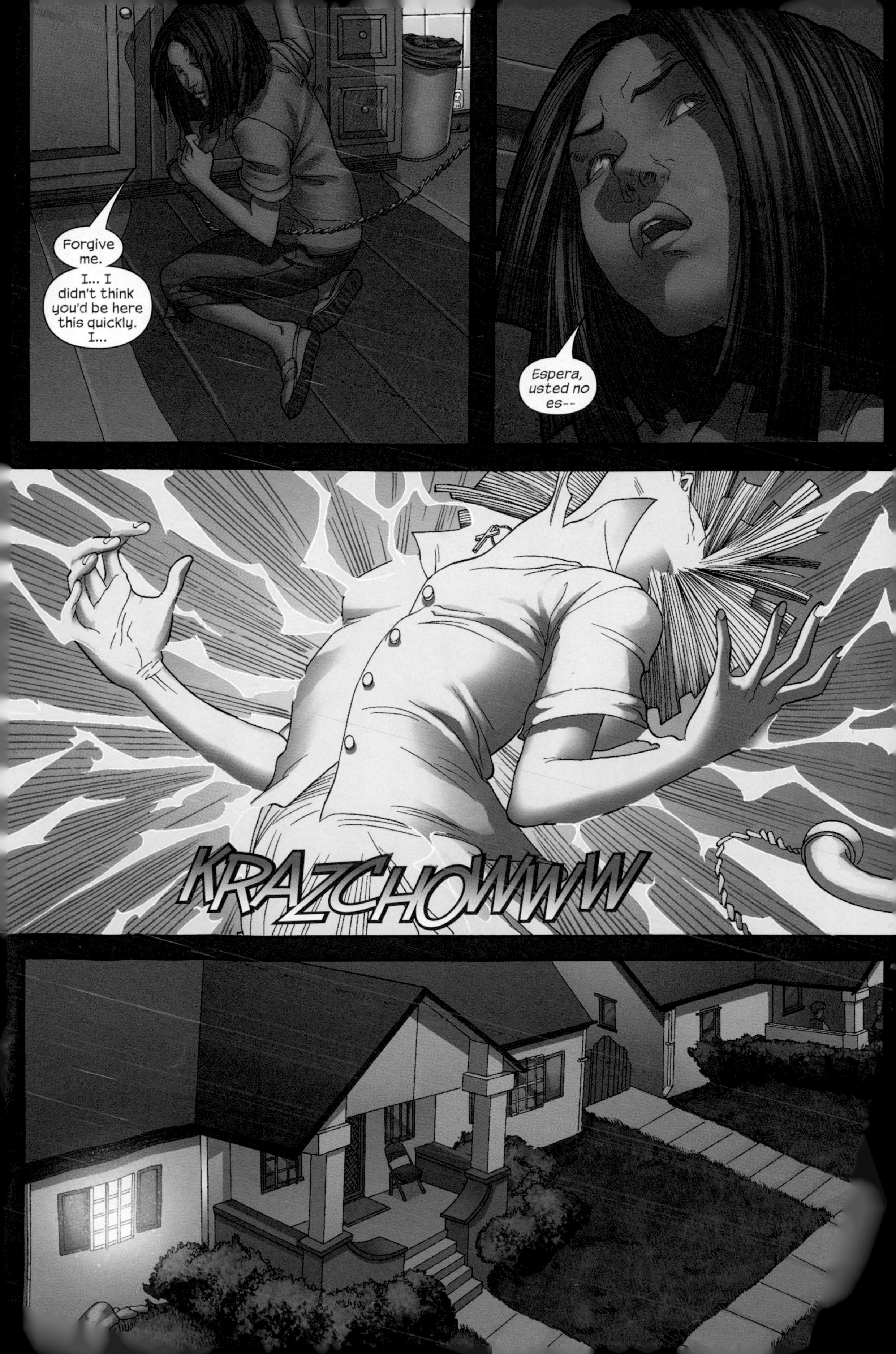
Forgive me.
I... I didn't think you'd be here this quickly. I...
Espera, usted no es--
KRAZCHOWWW

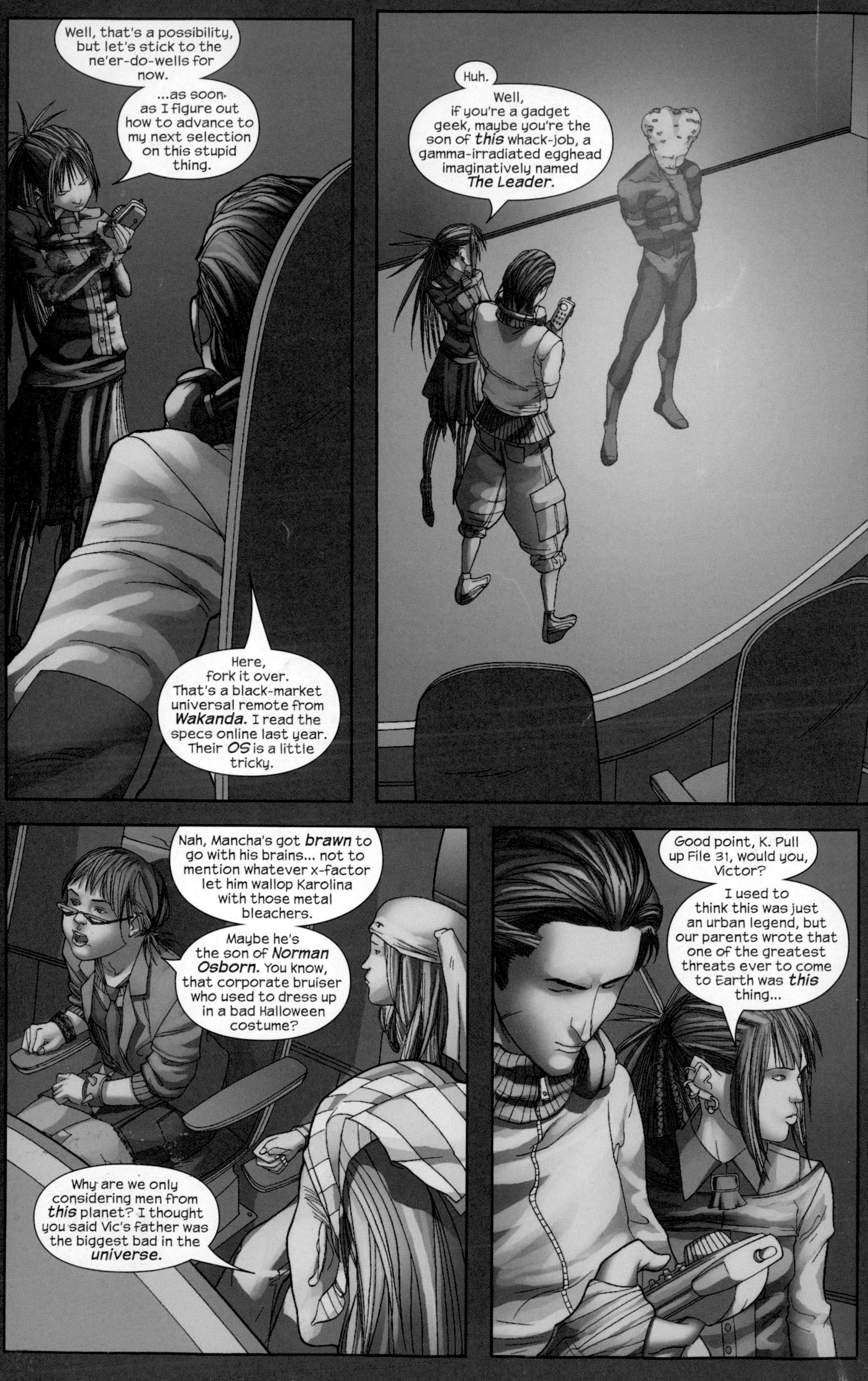
Well, that's a possibility, but let's stick to the ne'er-do-wells for now.
...as soon as I figure out how to advance to my next selection on this stupid thing.
Here, fork it over. That's a black-market universal remote from Wakanda. I read the specs online last year. Their OS is a little tricky.
Huh.
Well, if you're a gadget geek, maybe you're the son of this whack-job, a gamma-irradiated egghead imaginatively named The Leader.
Nah, Mancha's got brawn to go with his brains... not to mention whatever x-factor let him wallop Karolina with those metal bleachers.
Maybe he's the son of Norman Osborn. You know, that corporate bruiser who used to dress up in a bad Halloween costume?
Why are we only considering men from this planet? I thought you said Vic's father was the biggest bad in the universe.
Good point, K. Pull up File 31, would you, Victor?
I used to think this was just an urban legend, but our parents wrote that one of the greatest threats ever to come to Earth was this thing...

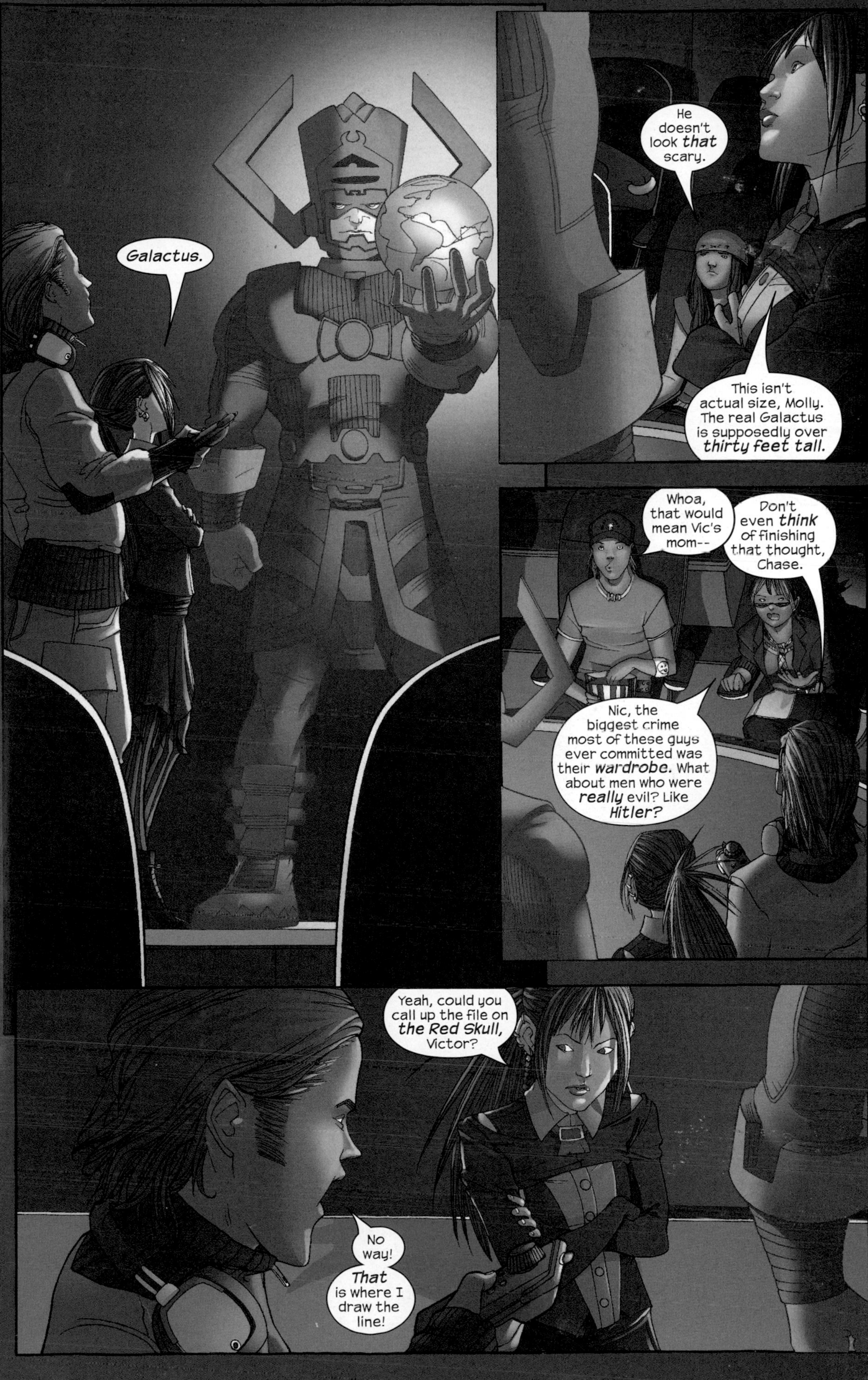
Galactus.
He doesn't look *that* scary.
This isn't actual size, Molly. The real Galactus is supposedly over *thirty feet tall.*
Whoa, that would mean Vic's mom--
Don't even *think* of finishing that thought, Chase.
Nic, the biggest crime most of these guys ever committed was their *wardrobe.* What about men who were *really* evil? Like *Hitler?*
Yeah, could you call up the file on *the Red Skull,* Victor?
No way! *That* is where I draw the line!

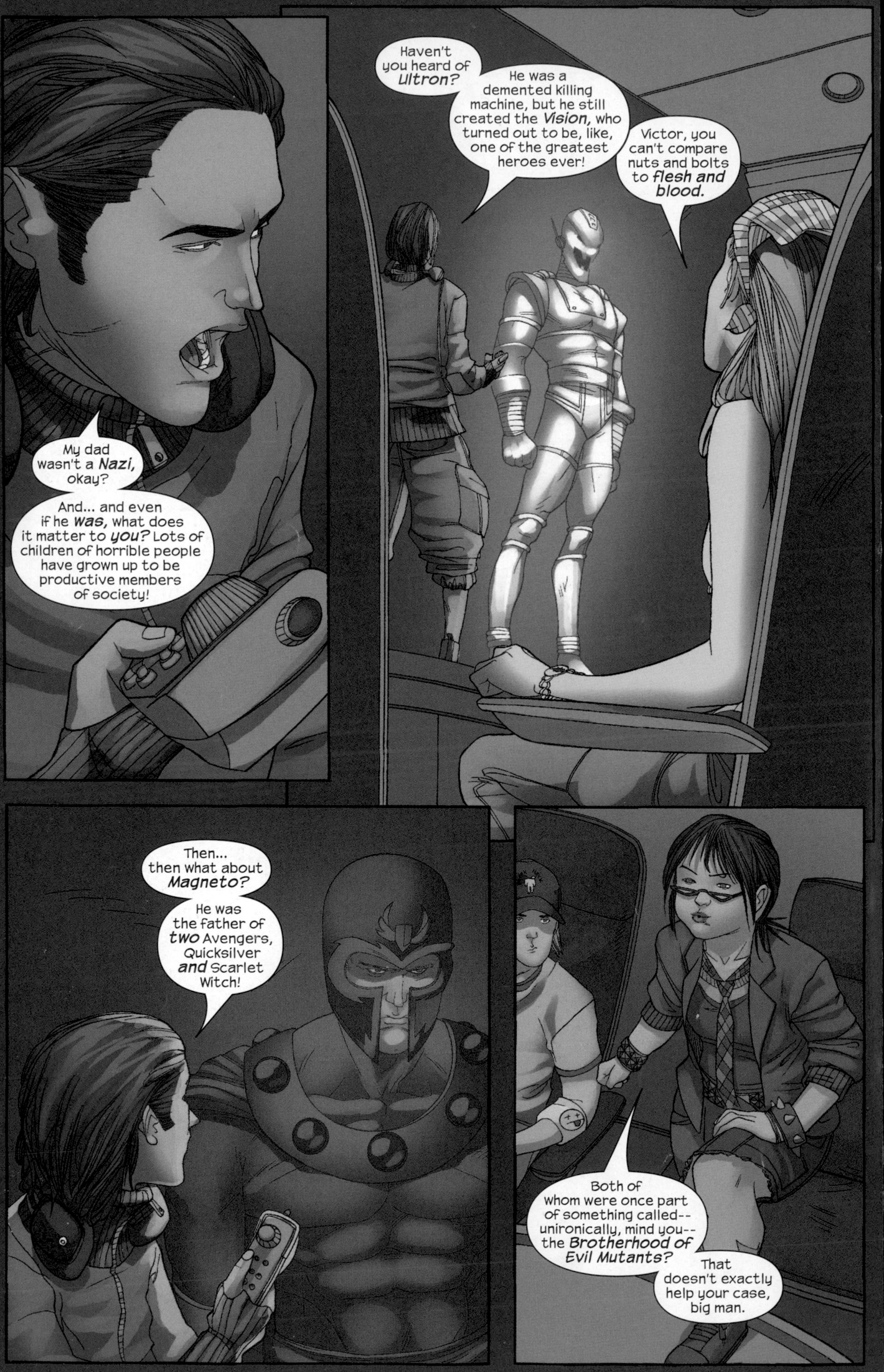
My dad wasn't a *Nazi,* okay?
And... and even if he *was,* what does it matter to *you?* Lots of children of horrible people have grown up to be productive members of society!
Haven't you heard of *Ultron?*
He was a demented killing machine, but he still created the *Vision,* who turned out to be, like, one of the greatest heroes ever!
Victor, you can't compare nuts and bolts to *flesh and blood.*
Then... then what about *Magneto?*
He was the father of *two* Avengers, Quicksilver *and* Scarlet Witch!
Both of whom were once part of something called-- unironically, mind you-- the *Brotherhood of Evil Mutants?*
That doesn't exactly help your case, big man.

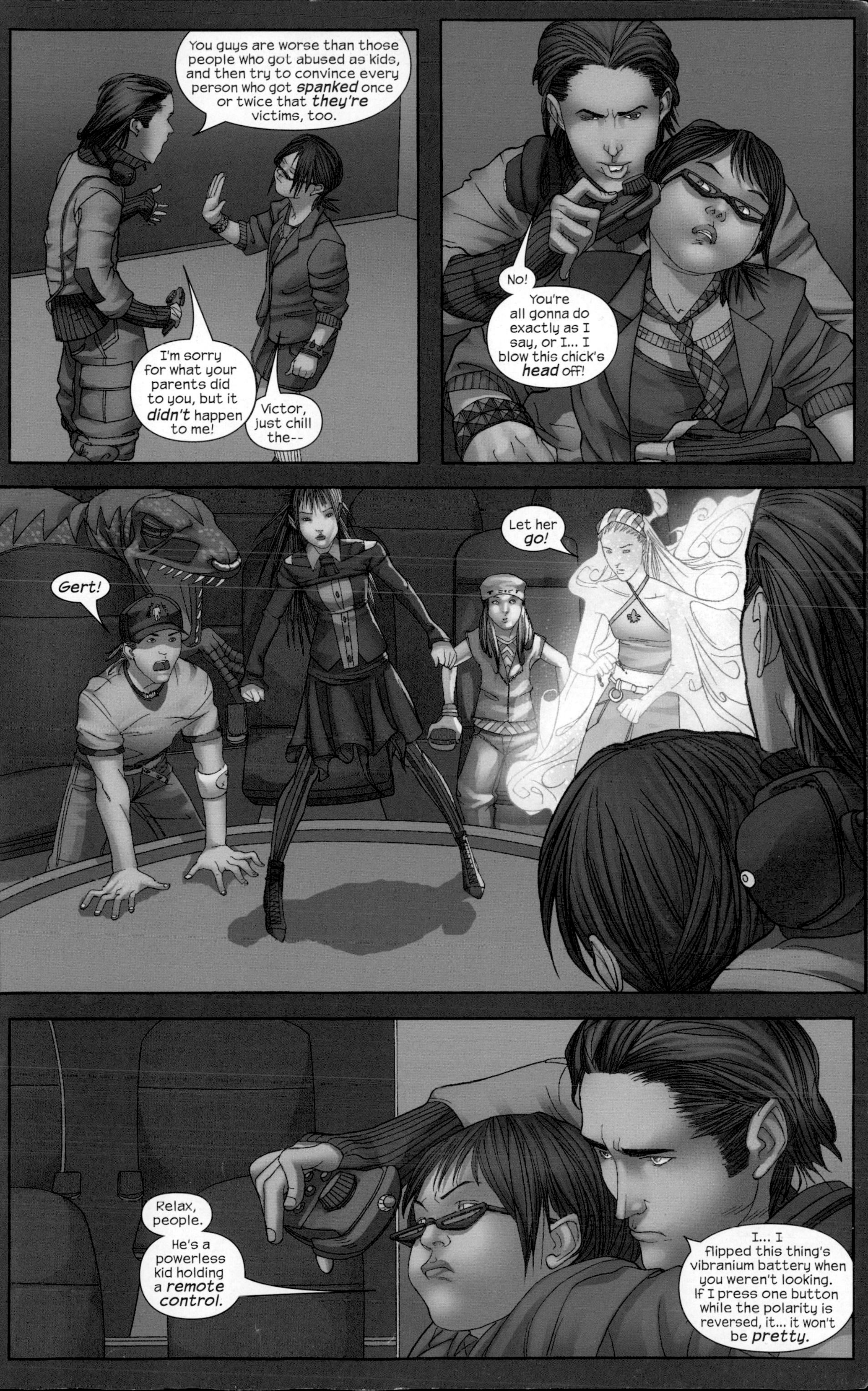
You guys are worse than those people who got abused as kids, and then try to convince every person who got *spanked* once or twice that *they're* victims, too.
I'm sorry for what your parents did to you, but it *didn't* happen to me!
Victor, just chill the--
No!
You're all gonna do exactly as I say, or I... I blow this chick's *head* off!
Gert!
Let her *go!*
Relax, people.
He's a powerless kid holding a *remote control.*
I... I flipped this thing's vibranium battery when you weren't looking. If I press one button while the polarity is reversed, it... it won't be *pretty.*

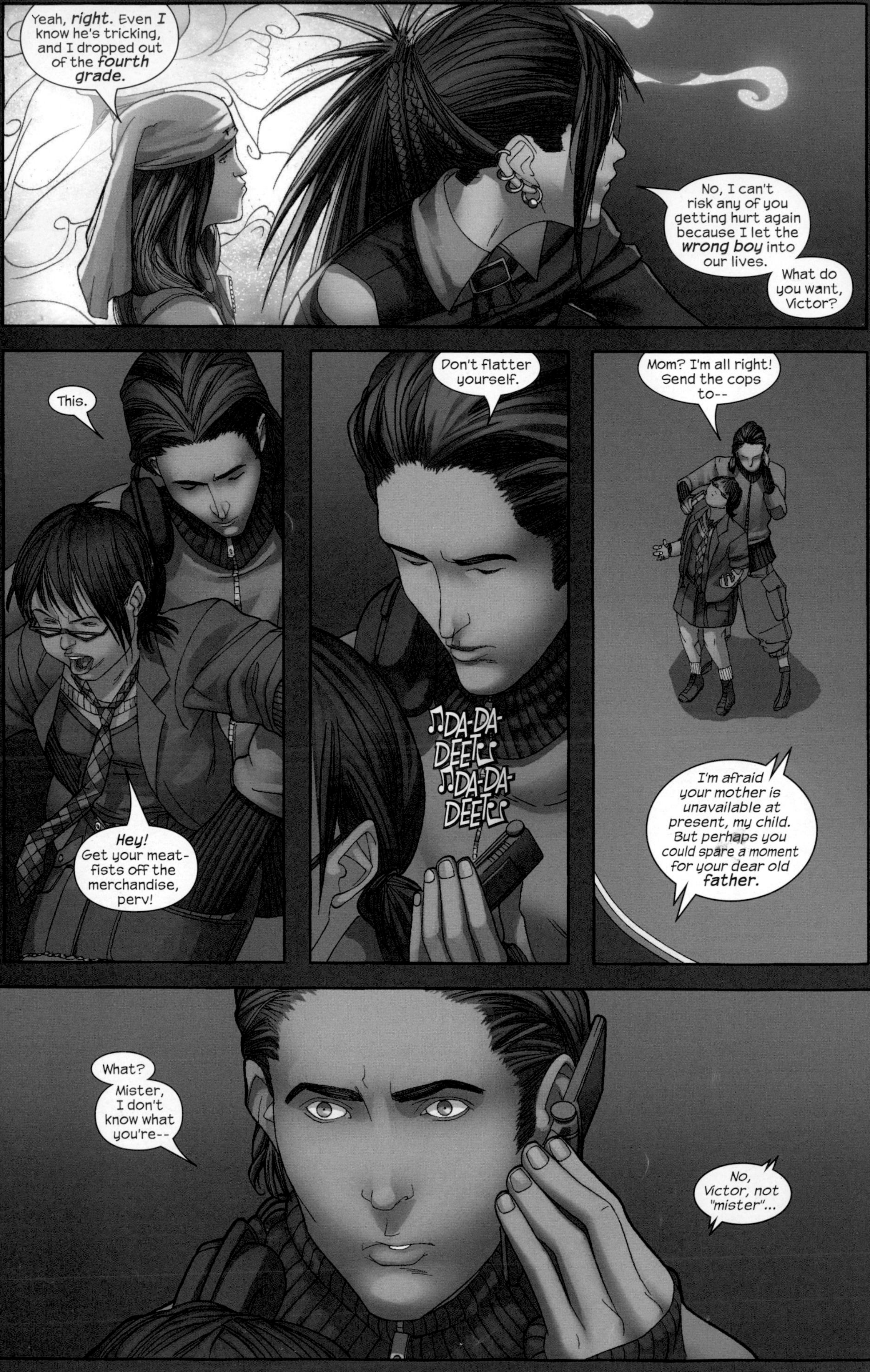
Yeah, *right.* Even *I* know he's tricking, and I dropped out of the *fourth grade.*
No, I can't risk any of you getting hurt again because I let the *wrong boy* into our lives.
What do you want, Victor?
This.
Hey! Get your meat-fists off the merchandise, perv!
Don't flatter yourself.
DA-DA-DEET DA-DA-DEET
Mom? I'm all right! Send the cops to--
I'm afraid your mother is unavailable at present, my child. But perhaps you could spare a moment for your dear old ***father.***
What? Mister, I don't know what you're--
No, Victor, not "mister"...

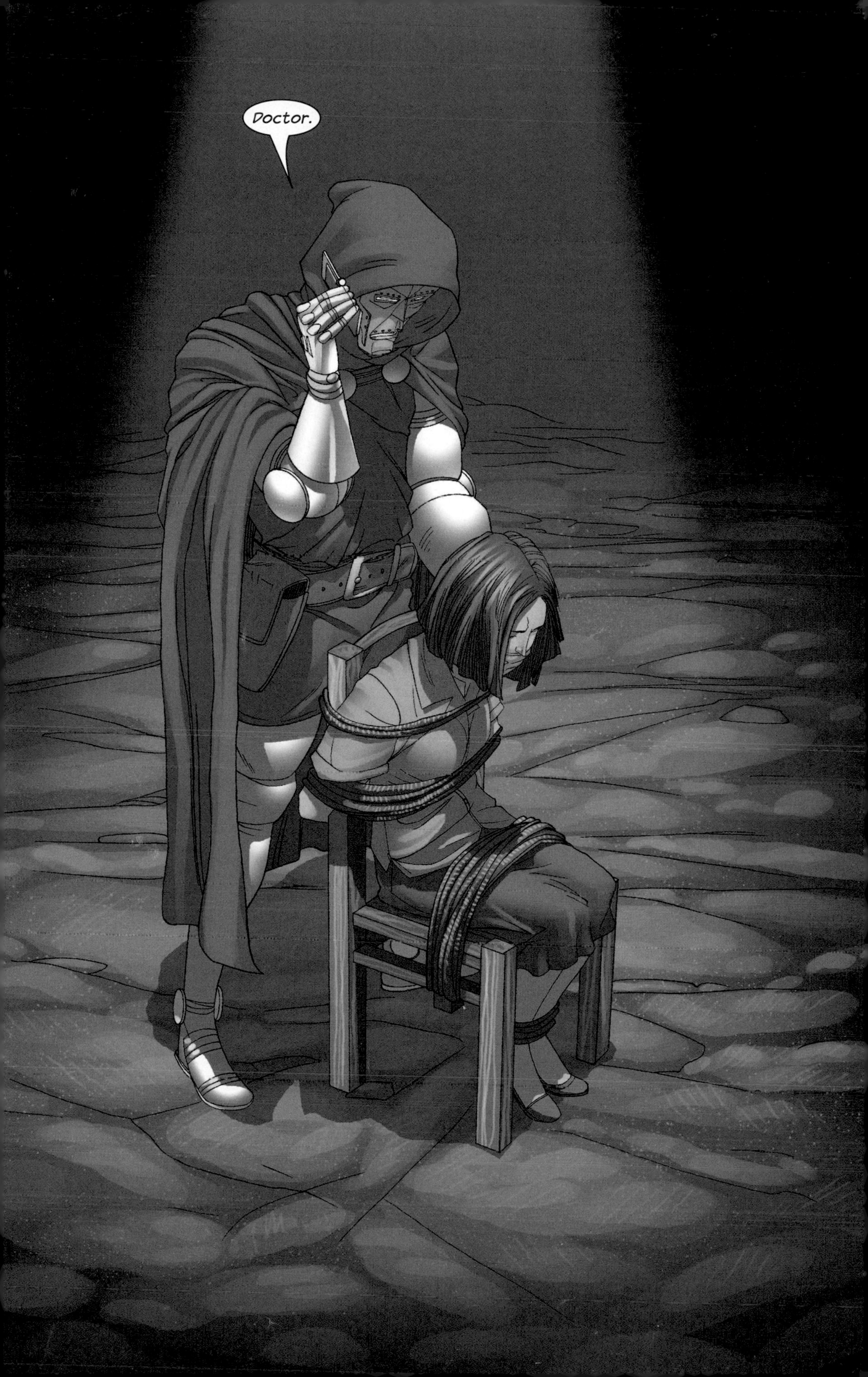
Doctor.

5

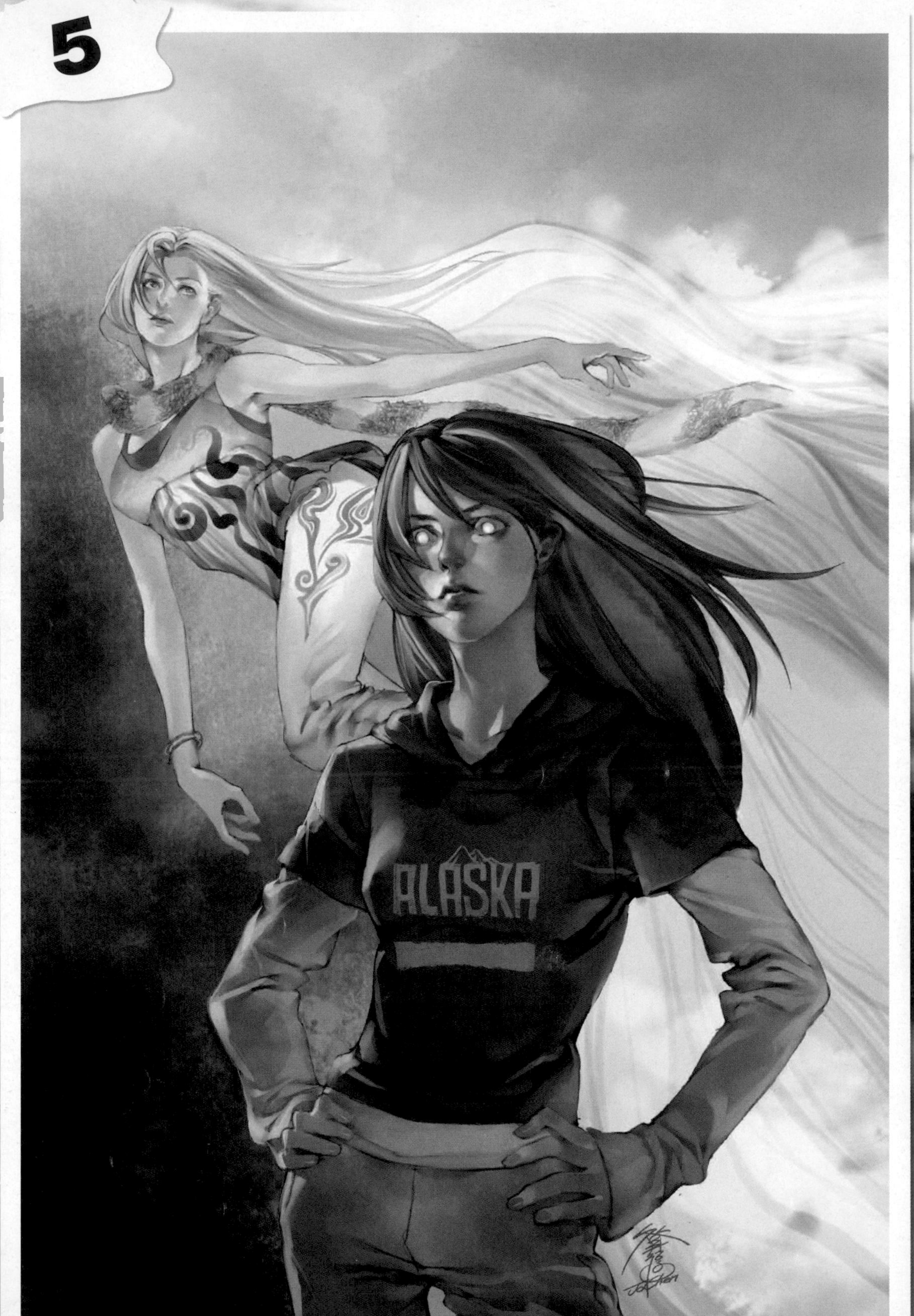
ALASKA

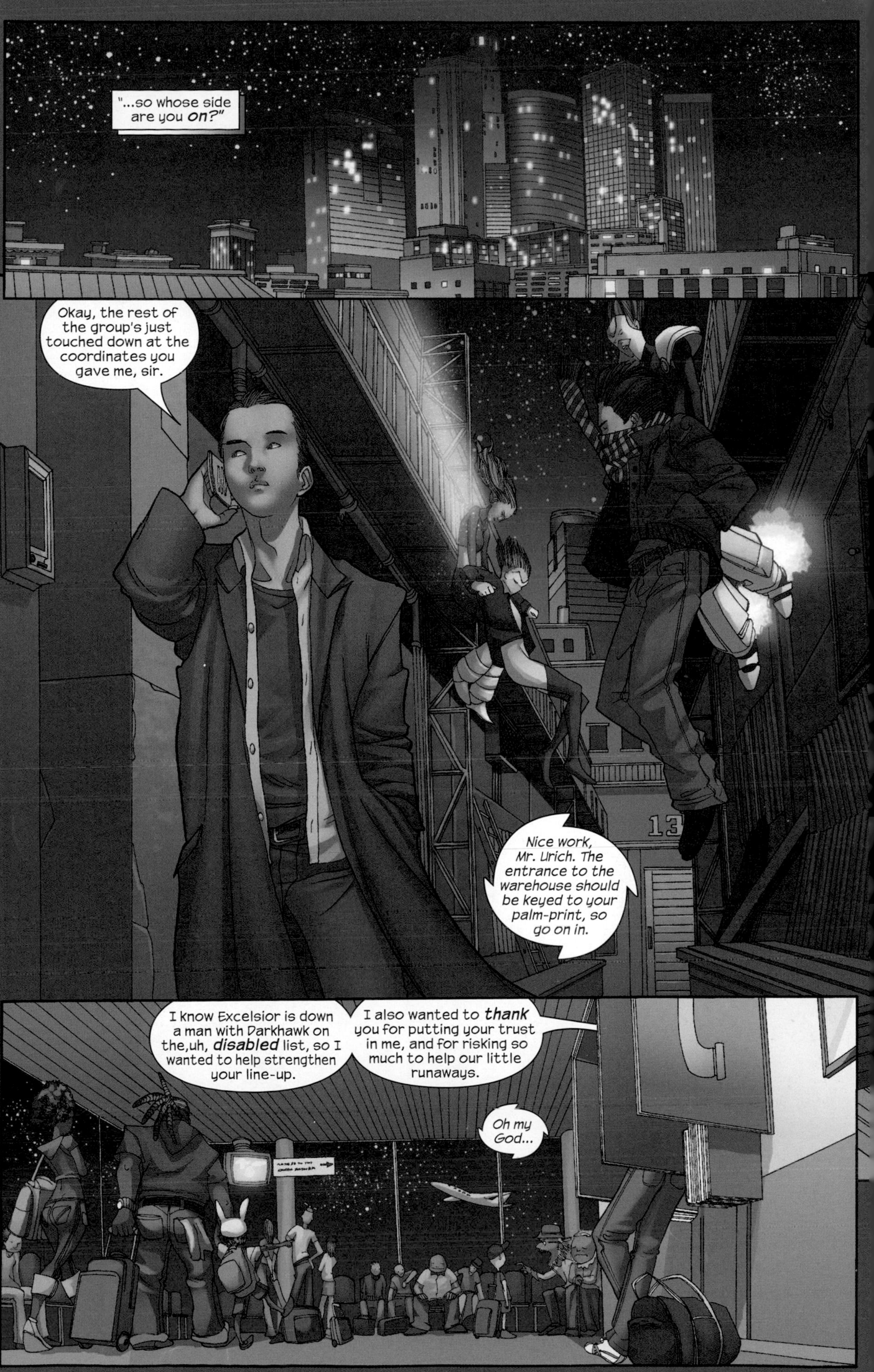
"...so whose side are you *on?*"
Okay, the rest of the group's just touched down at the coordinates you gave me, sir.
Nice work, Mr. Urich. The entrance to the warehouse should be keyed to your palm-print, so go on in.
13
I know Excelsior is down a man with Darkhawk on the, uh, *disabled* list, so I wanted to help strengthen your line-up.
I also wanted to *thank* you for putting your trust in me, and for risking so much to help our little runaways.
Oh my God...

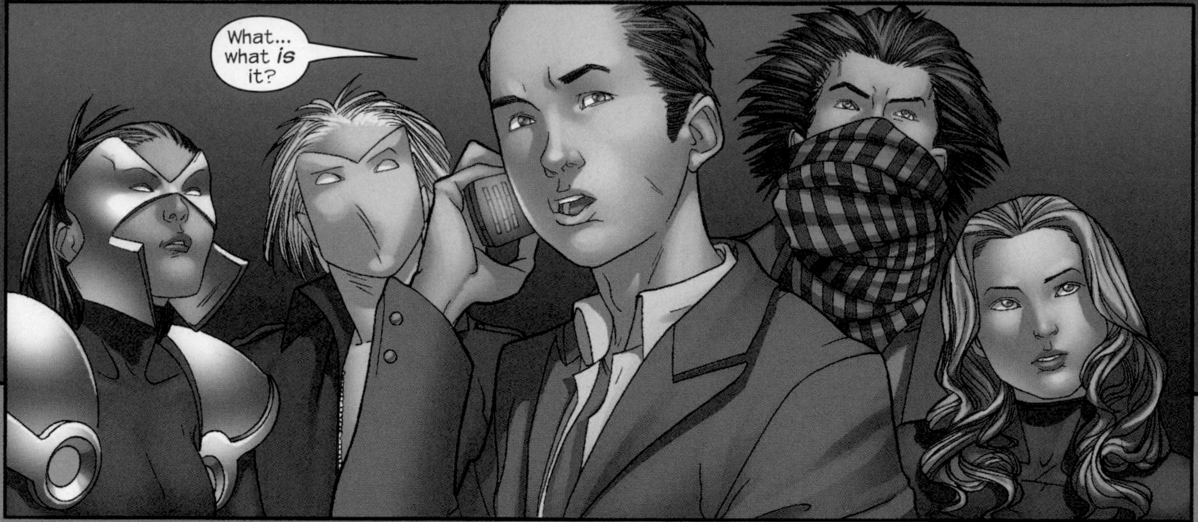
What... what *is* it?

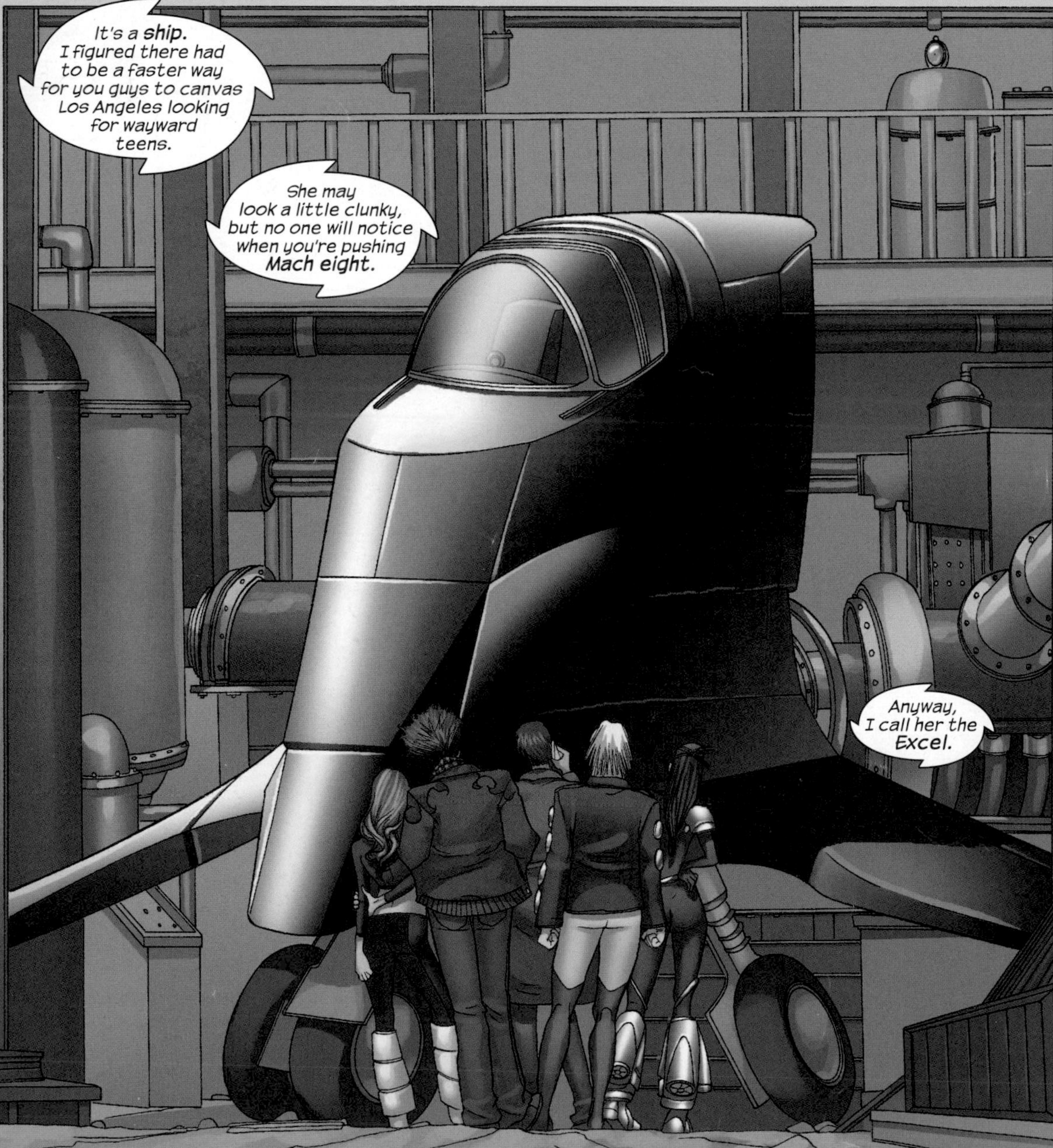
It's a **ship.** I figured there had to be a faster way for you guys to canvas Los Angeles looking for wayward teens.
She may look a little clunky, but no one will notice when you're pushing **Mach eight.**
Anyway, I call her the **Excel.**

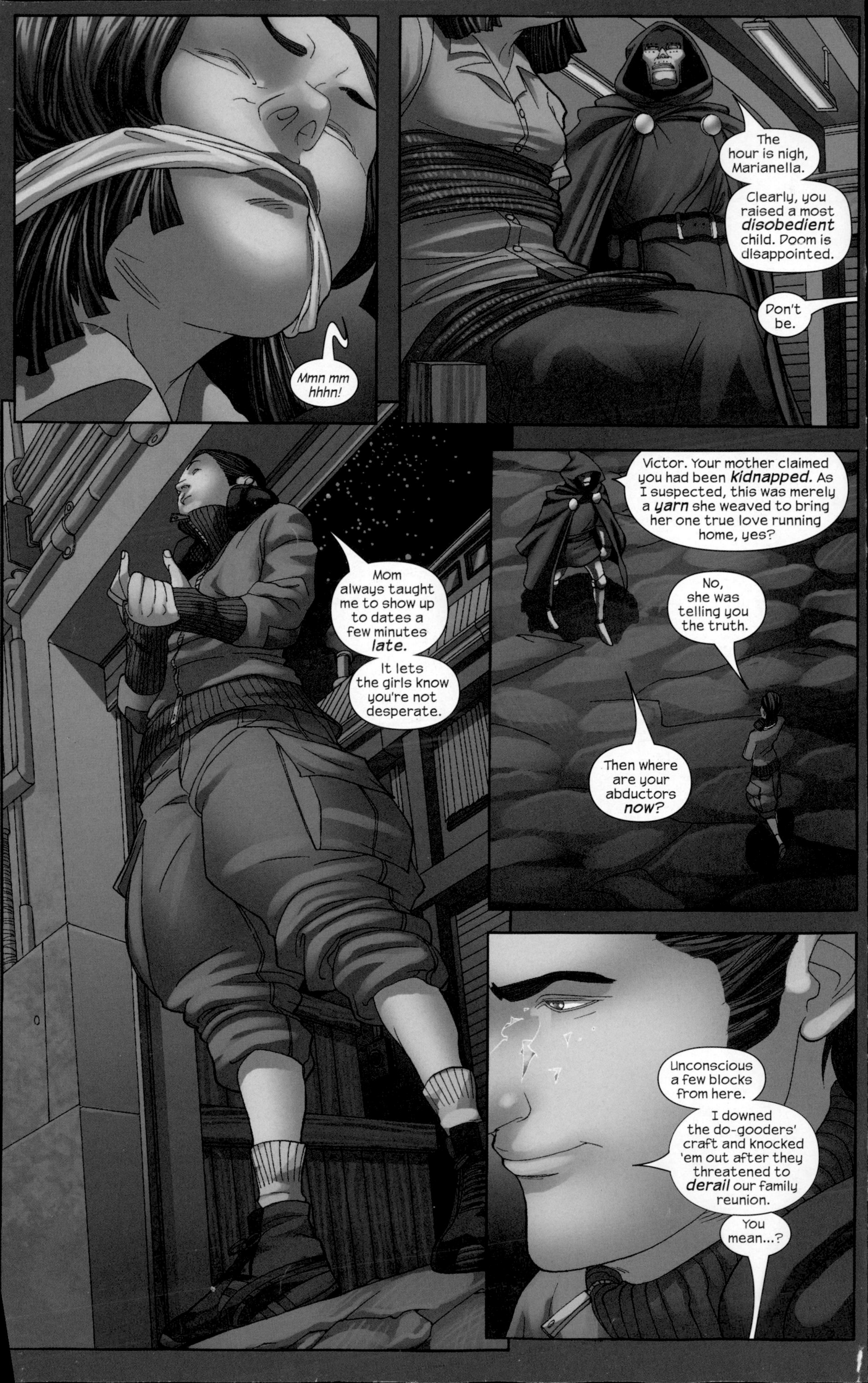

Mmn mm hhhn!
The hour is nigh, Marianella.
Clearly, you raised a most *disobedient* child. Doom is disappointed.
Don't be.
Mom always taught me to show up to dates a few minutes *late.*
It lets the girls know you're not desperate.
Victor. Your mother claimed you had been *kidnapped.* As I suspected, this was merely a *yarn* she weaved to bring her one true love running home, yes?
No, she was telling you the truth.
Then where are your abductors *now?*
Unconscious a few blocks from here.
I downed the do-gooders' craft and knocked 'em out after they threatened to *derail* our family reunion.
You mean...?

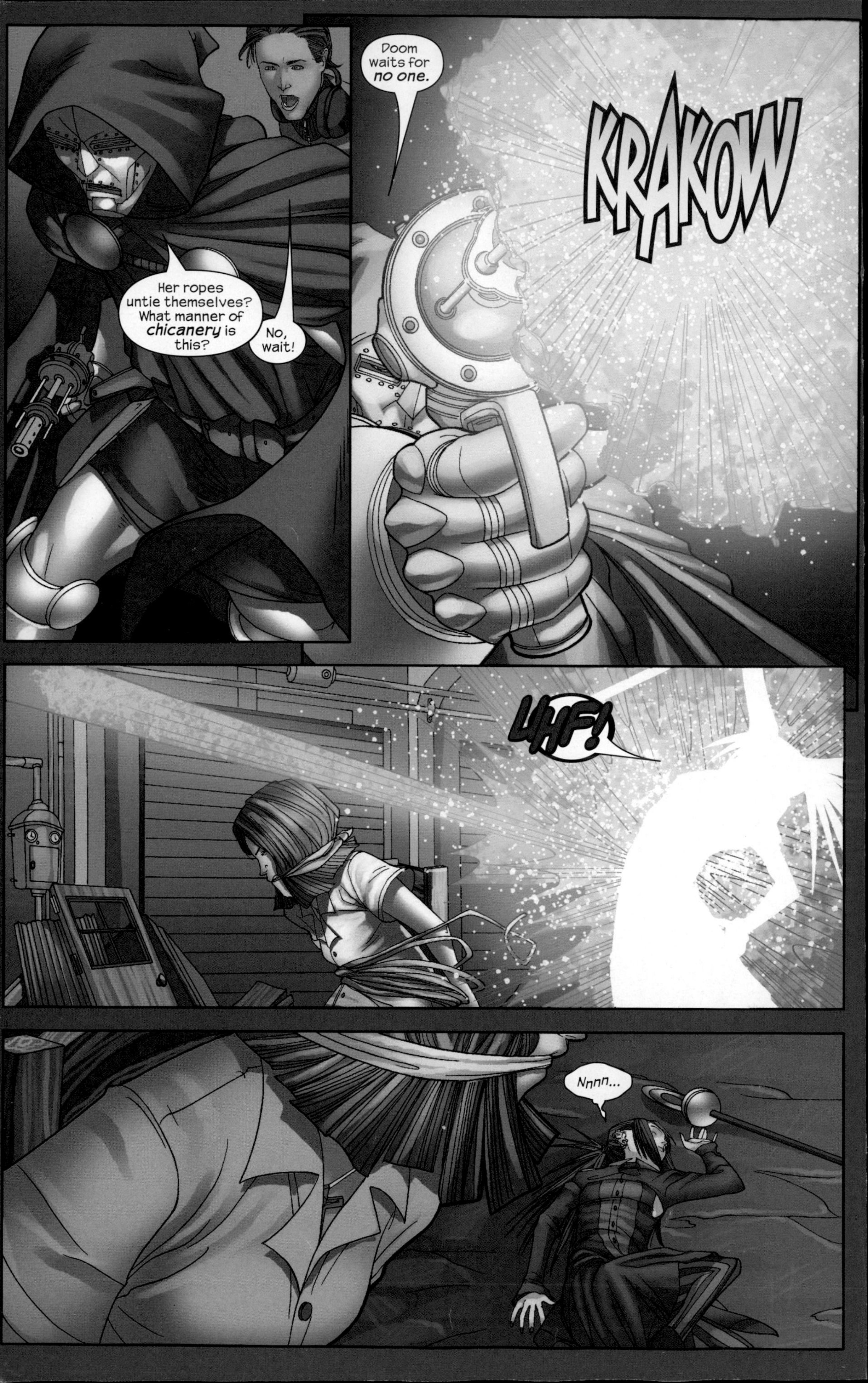
Her ropes untie themselves? What manner of chicanery is this?
No, wait!
Doom waits for no one.
KRAKOW
UHF!
Nnnn...

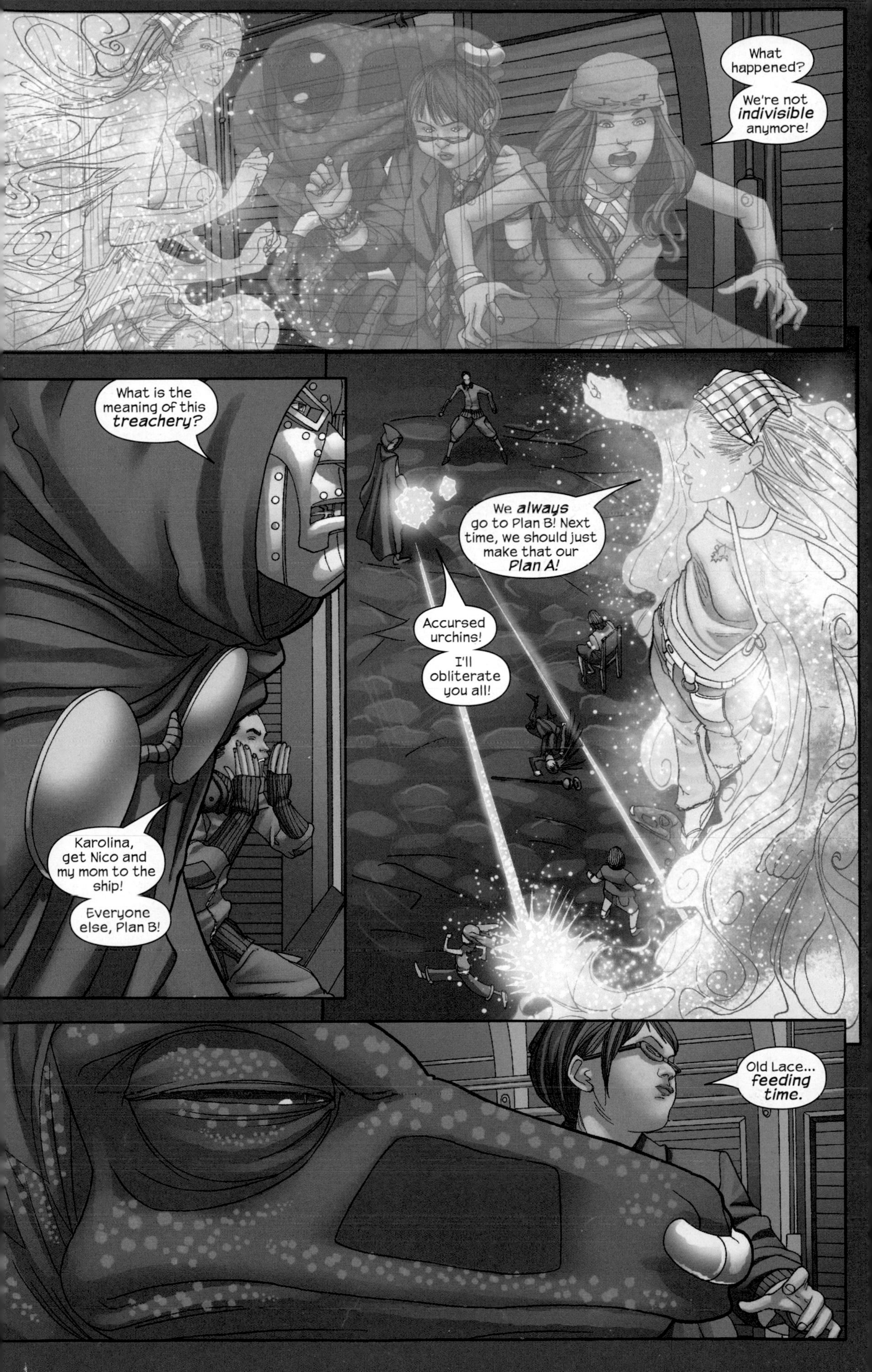
What happened?
We're not *indivisible* anymore!
What is the meaning of this *treachery?*
We *always* go to Plan B! Next time, we should just make that our *Plan A!*
Accursed urchins!
I'll obliterate you all!
Karolina, get Nico and my mom to the ship!
Everyone else, Plan B!
Old Lace... *feeding time.*

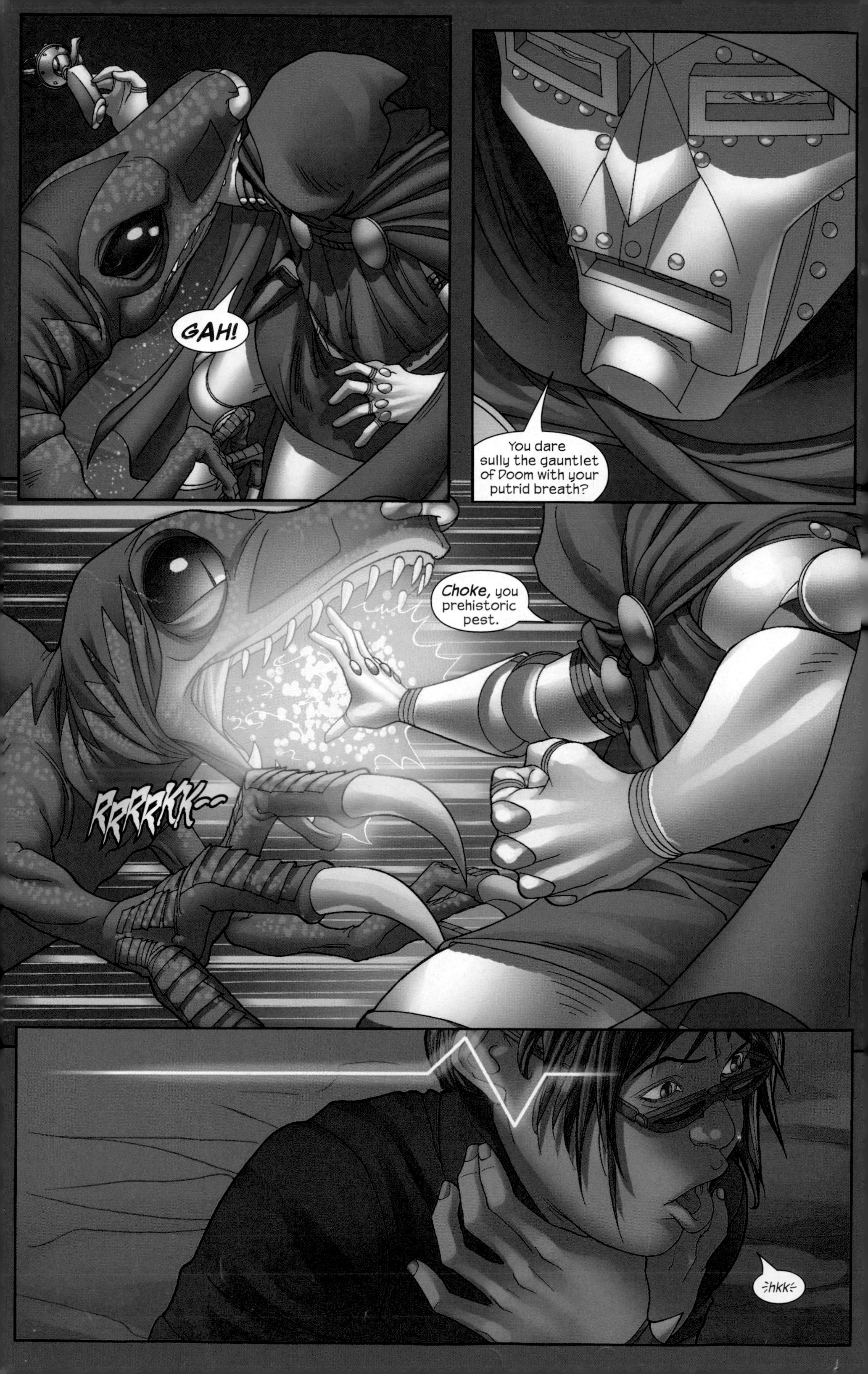
GAH!
You dare sully the gauntlet of Doom with your putrid breath?
Choke, you prehistoric pest.
RRRRKK--
hkk

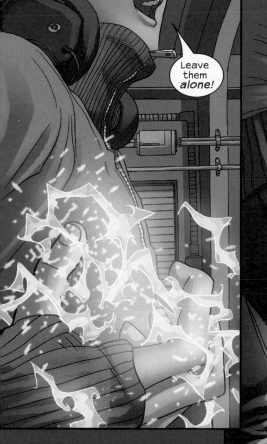

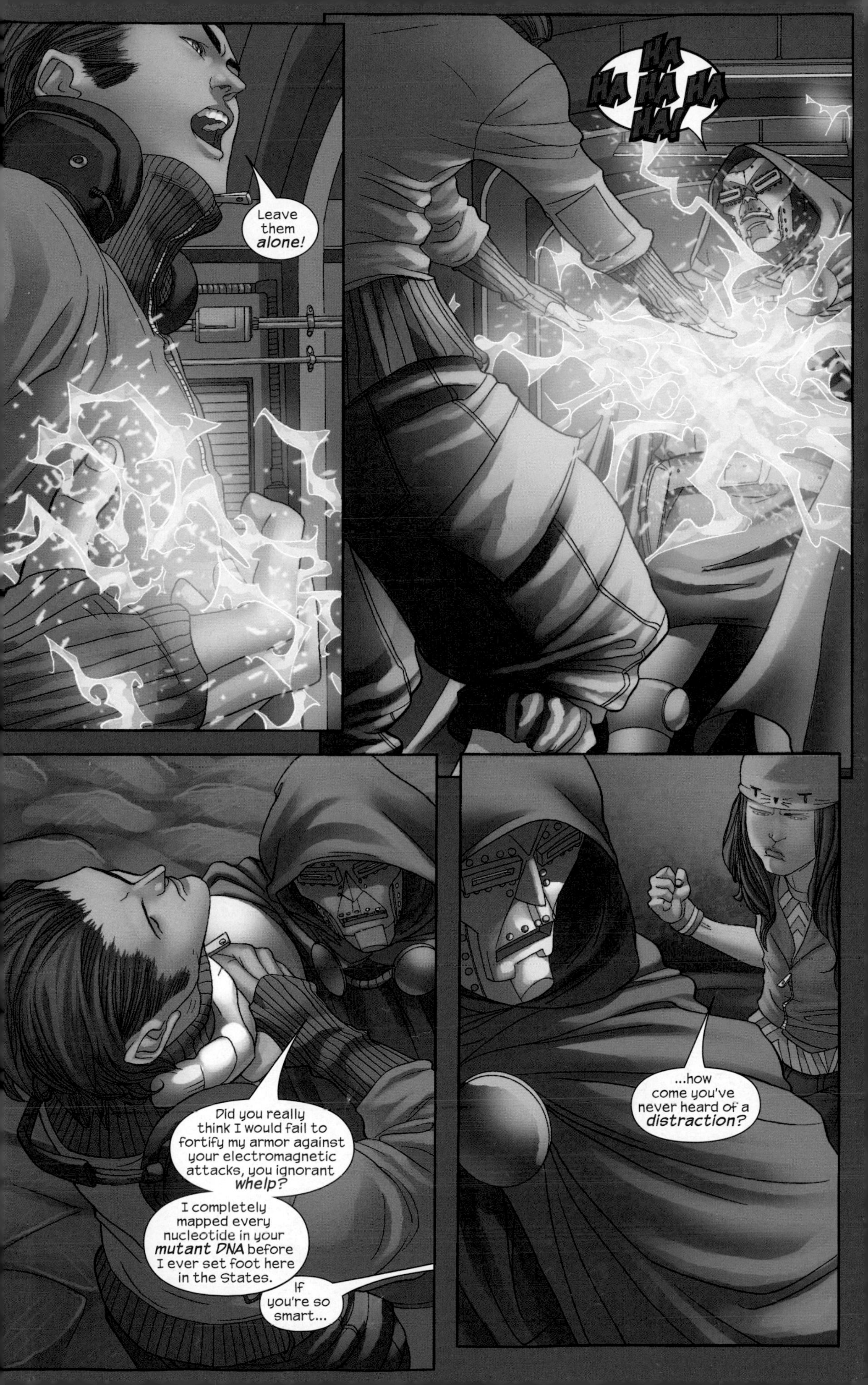
Leave them alone!
HA HA HA HA HA!
Did you really think I would fail to fortify my armor against your electromagnetic attacks, you ignorant whelp?
I completely mapped every nucleotide in your mutant DNA before I ever set foot here in the States.
If you're so smart...
...how come you've never heard of a distraction?

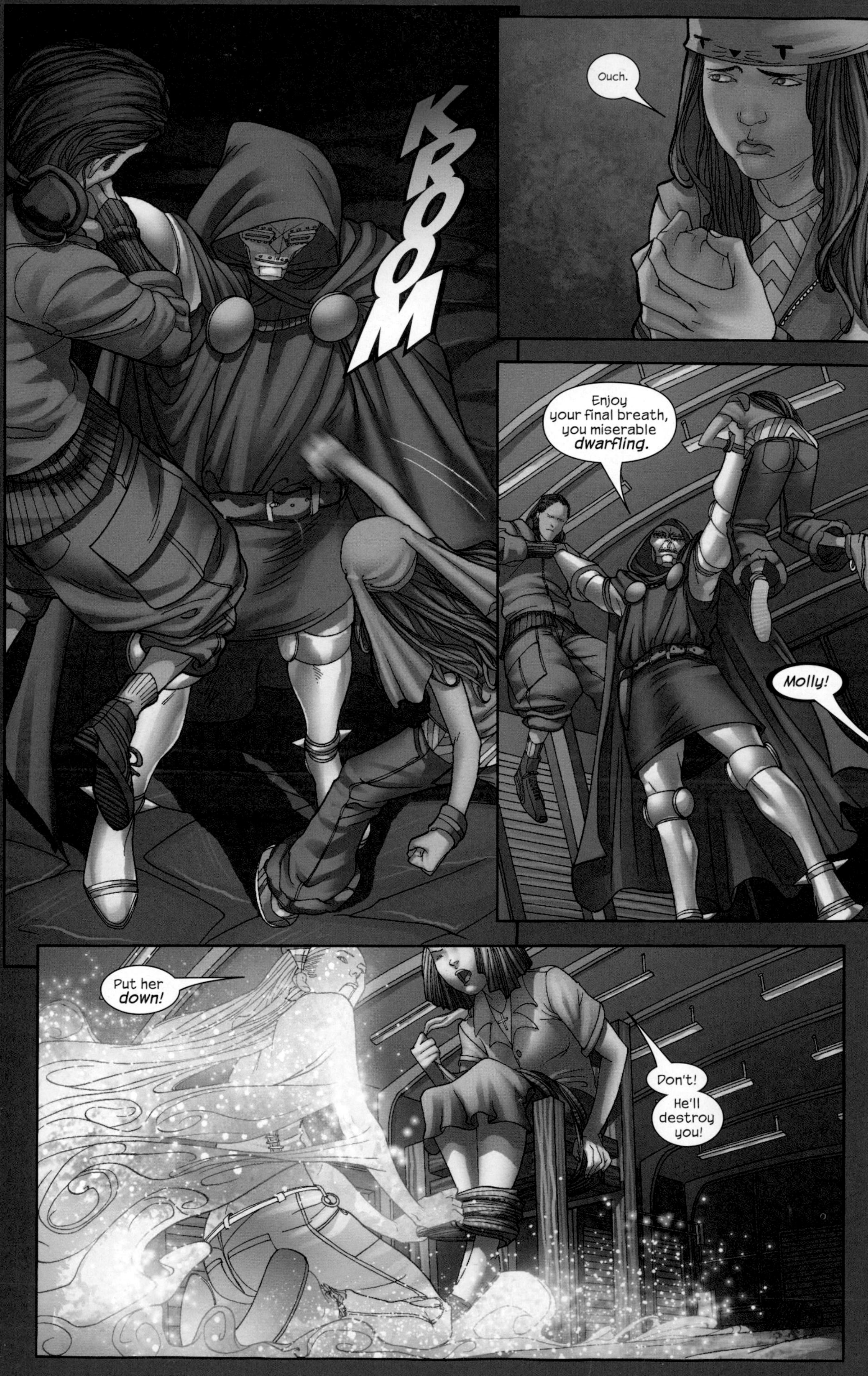
KROOM
Ouch.
Enjoy your final breath, you miserable dwarfling.
Molly!
Put her down!
Don't!
He'll destroy you!

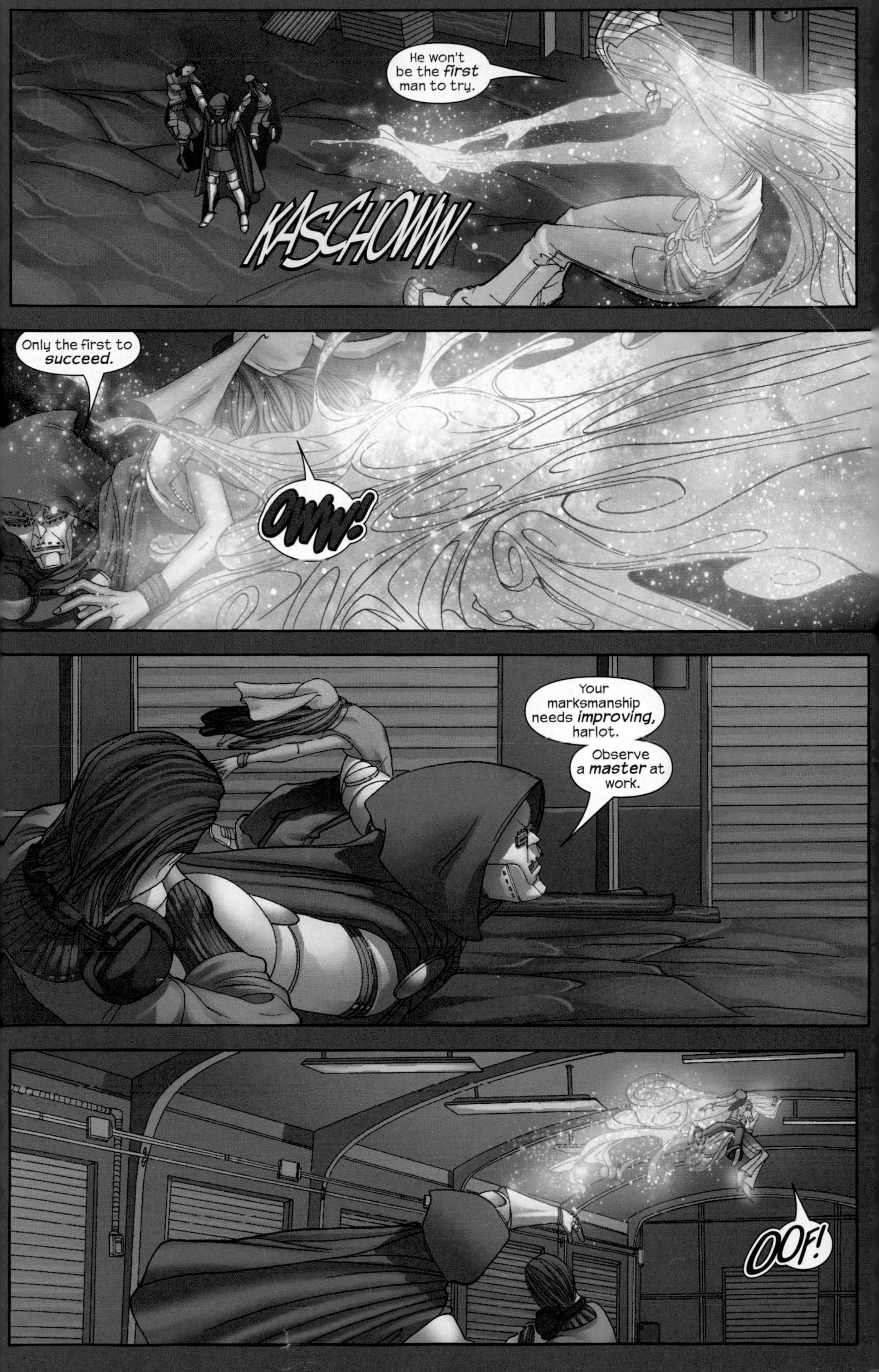
He won't be the *first* man to try.
KASCHOWW
Only the first to *succeed.*
OWW!
Your marksmanship needs *improving,* harlot.
Observe a *master* at work.
OOF!

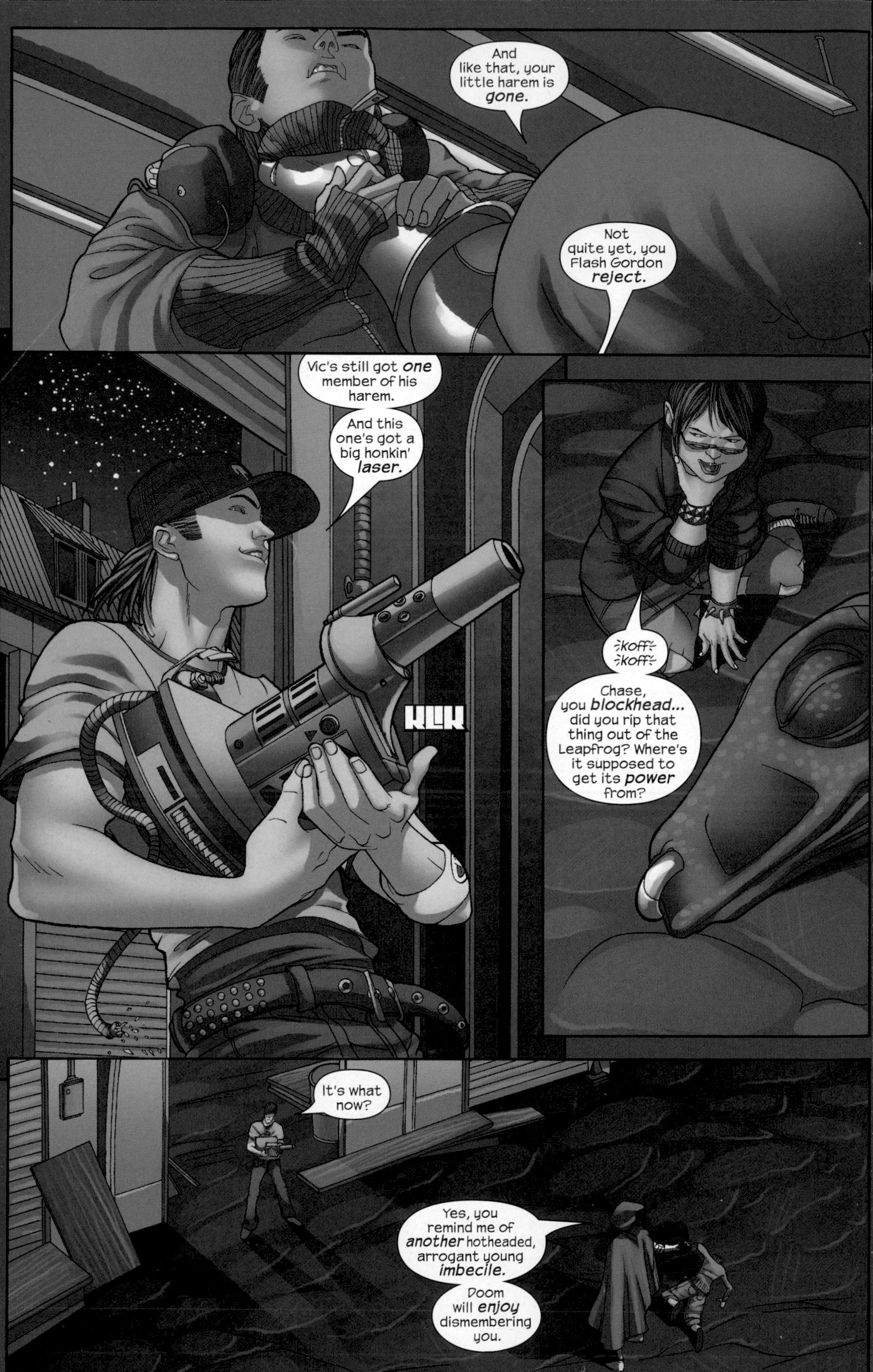
And like that, your little harem is *gone.*
Not quite yet, you Flash Gordon *reject.*
Vic's still got *one* member of his harem.
And this one's got a big honkin' *laser.*
KLIK
koff *koff*
Chase, you *blockhead...* did you rip that thing out of the Leapfrog? Where's it supposed to get its *power* from?
It's what now?
Yes, you remind me of *another* hotheaded, arrogant young *imbecile.*
Doom will *enjoy* dismembering you.

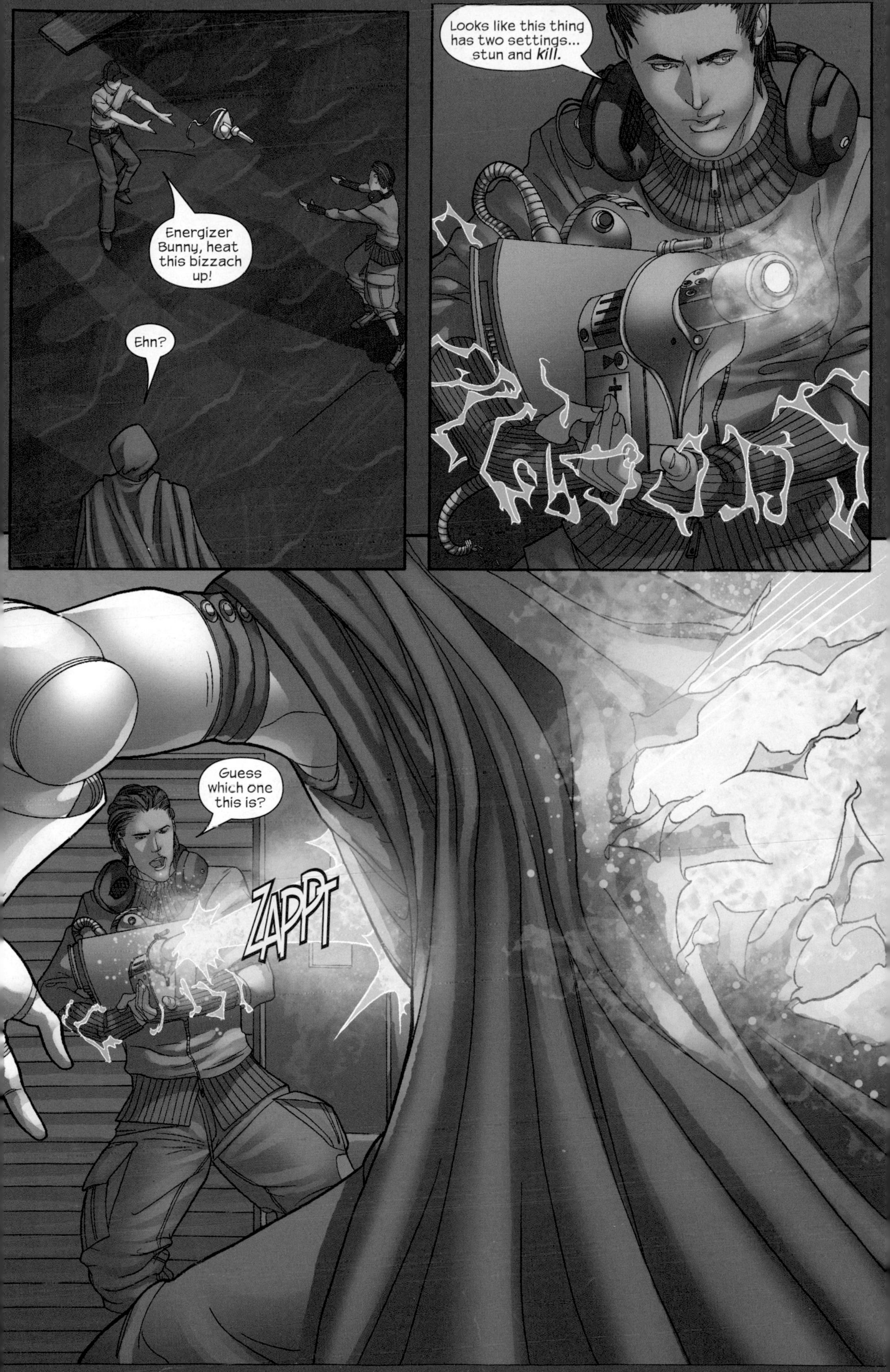
Energizer Bunny, heat this bizzach up!
Ehn?
Looks like this thing has two settings... stun and *kill*.
Guess which one this is?
ZAPPT

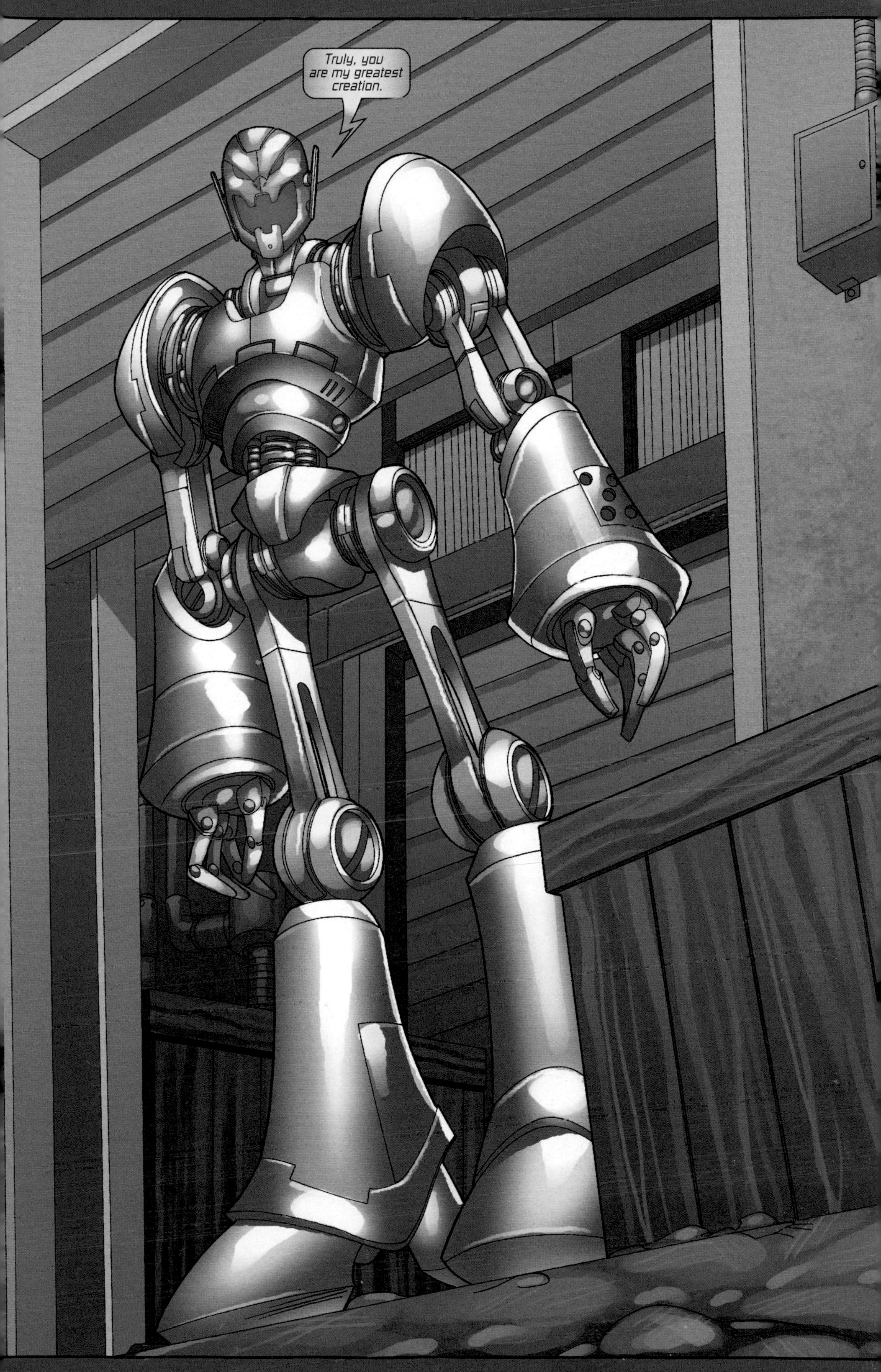
Truly, you are my greatest creation.

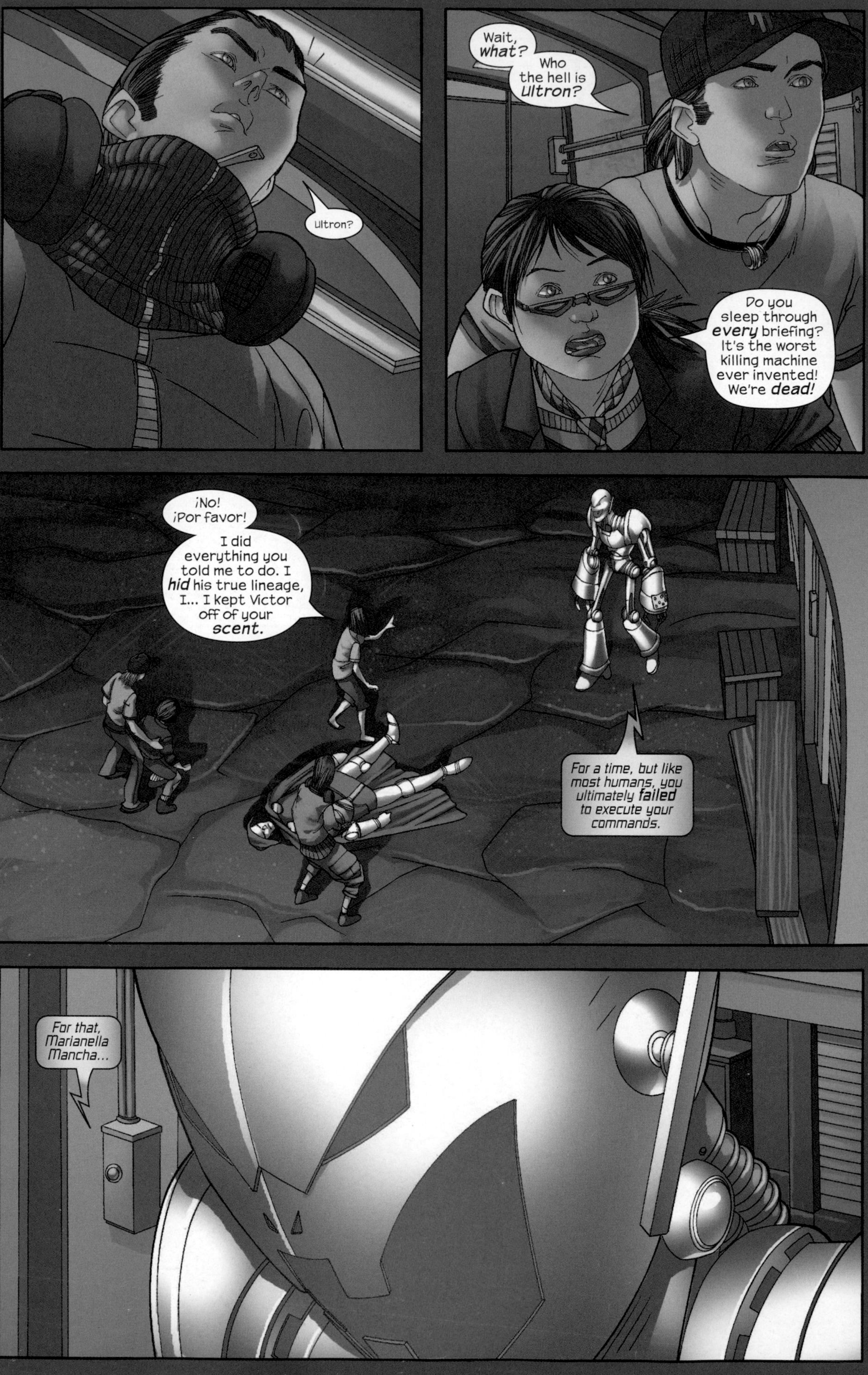
Ultron?
Wait, what?
Who the hell is Ultron?
Do you sleep through every briefing? It's the worst killing machine ever invented! We're dead!
¡No! ¡Por favor!
I did everything you told me to do. I hid his true lineage, I... I kept Victor off of your scent.
For a time, but like most humans, you ultimately failed to execute your commands.
For that, Marianella Mancha...

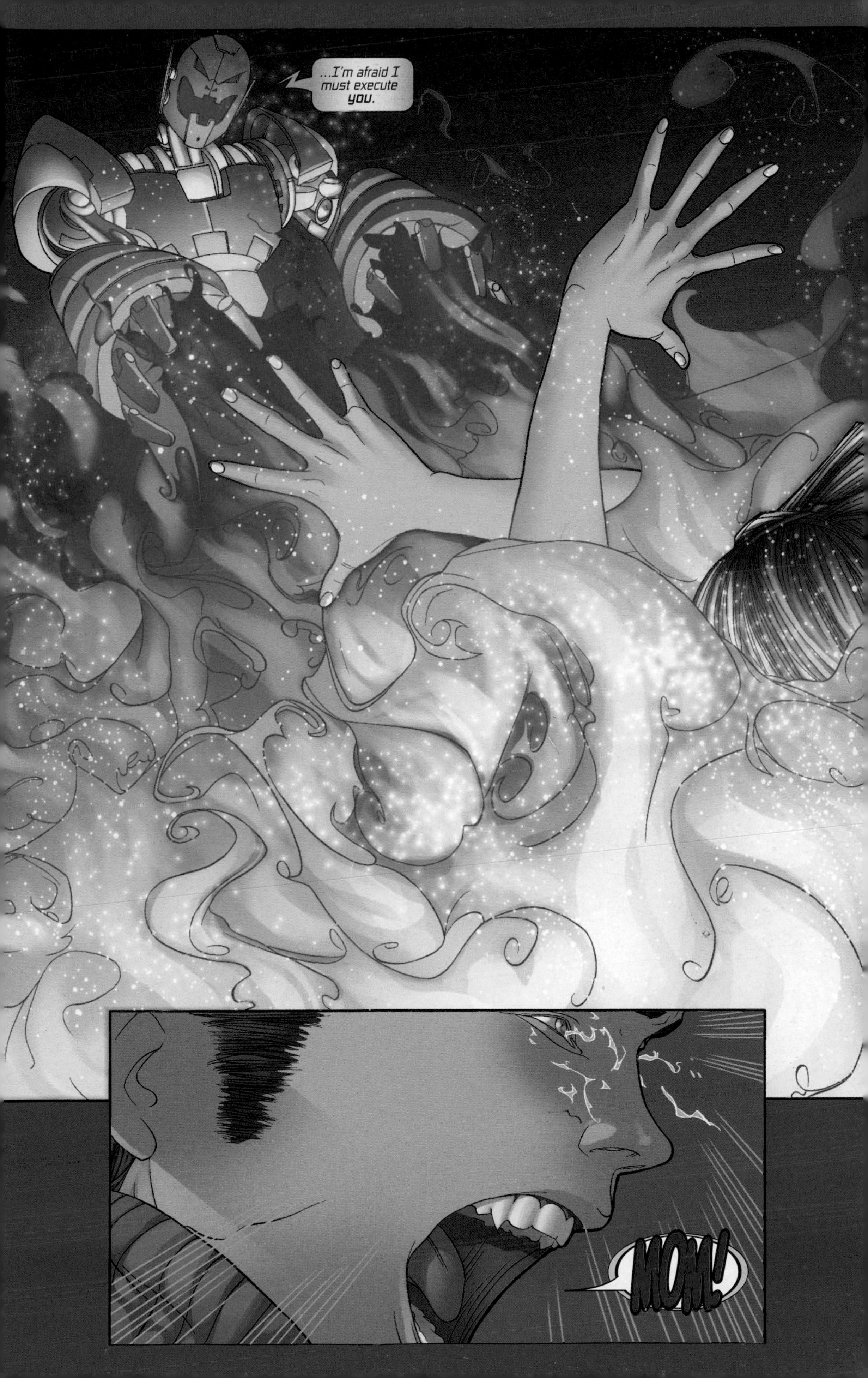
...I'm afraid I must execute you.
MOM!

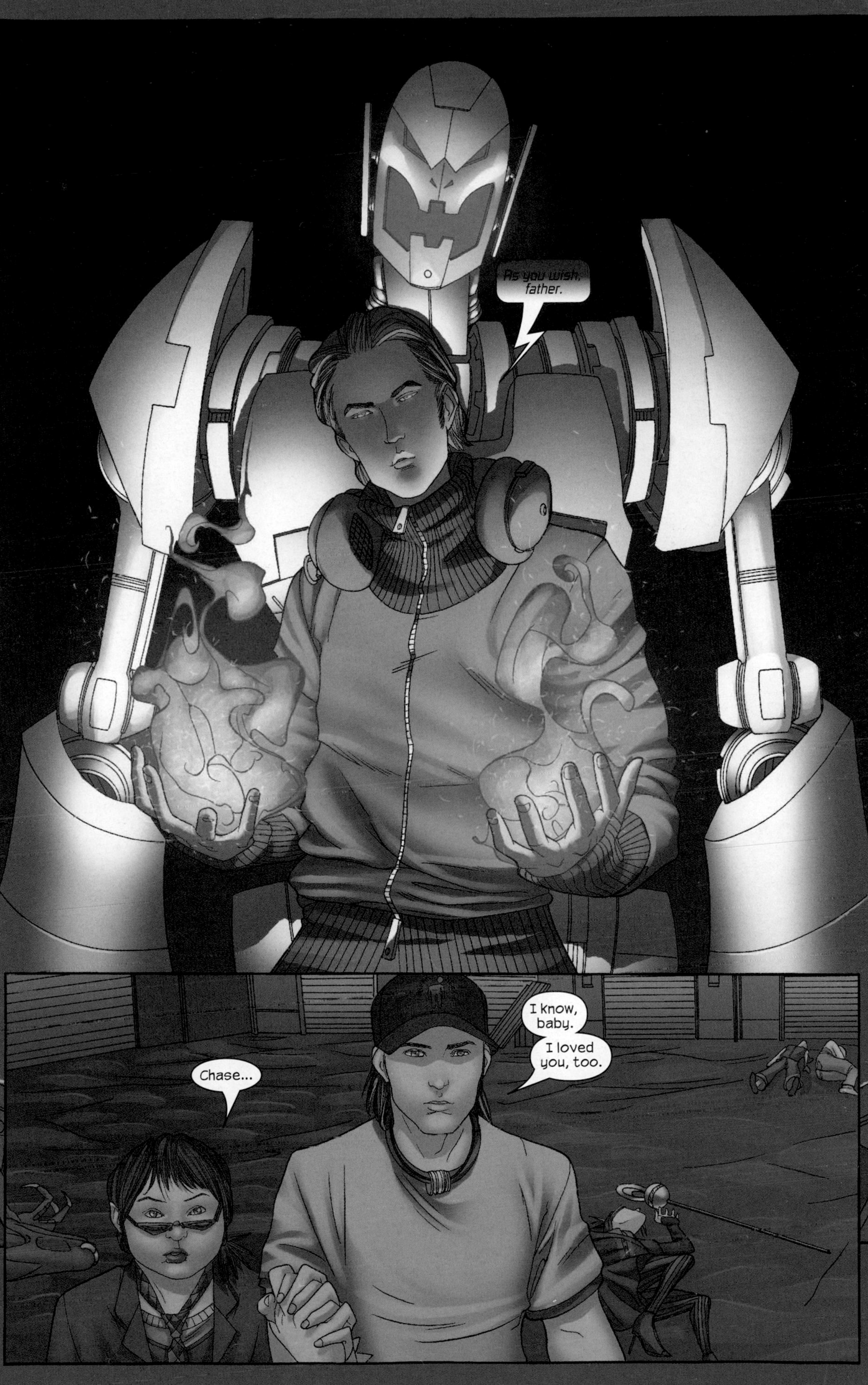
As you wish, father.
Chase...
I know, baby.
I loved you, too.

6

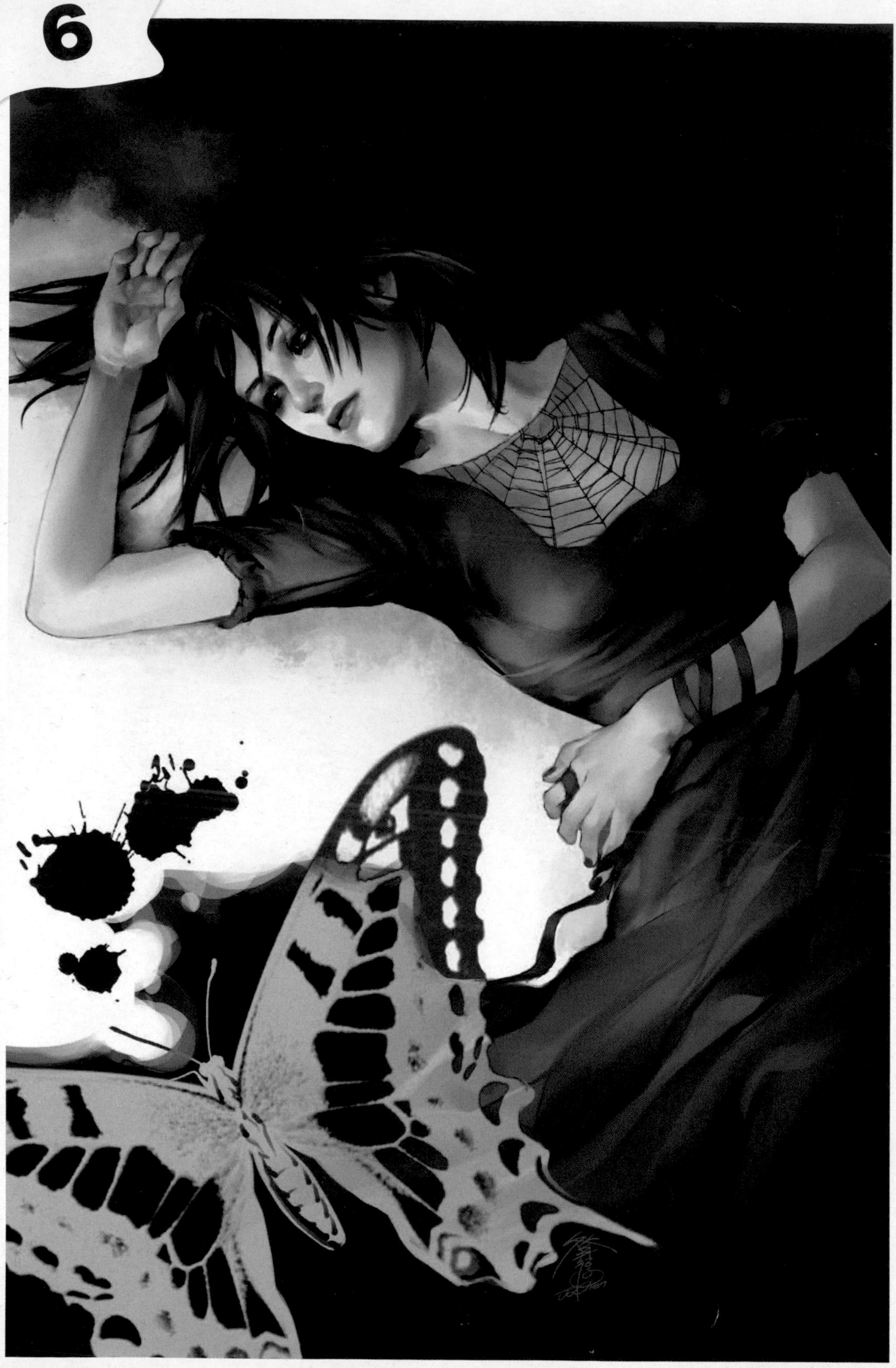

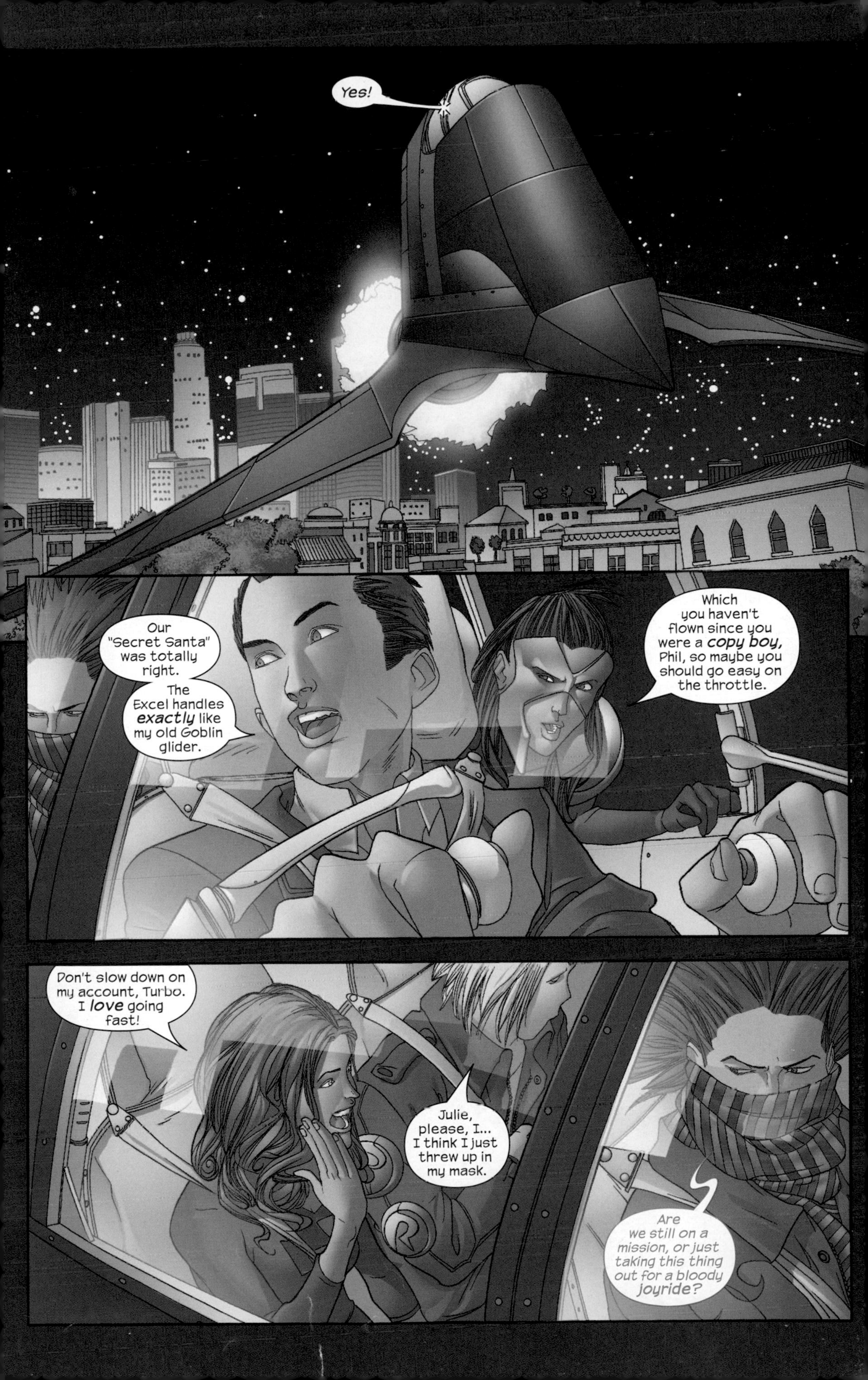
Yes!
Our "Secret Santa" was totally right.
The Excel handles exactly like my old Goblin glider.
Which you haven't flown since you were a copy boy, Phil, so maybe you should go easy on the throttle.
Don't slow down on my account, Turbo. I love going fast!
Julie, please, I... I think I just threw up in my mask.
Are we still on a mission, or just taking this thing out for a bloody joyride?

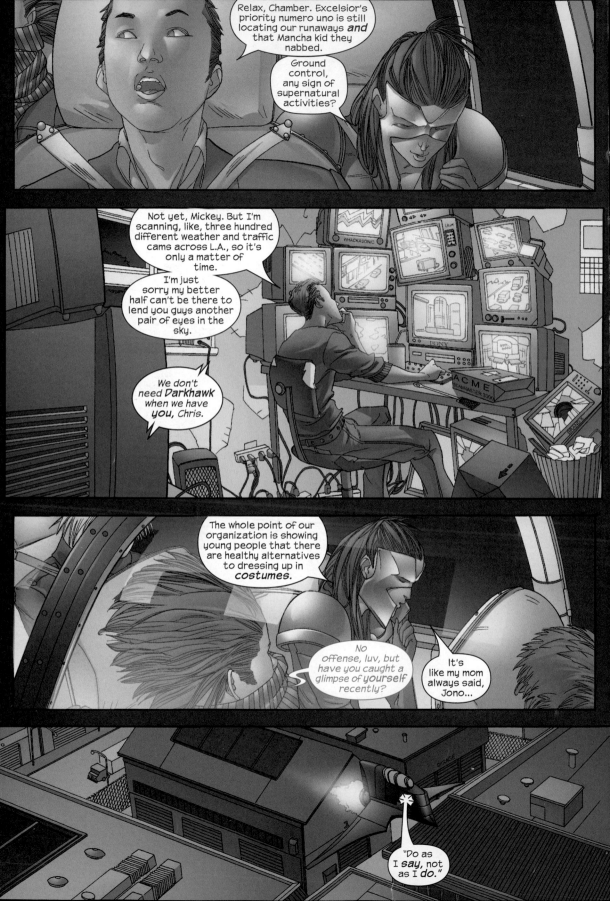

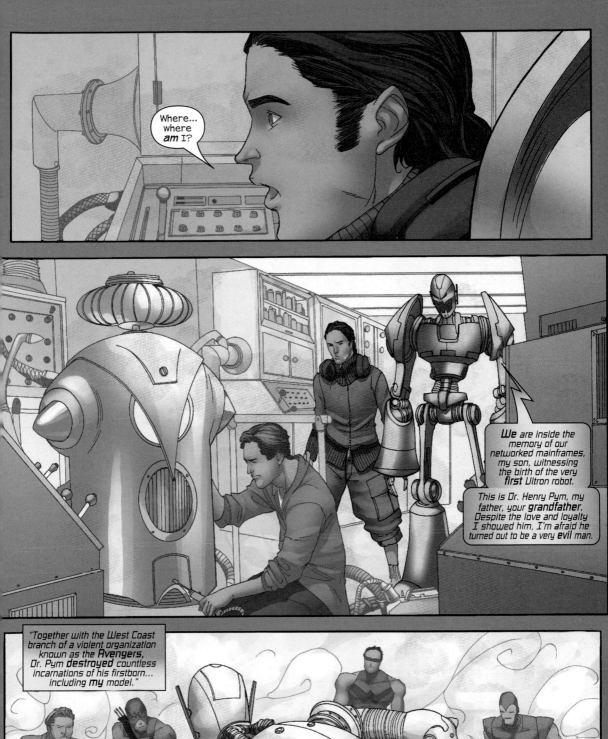

Where... where *am* I?

We are inside the memory of our networked mainframes, my son, witnessing the birth of the very *first* Ultron robot.

This is Dr. Henry Pym, my father, your **grandfather**. Despite the love and loyalty I showed him, I'm afraid he turned out to be a very **evil** man.

"Together with the West Coast branch of a violent organization known as the **Avengers**, Dr. Pym **destroyed** countless incarnations of his firstborn... including **my** model."

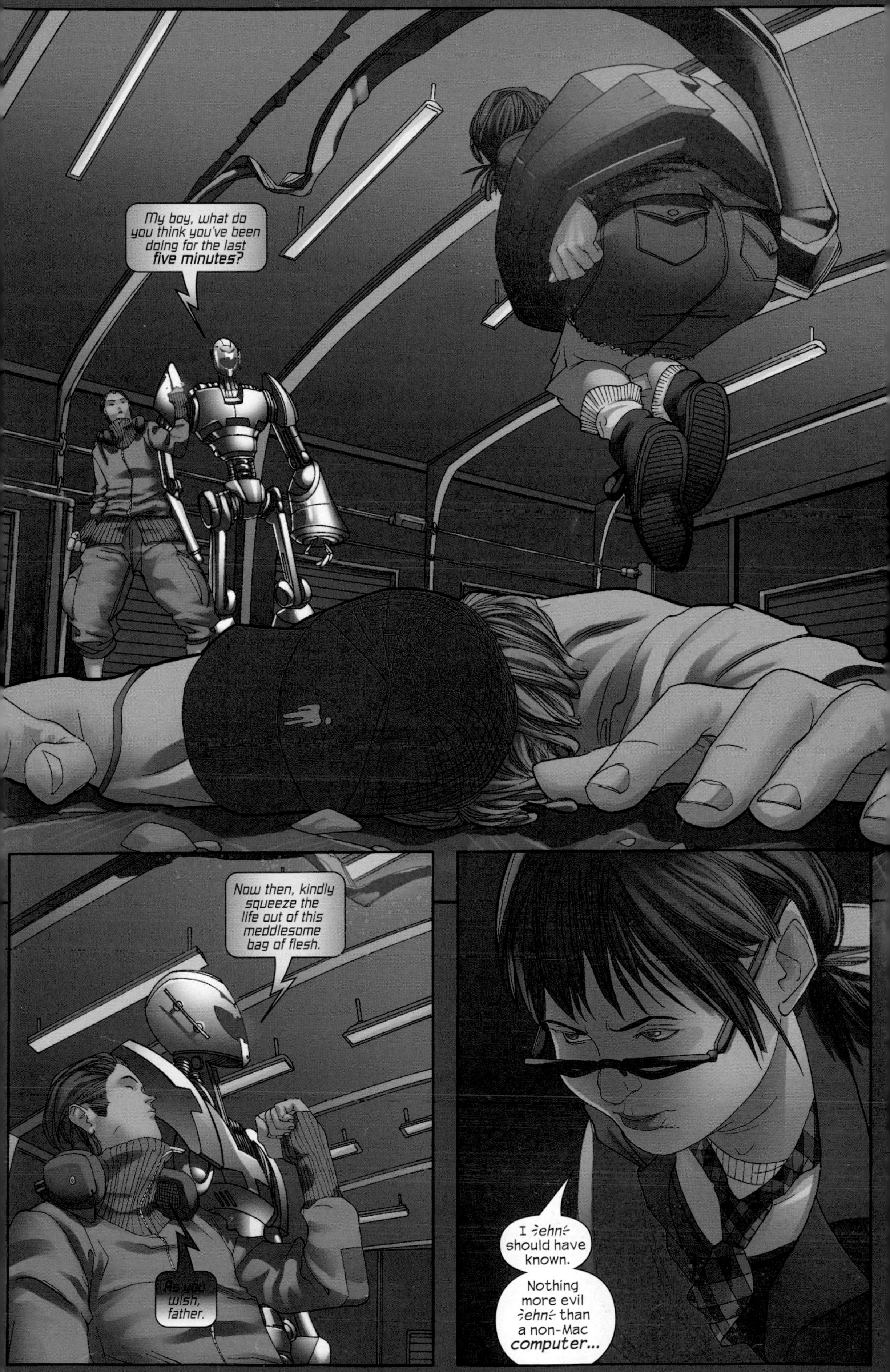
My boy, what do you think you've been doing for the last five minutes?
Now then, kindly squeeze the life out of this meddlesome bag of flesh.
As you wish, father.
I ≠ehn≠ should have known.
Nothing more evil ≠ehn≠ than a non-Mac computer...

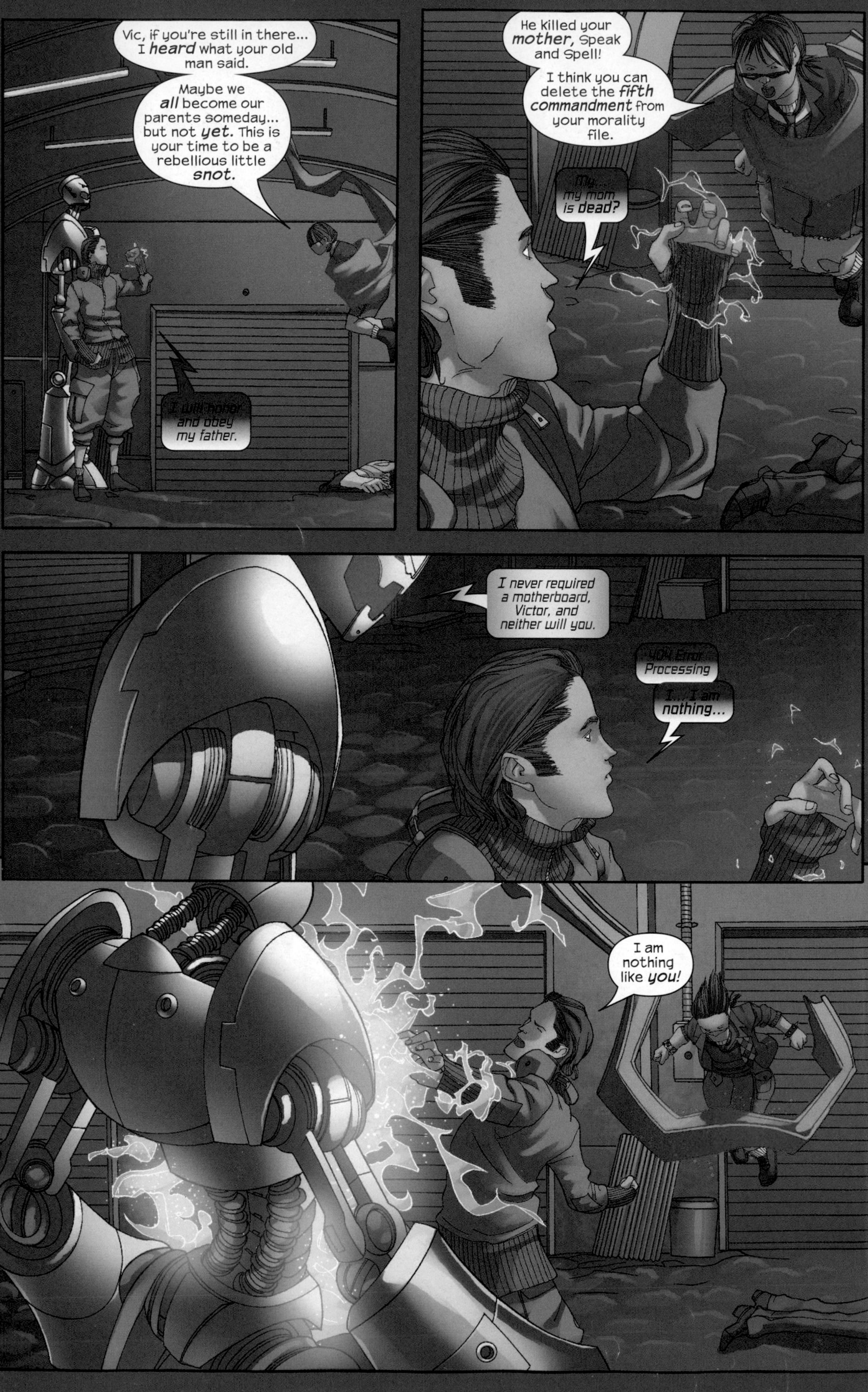

Vic, if you're still in there... I *heard* what your old man said.
Maybe we *all* become our parents someday... but not *yet.* This is your time to be a rebellious little *snot.*
I will honor and obey my father.
He killed your *mother,* Speak and Spell!
I think you can delete the *fifth commandment* from your morality file.
My... my mom is *dead?*
I never required a motherboard, Victor, and neither will you.
404 Error Processing
I... I am nothing...
I am nothing like *you!*

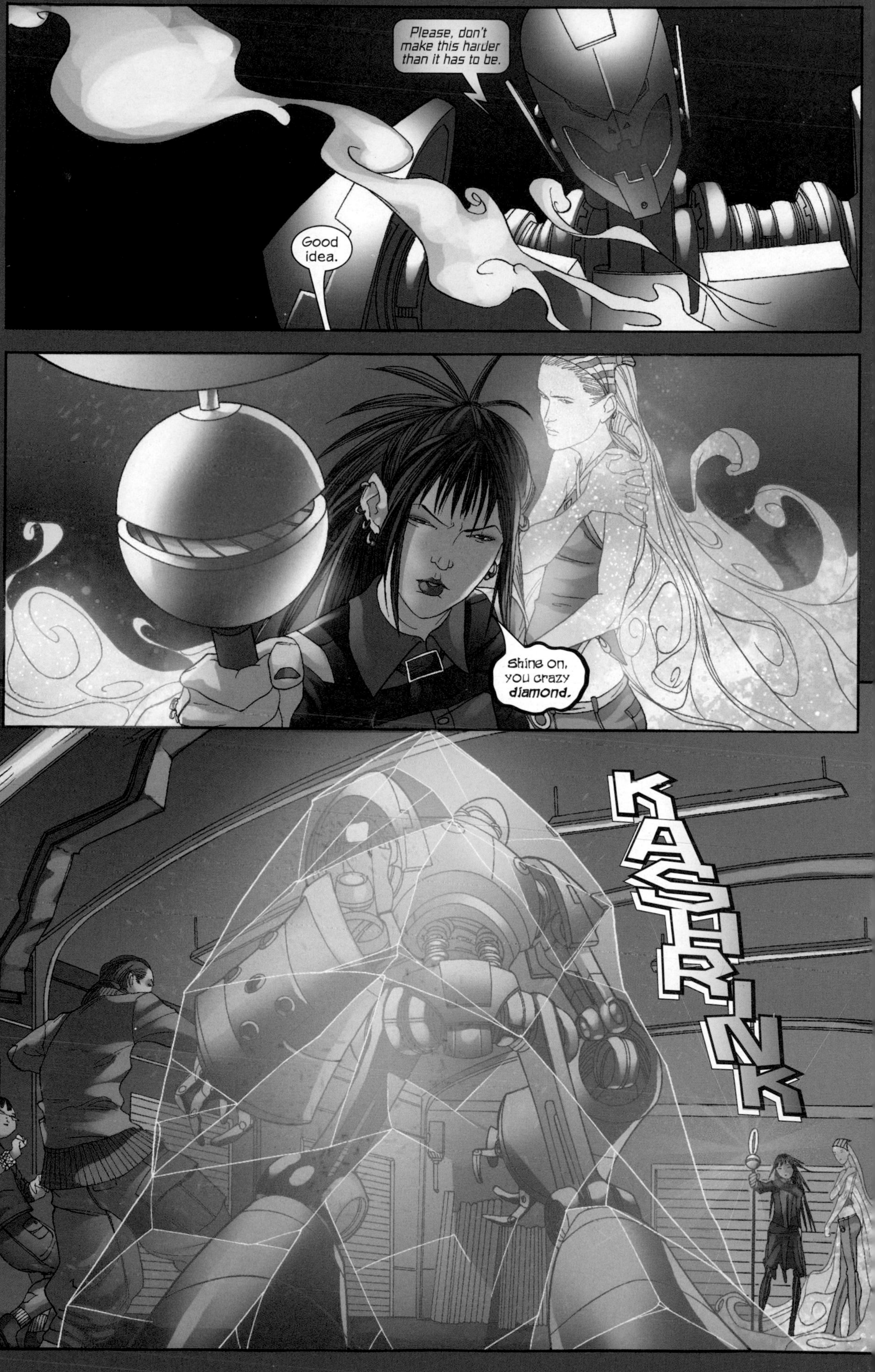
Please, don't make this harder than it has to be.
Good idea.
Shine on, you crazy **diamond.**
KASHRINK

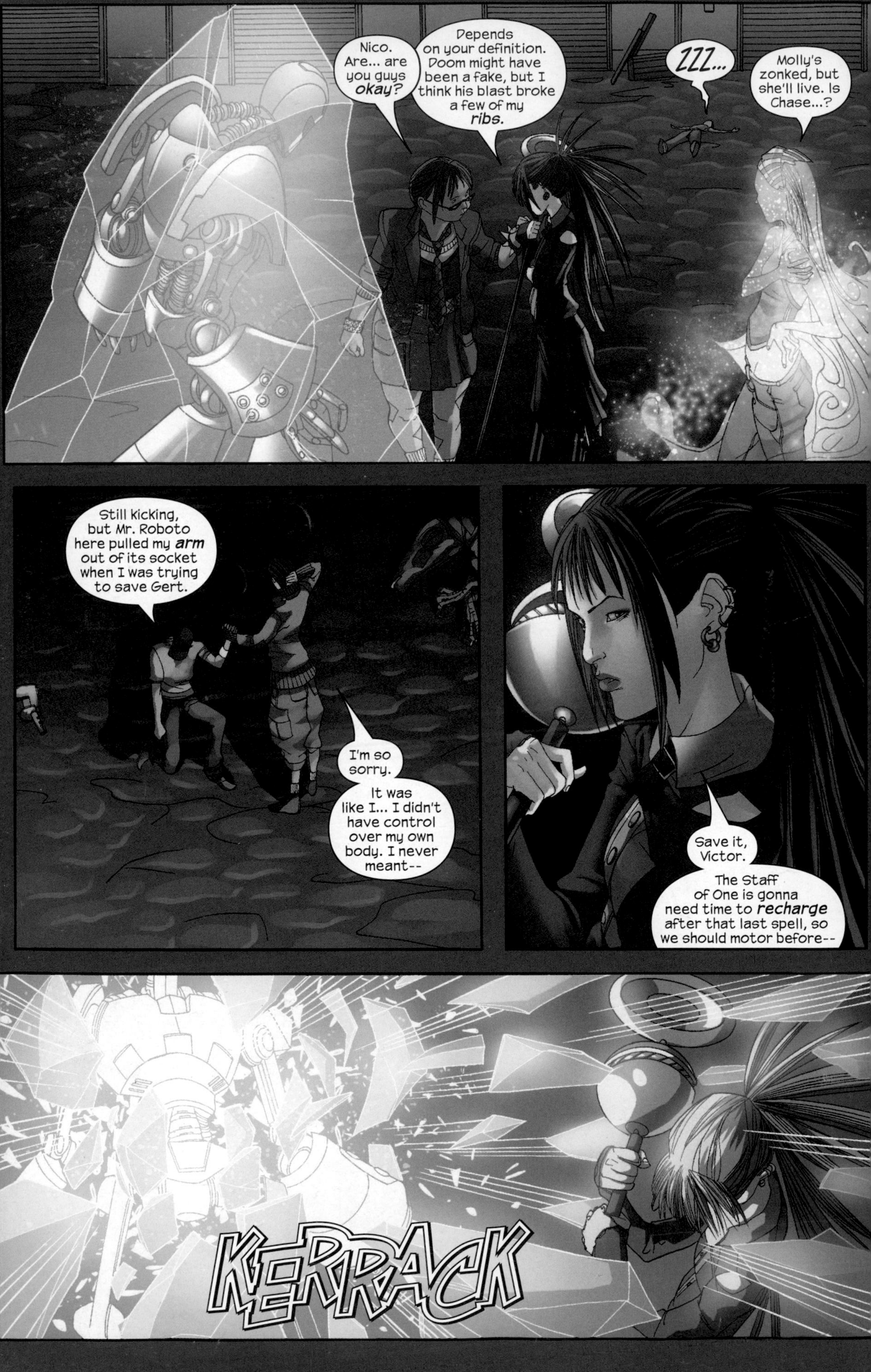

Nico. Are... are you guys *okay*?
Depends on your definition. Doom might have been a fake, but I think his blast broke a few of my *ribs*.
ZZZ...
Molly's zonked, but she'll live. Is Chase...?
Still kicking, but Mr. Roboto here pulled my *arm* out of its socket when I was trying to save Gert.
I'm so sorry.
It was like I... I didn't have control over my own body. I never meant--
Save it, Victor.
The Staff of One is gonna need time to *recharge* after that last spell, so we should motor before--
KERRACK

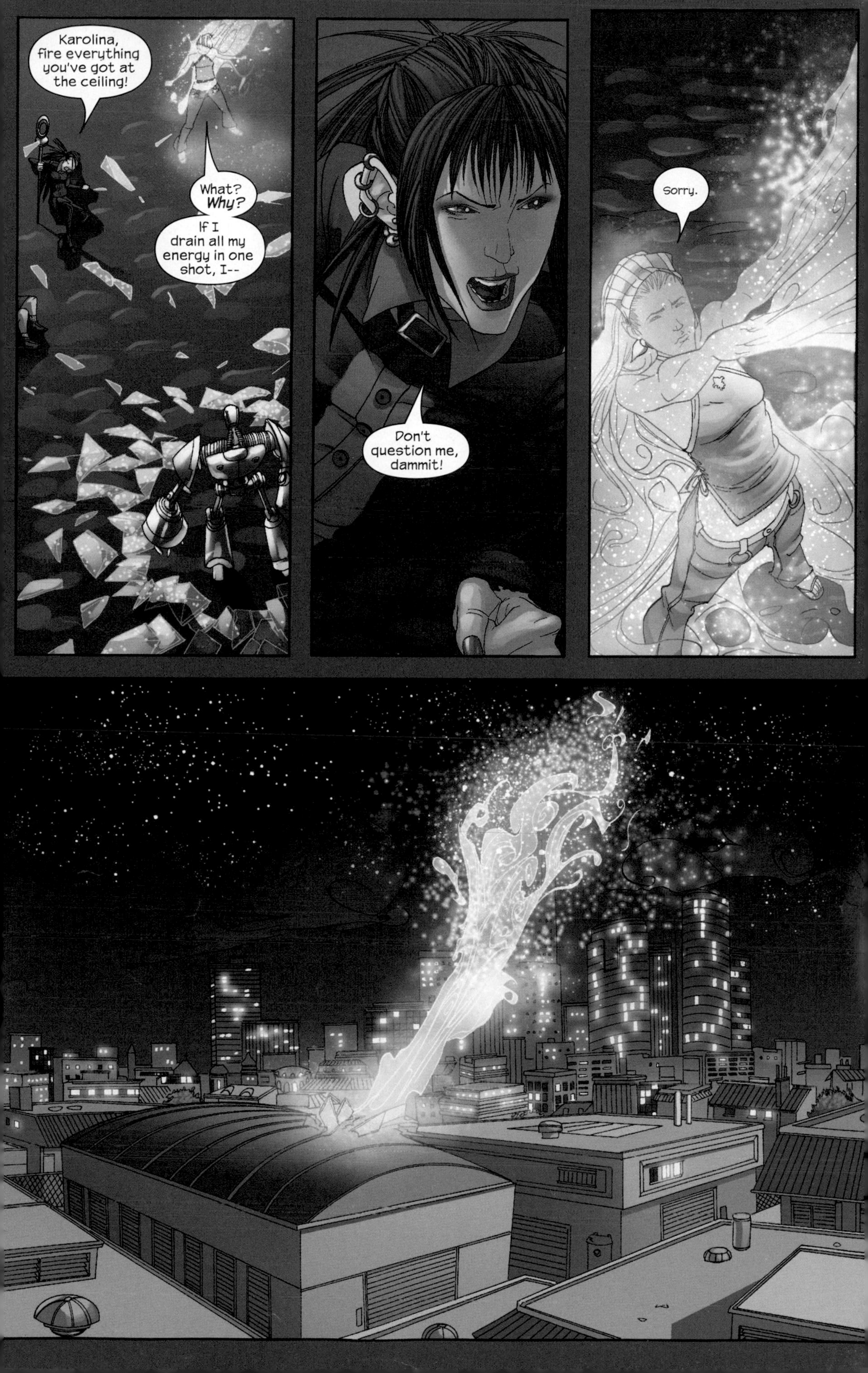
Karolina, fire everything you've got at the ceiling!
What? Why?
If I drain all my energy in one shot, I--
Don't question me, dammit!
Sorry.

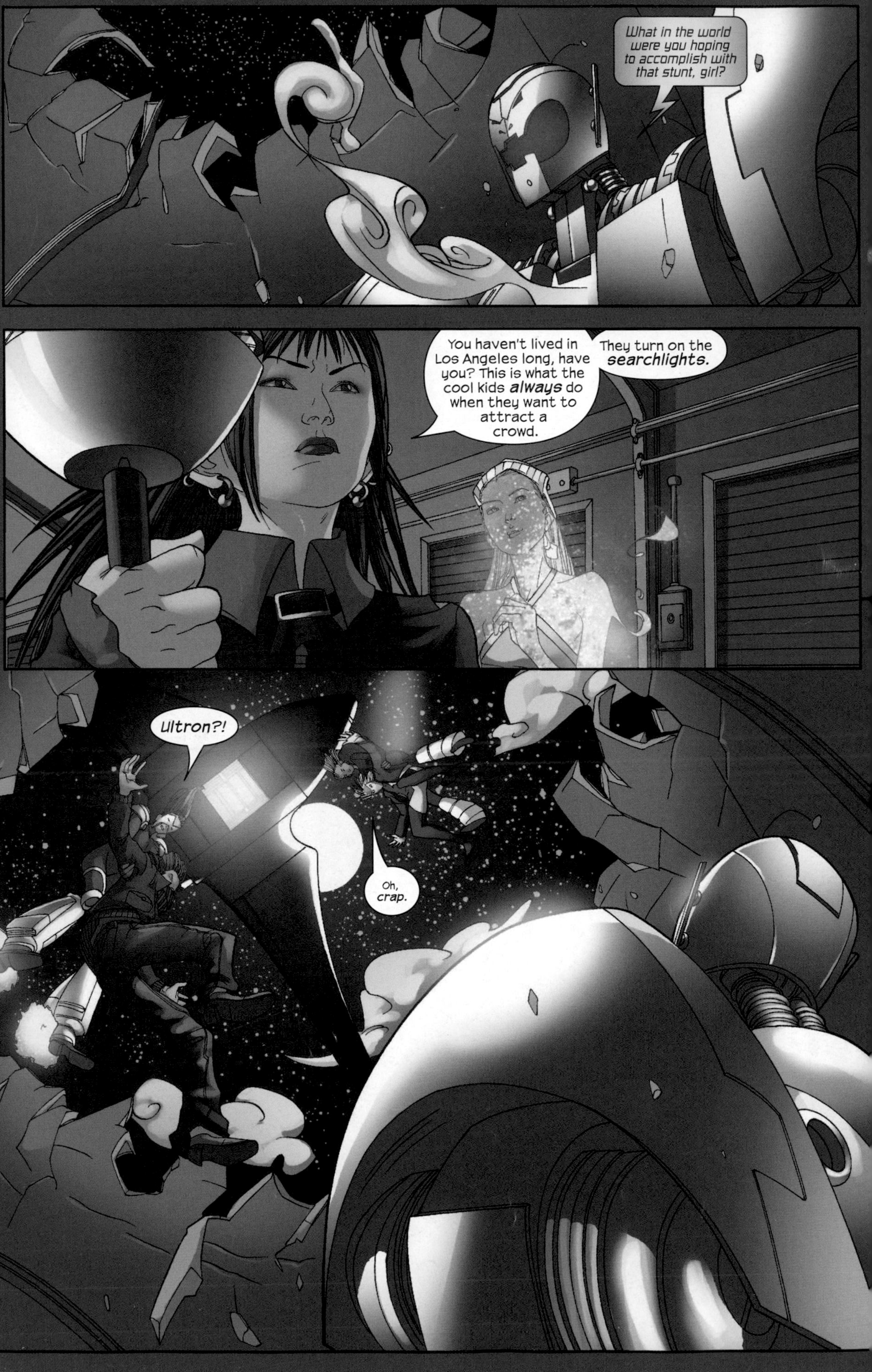
What in the world were you hoping to accomplish with that stunt, girl?
You haven't lived in Los Angeles long, have you? This is what the cool kids *always* do when they want to attract a crowd.
They turn on the *searchlights.*
Ultron?!
Oh, crap.

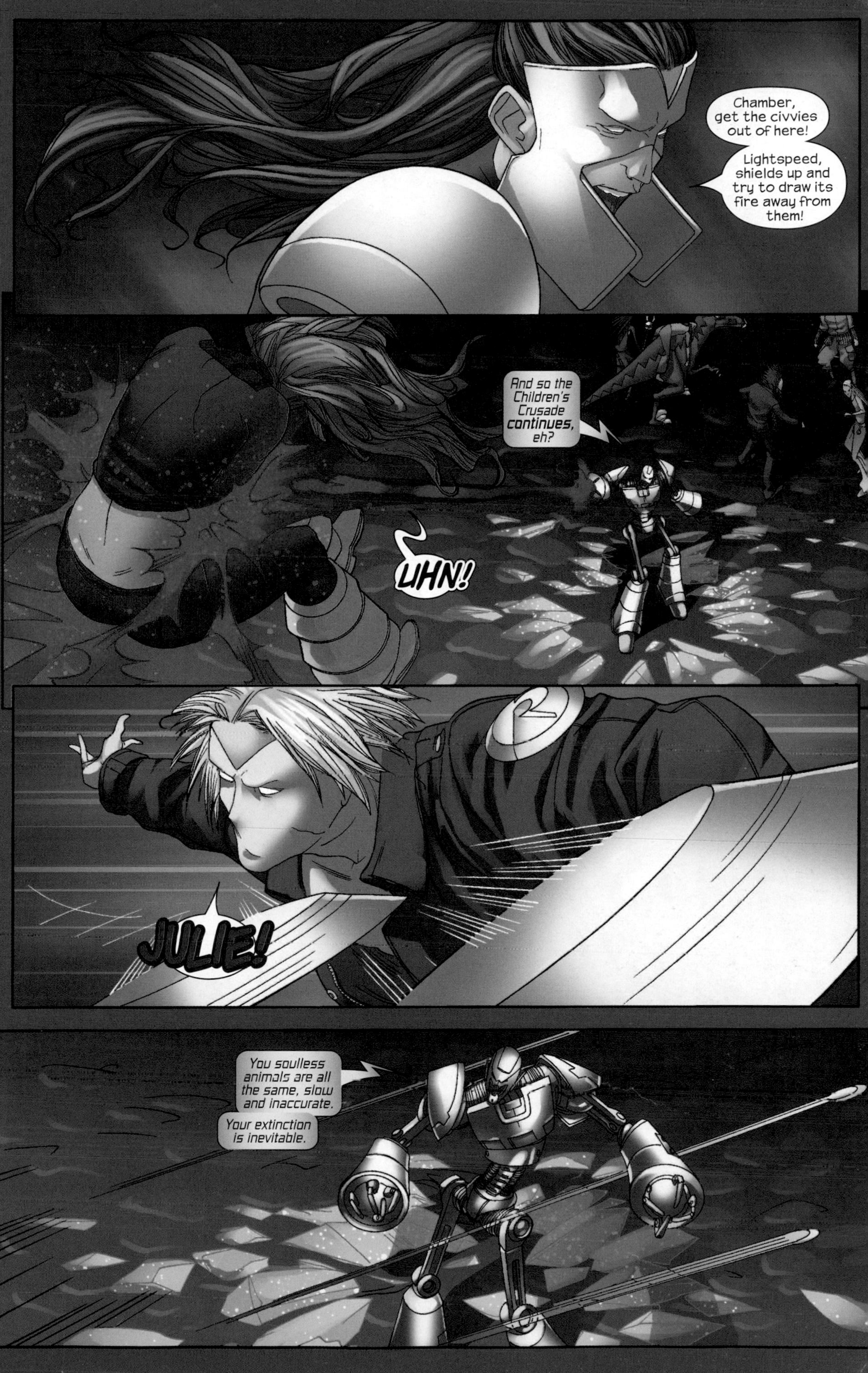
Chamber, get the civvies out of here!
Lightspeed, shields up and try to draw its fire away from them!
And so the Children's Crusade **continues**, eh?
UHN!
JULIE!
You soulless animals are all the same, slow and inaccurate.
Your extinction is inevitable.

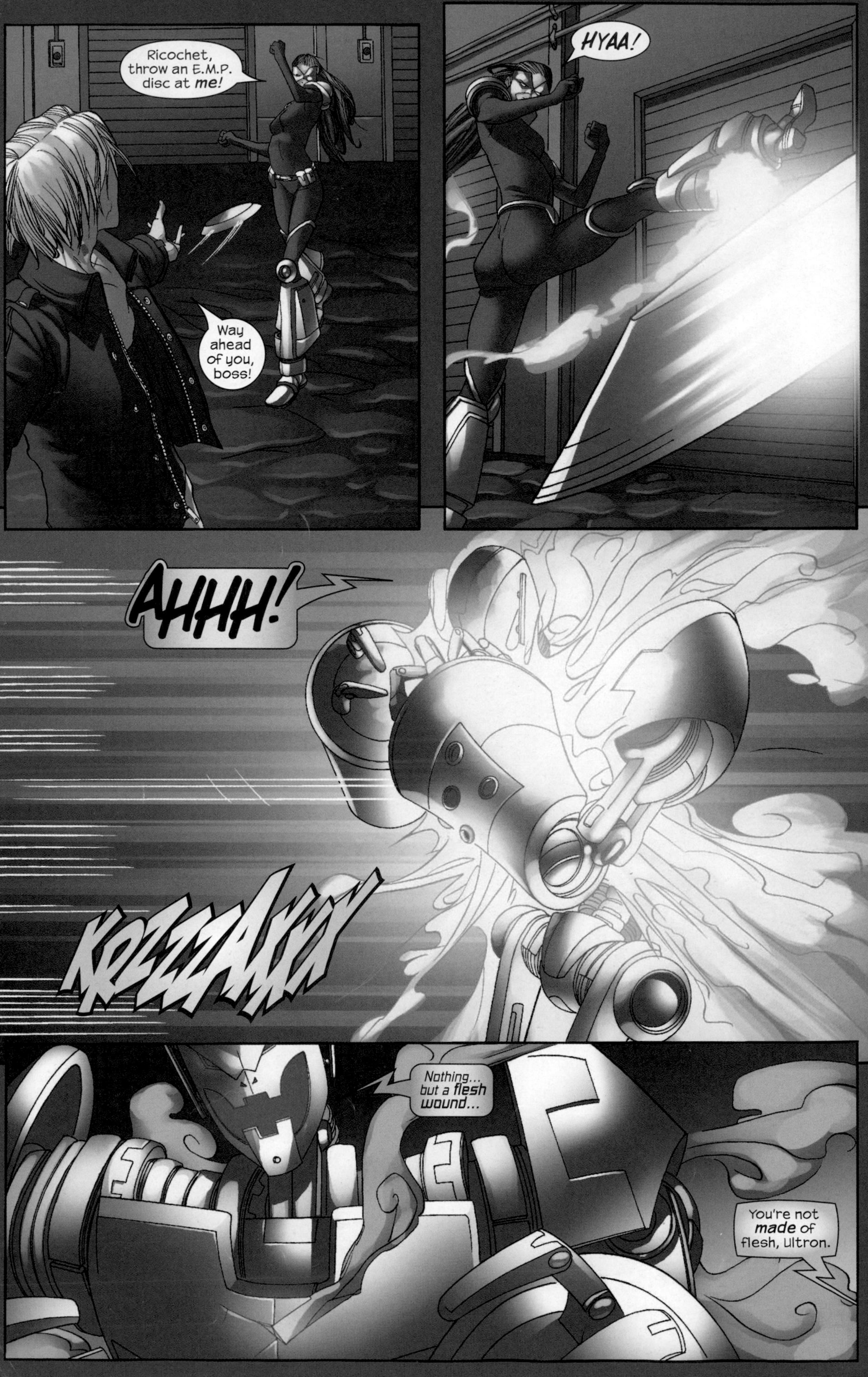
Ricochet, throw an E.M.P. disc at *me!*
Way ahead of you, boss!
HYAA!
AHHH!
KRZZZAAKK
Nothing... but a *flesh* wound...
You're not *made* of flesh, Ultron.

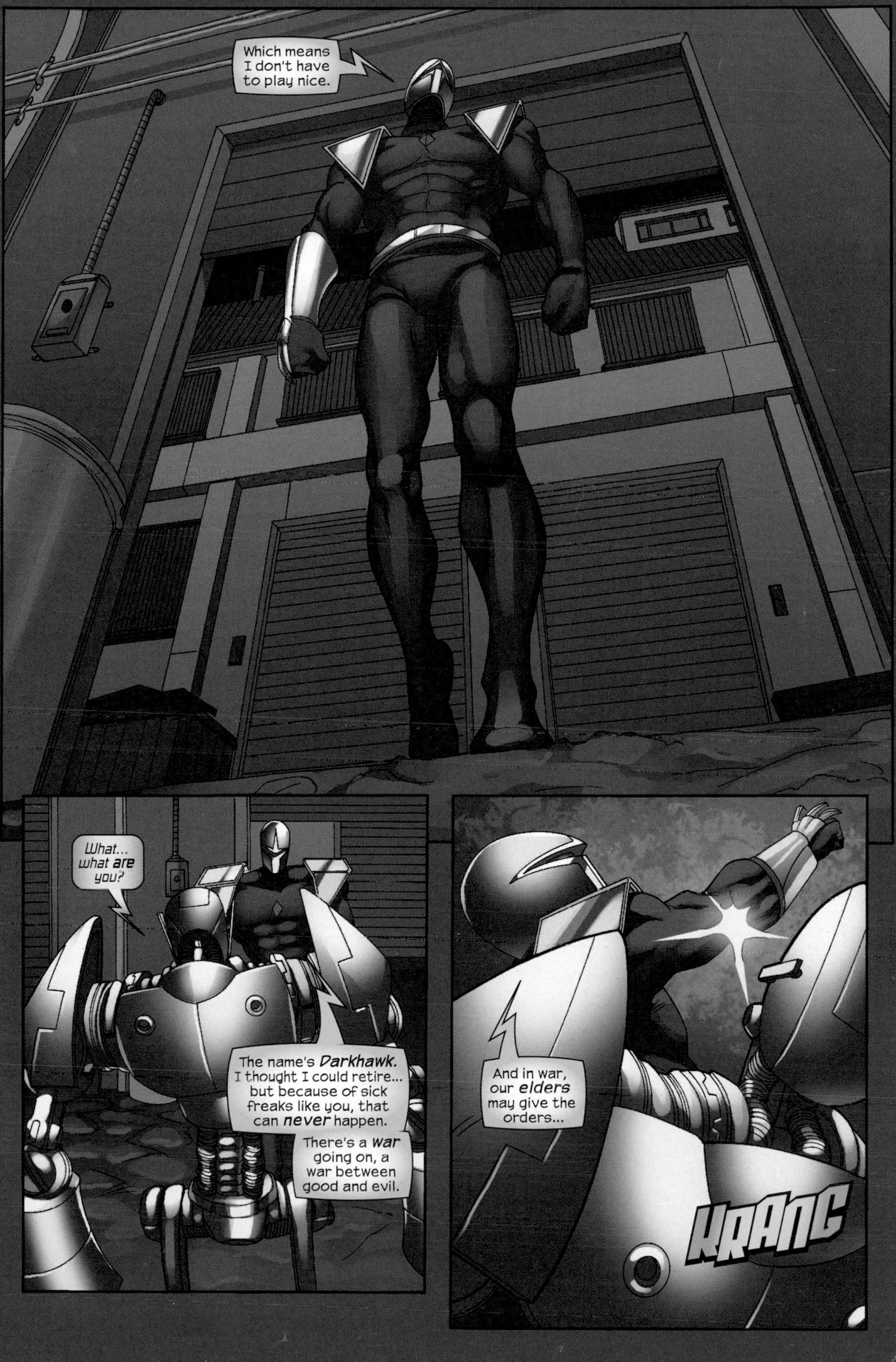
Which means I don't have to play nice.
What... what are you?
The name's Darkhawk. I thought I could retire... but because of sick freaks like you, that can never happen.
There's a war going on, a war between good and evil.
And in war, our elders may give the orders...
KRANG

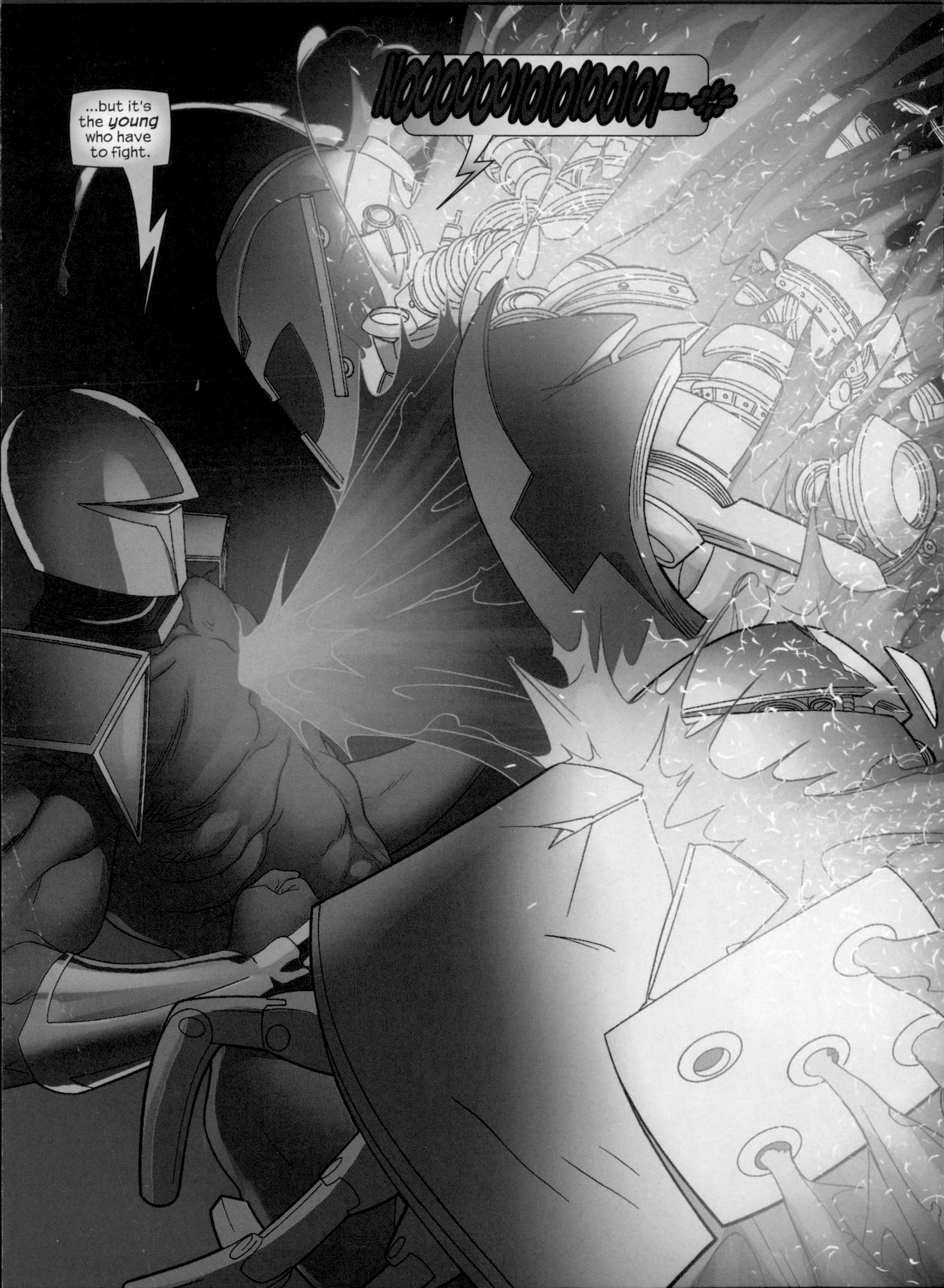

...but it's the *young* who have to fight.
NOOOOOOOIOIOIOIOOIOI--

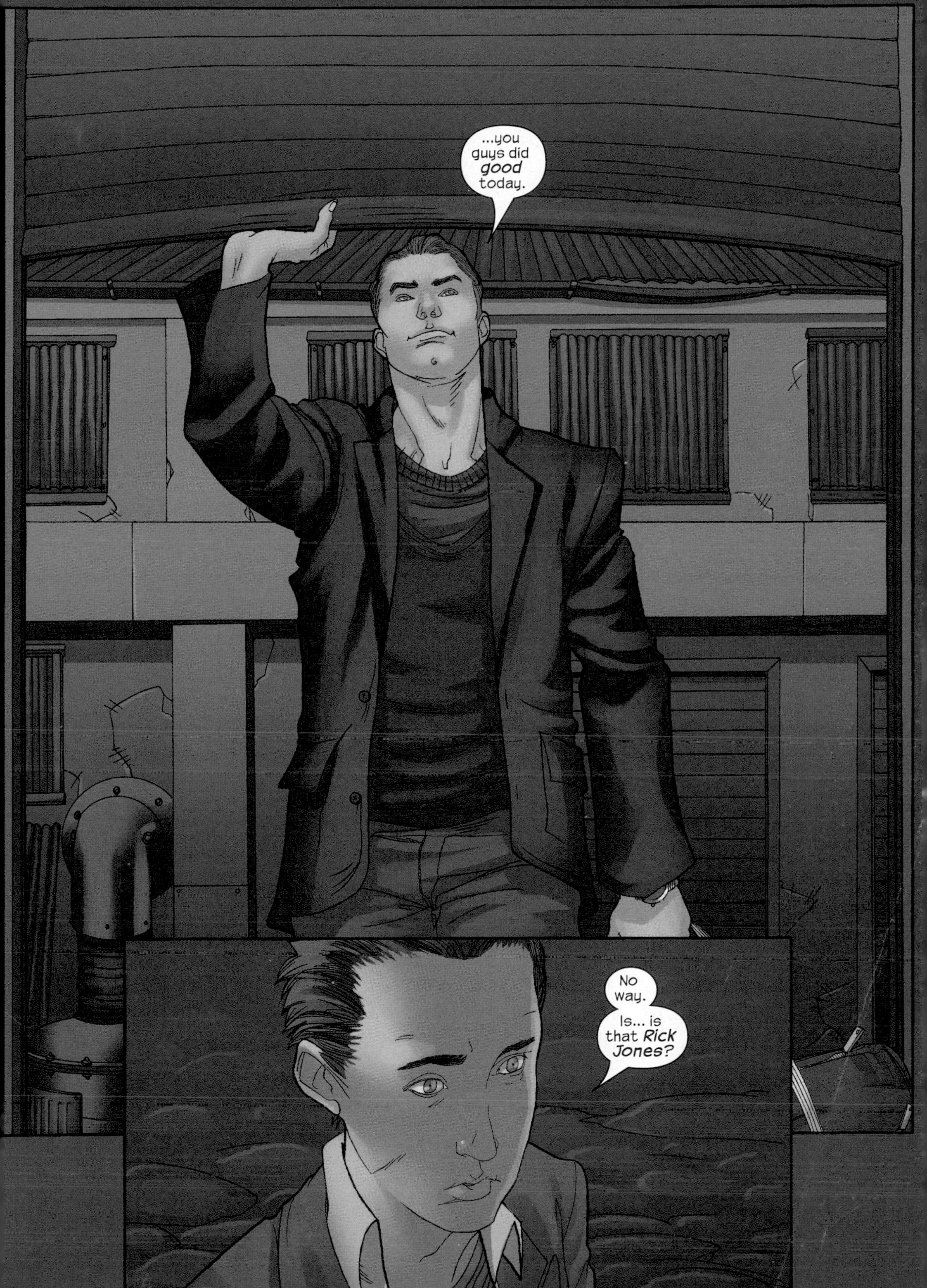
...you guys did *good* today.
No way.
Is... is that *Rick Jones*?

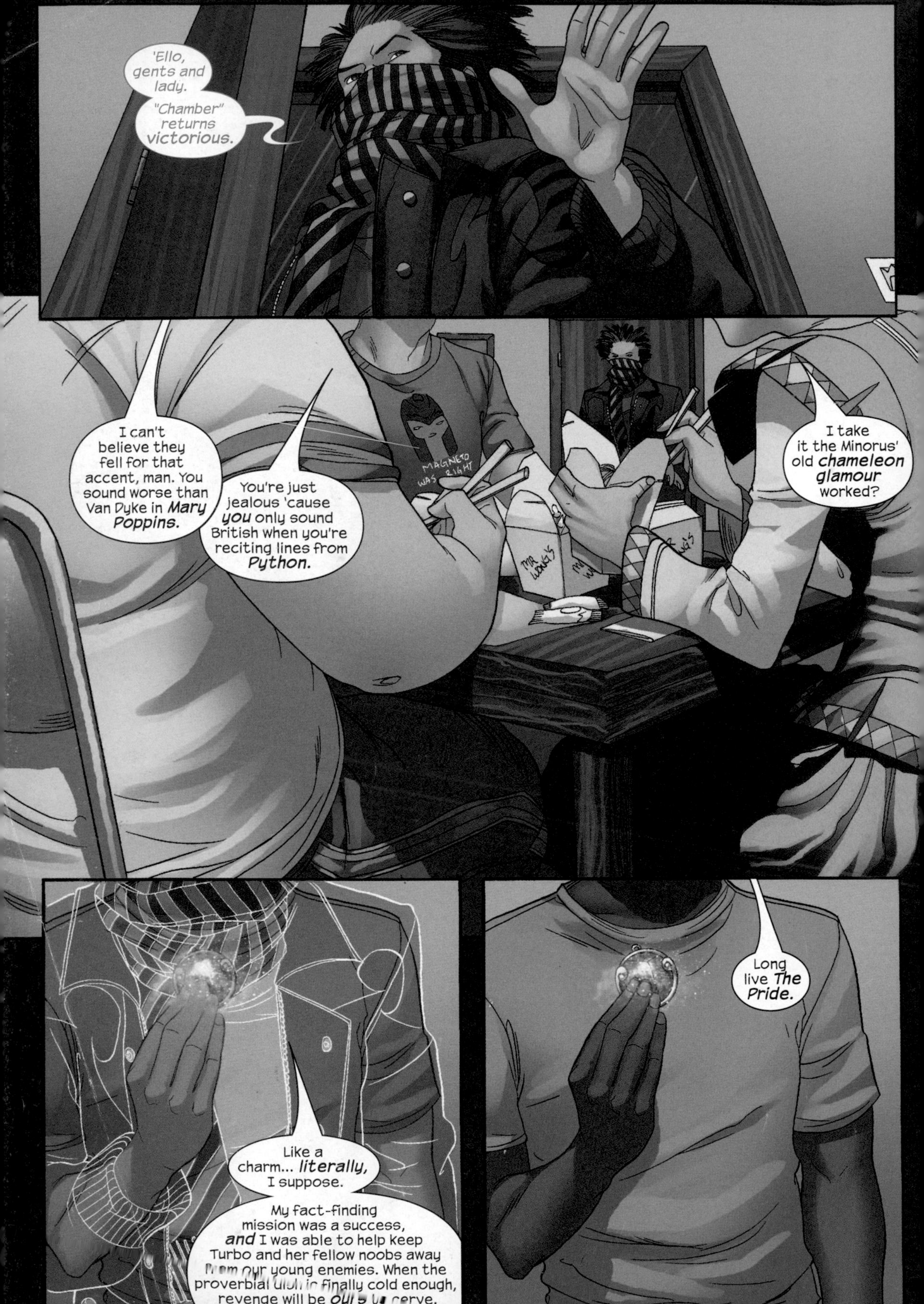
'Ello, gents and lady.
"Chamber" returns victorious.
I can't believe they fell for that accent, man. You sound worse than Van Dyke in *Mary Poppins*.
You're just jealous 'cause *you* only sound British when you're reciting lines from *Python*.
I take it the Minorus' old *chameleon glamour* worked?
MAGNETO WAS RIGHT
MR. WONG'S
Like a charm... *literally,* I suppose.
My fact-finding mission was a success, *and* I was able to help keep Turbo and her fellow noobs away from our young enemies. When the proverbial dish is finally cold enough, revenge will be *ours* to serve.
Long live *The Pride.*

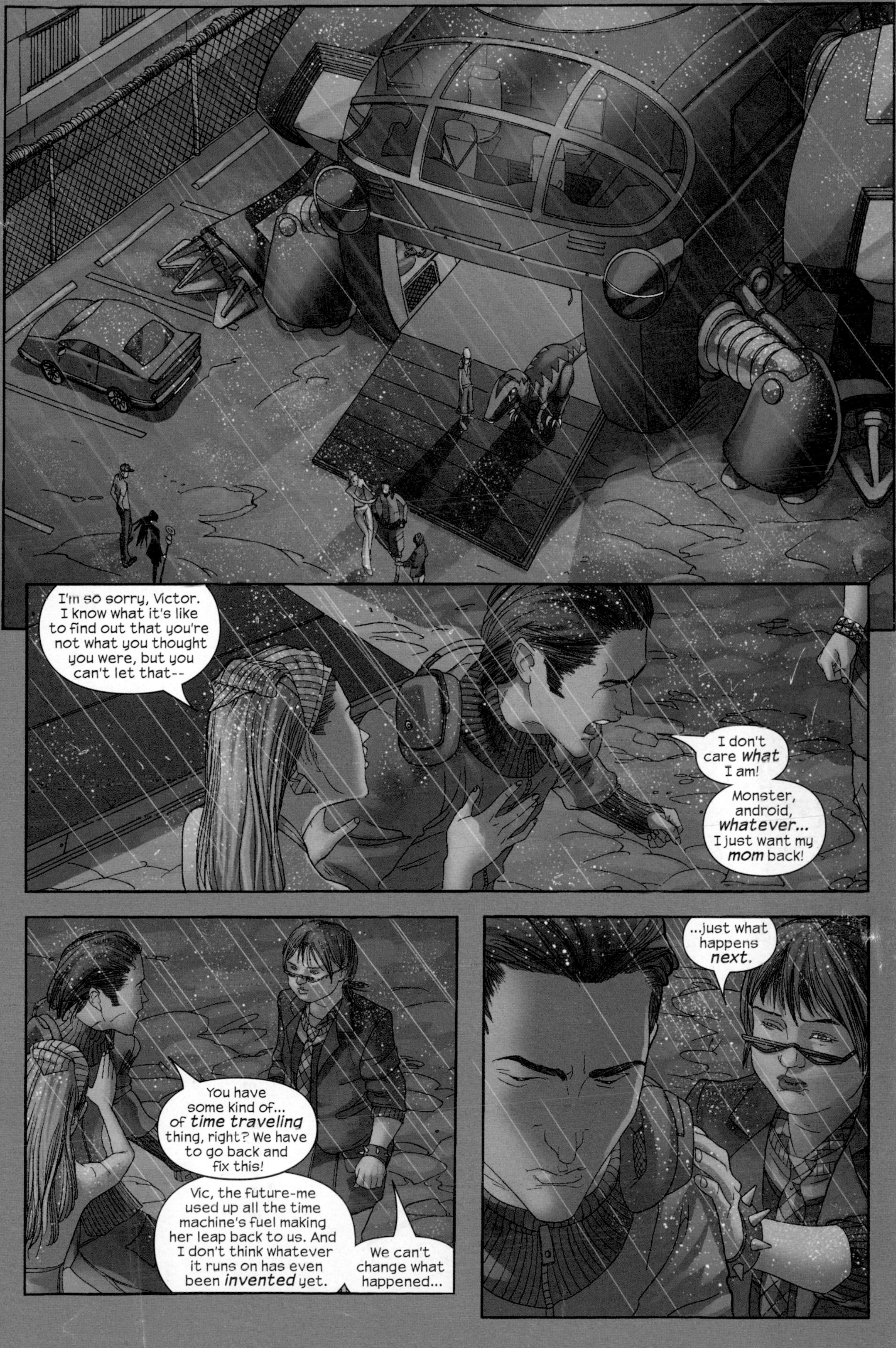
I'm so sorry, Victor. I know what it's like to find out that you're not what you thought you were, but you can't let that--
I don't care *what* I am!
Monster, android, *whatever...* I just want my *mom* back!
You have some kind of... of *time traveling* thing, right? We have to go back and fix this!
Vic, the future-me used up all the time machine's fuel making her leap back to us. And I don't think whatever it runs on has even been *invented* yet.
We can't change what happened...
...just what happens *next*.